THE POETRY OF W. D. SNODGRASS

UNDER DISCUSSION

Donald Hall, General Editor

The Poetry of
W. D. Snodgrass

Everything Human

Edited by Stephen Haven

Ann Arbor
THE UNIVERSITY OF MICHIGAN PRESS

Copyright © by the University of Michigan 1993
All rights reserved
Published in the United States of America by
The University of Michigan Press
Manufactured in the United States of America

1996   1995   1994   1993   4   3   2   1

Library of Congress Cataloging-in-Publication Data

The Poetry of W.D. Snodgrass : everything human / edited by Stephen
    Haven.
        p.   cm.—(Under discussion)
    Includes bibliographical references.
    ISBN 0-472-10252-4 (alk. paper)
        1. Snodgrass, W. D. (William De Witt), 1926–   —Criticism and
    interpretation.   I. Haven, Stephen.   II. Series.
    PS3537.N32Z8   1993
    811'.54—dc20   93-18171
                                                          CIP

A CIP catalogue record for this book is available from the British Library.

Thanks to Robert Phillips and to David Wojahn for
their advice and encouragement in the early stages of
this project. Thanks to Donald Hall for his guidance
in shaping a manuscript into a book, and to Ashland
University for its financial assistance. Special thanks to
W. D. and Kathleen Snodgrass.

All passages quoted from the poetry of W. D. Snod-
grass are reprinted with the permission of Soho Press.

Contents

Part Three   Essays: The First Three Books

Part Four   Reviews 1975–89: *In Radical Pursuit, The Führer Bunker, Selected Poems,* and Fine Press Editions

A W. D. Snodgrass Chronology

1926   Born 5 January in Wilkinsburg, Pennsylvania.

1928   Moves with family to Beaver Falls, Pennsylvania.

1943–44   Studies at Geneva College, Beaver Falls, Pennsylvania.

1944–45   Drafted into the United States Navy. Serves in the Pacific.

1946   Continues studies at Geneva College. Marries Lila Jean Hank.

1947   Continues undergraduate studies at the University of Iowa.

1949   B.A. degree from the University of Iowa.

1950   Cynthia Jean Snodgrass born (the daughter of the "Heart's Needle" sequence).

1951   M.A. degree in English from the University of Iowa. Publishes poems in journals for the first time, in *Experiment: A Quarterly of New Poetry* and *Western Review*.

1953   Divorced from Lila Jean Hank. Begins work on the "Heart's Needle" sequence. Receives M.F.A. degree in Poetry from the University of Iowa Writers' Workshop.

1953–54   Publishes poems in *Botteghe Oscure, Partisan Review,* and the *New Yorker.*

1954   Marries Janice Marie Ferguson Wilson.

1955   Leader of the Moorehead Writers' Conference Poetry Workshop, Moorehead, Kentucky.

1955–57   Teaches English as an instructor at Cornell University. Poems published in *Perspective, Epoch, Paris Review,* and the *Hudson Review.*

1957   Sections II, IV, VI, VIII, and X of "Heart's Needle" sequence published in *New Poets of England and America,* ed. Donald Hall, Robert Pack, and Louis Simpson. "April In-

---

See bibliography for publishers of the books listed in this chronology.

ventory" and "The Marsh" are also reprinted in the anthology from earlier journal publications. Receives letter from Robert Lowell praising the anthologized poems and offering help in finding a book publisher. Second child, Russell Bruce Snodgrass, born.

1957–58   Teaches English as an instructor at the University of Rochester.

1958   Wins *Hudson Review* Fellowship in Poetry and Ingram Merrill Foundation Poetry Prize. Leads poetry workshop at the Antioch Writers' Conference.

1959   *Heart's Needle* published. Becomes Assistant Professor of English, Wayne State University. Receives Longview Foundation Award.

1960   Wins Pulitzer Prize in Poetry for *Heart's Needle*. Receives citation from the Poetry Society of America and a grant from the National Institute of Arts and Letters.

1961   Receives the British Guiness Award for Poetry.

1962   Twice included in the 2d edition of *New Poets of England and America,* ed. Donald Hall and Robert Pack, one group of poems under his own name and one group under a pseudonym, S. S. Gardons. The Gardons pieces are part of a sequence of eight poems, eventually collected under the title *Remains,* about the death of Snodgrass's sister.

1963   Awarded a Ford Foundation Grant.

1966   Divorced from Janice Marie Ferguson Wilson. Wins Miles Poetry Award.

1967   Publishes *Gallows Songs,* translations (in collaboration with Lore Segal) from the poetry of Christian Morgenstern. Marries Camille Rykowski.

1968   Publishes *After Experience.* Becomes professor in English and Speech at Syracuse University.

1969   Publishes pamphlet *Spaulding Distinguished Lectures.*

1970   Publishes *Remains* under the pseudonym S. S. Gardons (limited ed.).

1972   Appointed member of the National Institute of Arts and Letters. Wins Guggenheim Fellowship.

1973   Appointed Fellow of the Academy of American Poets.

1975   Publishes collection of lectures and essays, *In Radical Pursuit.*

1977   Publishes *The Führer Bunker* as a cycle of poems in prog-
       ress. Featured, with photograph on cover, in *American Po-
       etry Review*. Publishes collection of translations, *Six Trouba-
       dour Songs* (limited ed.). Continues to translate songs
       (sometimes set to original music) from many different lan-
       guages. Divorced from Camille Rykowski.

1978   Visiting Distinguished Professor, Old Dominion Univer-
       sity. Publishes *Traditional Hungarian Songs* (limited ed.).

1979   Accepts professorship at the University of Delaware. Re-
       mains at Delaware through the present day (1992).

1979   Publishes *If Birds Build with Your Hair* (limited ed.).

1981   New York stage production of *The Führer Bunker*.
       Adapted by Snodgrass, directed by Carl Weber. American
       Place Theater, April–June. Publishes *These Trees Stand*
       (limited ed.).

1982   Publishes second collection in *The Führer Bunker* cycle:
       Heinrich Himmler: Platoons and Files (limited ed.). Begins
       collaborating with the painter, DeLoss McGraw. Two full-
       length collections eventually result from the collaboration
       as well as a number of limited, fine press editions.

1983   Publishes third collection in *The Führer Bunker* cycle:
       Magda Goebbels (limited ed.). Publishes *Six Minnesinger
       Songs* (limited ed.) and *The Boy Made of Meat* (limited
       ed.), a poem for children.

1984   Publishes *Antonio Vivaldi: The Four Seasons* (song transla-
       tions, limited ed.) and *D. D. Byrde Callyng Jennie Wrenn*
       (limited ed.).

1985   *Remains* reissued under Snodgrass's own name. Widely
       available to the poetry public for the first time. Marries
       Kathleen Brown.

1986   Publishes *A Locked House* (limited ed.) and three limited
       editions with colored lithographs and illustrations by De-
       Loss McGraw: *A Colored Poem, The House the Poet Built,*
       and *The Kinder Capers*.

1987   Publishes *Selected Poems: 1957–1987*. Gavin Ewart, review-
       ing the book for the *New York Times*, calls Snodgrass
       "one of the six best poets now writing in English." Stage
       production of *The Führer Bunker*, adapted by Snodgrass
       and Annette Martin, directed by Martin: Eastern Michi-
       gan University, Ypsilanti, Michigan, 3–11 April.

1988   Publishes *W. D.'s Midnight Carnival,* a collaborative book of poems and paintings with painter DeLoss McGraw; *The Midnight Carnival,* a limited edition with etchings by DeLoss McGraw; the pamphlet *Lullaby: The Comforting of Cock Robin;* and *To Shape a Song,* a limited edition with illustrations by DeLoss McGraw. Visiting Professor, Cornell University, fall semester.

1989   Publishes *The Death of Cock Robin,* second full-length book of collaborations with DeLoss McGraw.

1990   Publishes "Autumn Variations" and "As a Child, Sleepless" in *Poetry.* Publishes *Autumn Variations* as a limited edition and also a limited edition of translations, *Star and Other Poems,* by Mihai Eminescu. Publishes new poems from *The Führer Bunker* cycle in *American Poetry Review.*

1991   Featured, with photograph on cover, in the *Southern Review* (Summer 1991). The issue includes new poems and "Pulse and Impulse," a two-part essay on poetics.

STEPHEN HAVEN

Introduction

The best-known part of W. D. Snodgrass's career is the earliest. Anyone committed to an interest in postwar American poetry knows that he studied in the Iowa Writers' Workshop in the early 1950s. From the early to mid-1950s his poems began appearing in such journals as *Partisan Review, Paris Review, Hudson Review,* and the *New Yorker.* After his work was included in the well-known 1957 Hall, Pack, and Simpson anthology, *New Poets of England and America,* he was on his way to a wider audience. Robert Lowell, Snodgrass's former teacher at Iowa, was so impressed with the anthologized poems that in an October 1957 letter he wrote to offer Snodgrass help in finding a publisher. He calls the poems "heart-felt" and "amazing technically" and claims that Snodgrass is "better than anyone in the book except Larkin."[1] Among others the anthology includes such talent as W. S. Merwin, Adrienne Rich, James Wright, Robert Bly, Anthony Hecht, Donald Justice, Donald Hall, James Merrill, Howard Nemerov, Richard Wilbur, and Lowell himself.

The poems are not only "heart-felt" and "amazing technically"; they are different. In "Seasoned Wood," Donald Hall's contribution to *Everything Human,* Hall describes the shock produced by the publication of Snodgrass's *Heart's Needle* and Lowell's *Life Studies.* If the personal lyrics of these two books are, as a genre, nothing new in English and American literature, few poets had so directly revealed in their poems the darker sides of their personal lives. Perhaps John Clare. But "Child of my winter, born / When the new fallen soldiers froze . . ." and "Tamed by Miltown we lie on mother's bed"? Domestic disharmony, divorce, child loss, and, in the case of Lowell, madness and incarceration. The distinct visions behind these two books are far cries from Eliot's ars poetica, so influential in the 1950s, that "the more perfect the artist, the more completely separate in him will be the man who suffers and the mind which creates."[2] In writing about the intimacies and betrayals of family life both poets were taking steps in the direction of a more emotionally intense poetry.

Snodgrass was thirty-one when Lowell wrote to him, thirty-three when *Heart's Needle* was published, and thirty-four when he received the 1960 Pulitzer Prize for Poetry. By the time *Heart's Needle* appeared he had been accepted as a peer by some of the most important postwar American poets (Lowell, Randall Jarrell, Theodore Roethke, and John Berryman among them). The book's impact on his own generation was also great. In *The Confessional Poets,* the first book-length study of confessional poetry (the chapter on Snodgrass appears here), Robert Phillips credits Snodgrass and Lowell as cofounders of the confessional school. Though Snodgrass has resisted this association with confessional poetry, and though much of the poetry eventually considered confessional differs considerably from Snodgrass's poetry of the 1950s, the personal lyric reintroduced in *Heart's Needle* arguably became the dominant poetry of the 1960s and 1970s. Snodgrass was a decade ahead of the age.

Such was the impact of Snodgrass's first book, all of it familiar history to poets, literary critics, and teachers of poetry. But illustrious beginnings in poetry can bring difficulties as well as blessings. The poetry public not only expected Snodgrass to match or outdo his early work, it expected subsequent volumes to be written in a similar vein. Because the second book was so different from the first, *After Experience* disappointed some of the admirers of *Heart's Needle,* even as the new book was highly praised by others. Almost every subsequent collection—*After Experience, Remains, The Führer Bunker, If Birds Build with Your Hair, A Locked House, The Death of Cock Robin,* and *W. D.'s Midnight Carnival*—represents a departure from earlier collections in terms of form and subject matter. Snodgrass is a poet of thematic continuity within an evolving formal change. He is the type of artist who cultivates change—like Picasso or William Carlos Williams—as opposed to the type, like John Crowe Ransom or Richard Wilbur, who spends a lifetime working within the different shades of one dominant style. From the beginning, to borrow a phrase from Williams, almost every one of Snodgrass's books "begins to begin again."

Everything Human largely consists of representative book reviews and critical essays. The book reviews were chosen mainly for their critical quality but occasionally for the light they shed on the range of immediate responses to Snodgrass's individual collections. More than one-third of the critical essays are previously unpublished. The division of *Everything Human* into early (secs. 1–3) and later work (secs. 4–5) presupposes a line of demarcation roughly around the time that the BOA Editions version of

The Führer Bunker was written and eventually published (1977). Such a division is both practical and superficial. Though few of Snodgrass's early critics and contemporaries could foresee, in the 1960s, the extent to which Snodgrass's poetic world of "personal" poetry would expand to include such apparently distant subject matter as the final days of the Third Reich, the continuity of Snodgrass's vision is increasingly clear to his more recent critics, and was anticipated in a few prescient essays of the late 1960s and early 1970s.

The related issues, for example, of sincerity and the embodiment of truth in poetry directly or indirectly thread throughout many of the critical responses to Snodgrass's work. Though few, if any, of the essays in this volume are completely, or even largely, concerned with these issues, they resurface time and again, most recently in X. J. Kennedy's "The Size of Snodgrass," in which Kennedy claims that Snodgrass "restored to formal poetry in America its ancient advantage of truth-telling." M. L. Rosenthal may have been the first to suggest criticism along these lines (and the first to use the term *confessional*) when, in a 24 October 1959 review published in the *Nation,* he quotes an older, anonymous poet as saying that in his poetry Snodgrass is "plainly and openly what he is."

The issues of truth and sincerity, of self-knowledge and its expression, continue to interest Snodgrass's critics in most of the essays published in the late 1960s to early 1970s. Snodgrass, himself, is at least partially responsible for this direction in the critical response to his work. All of the essays in section 3 of *Everything Human* quote some portion of the conclusion to Snodgrass's essay "Finding a Poem," first published in *Partisan Review* in 1959. Robert Phillips refers to this passage as Snodgrass's literary manifesto, in which Snodgrass himself raises the issue of sincerity:

> I am left, then, with a very old fashioned measure of a poem's worth—the depth of its sincerity. And it seems to me that the poets of our generation—those of us who have gone so far in criticism and analysis that we cannot ever turn back and be innocent again, who have such extensive resources for disguising ourselves from ourselves—that our only hope as artists is to continually ask ourselves, "Am I writing what I *really* think? Not what I think is acceptable; nor what my favorite intellectual would think in this situation; nor what I wish I felt. Only what I cannot help thinking." For I believe that the

only reality which a man can ever surely know is that self he cannot help being, though he will only know that self through its interactions with the world around it."

The passage is as interesting for its emphasis on the need for self-knowledge as it is for its recognition of the disguises of the self. "Early" critics have emphasized different parts of this statement, many accentuating the emotional honesty or sincerity in Snodgrass's early poetry, others, like Richard Howard, the masked self in those same poems. A more recent essay, David Wojahn's "Snodgrass's Borrowed Dog: S. S. Gardons and *Remains,*" was in part written as a refutation of the "prevailing tendency [of critics] in their writing . . . to see autobiographical poems *as* autobiography." In still another essay, "To Tell the Truth: The Poetry of W. D. Snodgrass," Gertrude White points out, by quoting a passage from Snodgrass's essay "Tact and the Poet's Force," that the embodiment of "truth" in Snodgrass's poetry has as much, if not more, to do with craft as with vision:

Why must ideas and emotions be repressed from conscious statement into details and facts; repressed again from facts into the texture of language, the choice of words, connotations; repressed finally into technical factors like rhyme and echoes of other words. . . . We are concerned here with problems of inmost belief and strong emotion . . . We simply do not credit people's conscious statements in these areas. And for very good reasons—most people simply do not use their conscious minds for the discernment or the revelation of the truth. They use their conscious minds to disguise themselves from others and from themselves.[3]

The age-old question of self-knowledge, then, seems to be one issue at the heart of Snodgrass's poetry. If, in Snodgrass's confessional period, the self appears largely in the context of its personal surroundings, the backdrop of the Korean War in *Heart's Needle* and suburban America in *After Experience* locate the self in relation to places and events beyond the poet's own interior world. As Snodgrass's subject matter, especially in *The Führer Bunker,* expands to place his personae more directly in social and historical contexts, the scope of his attempt to know the "self through its interactions with the world around it" vastly widens. As Laurence Goldstein notes in his essay included in this volume, the issue of sincerity also takes on an added dimension in *The Führer Bunker,* in which some of the poems' speakers are so skilled as rhetoricians as to convincingly feign sincerity. If, in *The Führer Bunker,* Snodgrass looks from a different angle at the issues of sincerity and inmost belief, the issues themselves remain consistently Snodgrassian.

There are, of course, many other elements in Snodgrass's work reflecting—to use X. J. Kennedy's words—"the wide sweep and fierce consistency of Snodgrass's poetry." The themes of will, choice, loyalty, betrayal, war, guilt, and family are as evident in *The Führer Bunker* as they are in *Heart's Needle.*[4] There is also an emotional range as wide as the thematic one. In Snodgrass's poetic vision there is a bunker in every flower and at least a few flowers in every bunker. *Everything Human* means to clarify the aesthetic unity informing Snodgrass's wide range of emotion and subject matter.

Finally, in a country where, almost traditionally, many of our most talented poets die in mid-career or stop producing after the flash of their first few brilliant books, it is our fortune that W. D. Snodgrass is alive and well and writing. The untimely deaths of poets of Snodgrass's generation (Anne Sexton and Sylvia Plath) and of the one before his (Berryman, Lowell, Jarrell, Roethke, Delmore Schwartz, and Weldon Kees) represent an immeasurable loss to the country. They have robbed us, at least in the case of these poets, of a poetry that represents the whole gamut of human experience—of the potential for poetry like Yeats's "The Circus Animals' Desertion," Frost's "Directive," Williams's "Asphodel," and Bishop's "One Art," poems that could only be written from the perspective of a long life. At the age of sixty-seven Snodgrass has reached such a vantage point. It is time to stop and appraise the entire scope of his work. *Everything Human* is the first of many steps in that direction.

NOTES

1. Robert Lowell's letter to W. D. Snodgrass, 24 October 1957. Lowell goes on in this letter to make references to *Life Studies,* in which he implicitly recognizes the impact of the "Heart's Needle" sequence on his own work: "I have been writing very hard myself lately and have written almost half a book since the middle of August, and feel I have just really begun to know how to get out what I want to say, what I've lived. You learned earlier."

2. T. S. Eliot, "Tradition and the Individual Talent." In *Selected Prose of T. S. Eliot,* ed. Frank Kermode (New York: Farrar, Strauss and Giroux, 1975), 41.

3. W. D. Snodgrass, "Tact and the Poet's Force," *In Radical Pursuit* (New York: Harper, 1975), 18–21. As quoted in Gertrude White's "To Tell the Truth: The Poems of W. D. Snodgrass," *Odyssey* 3, no. 2 (1979): 13.

4. In an interview with Paul Gaston, "W. D. Snodgrass and *The Führer Bunker,*" Snodgrass discusses these themes at length. See *Papers on Language and Literature* 13 (Summer 1977): 295–311; and 13 (Fall 1977): 401–12.

PART ONE *Reviews 1959–61:*
Heart's Needle

PHILIP BOOTH

From "Gunn and Snodgrass"

It would be hard to give comparable praise to any other new poems if an improbable poet named W. D. Snodgrass had not just published *Heart's Needle*. But like no other young American poet, Mr. Snodgrass can pace the conflict between his own emotion and the tensions of conventional metric.

His first book is almost entirely in the first-person singular, and the risk of his ten-part title poem (addressed to his daughter, after a divorce) is mirrored by the painful brilliance of his shorter lyrics. For every needle which has pricked his heart to the hurt and wonder of half-fulfilled human relationships, his mind has returned the sharp pathos of a fully formed poem.

He sustains this balance miraculously, walking with his daughter (and himself) through the museums, zoos, swamps, and campuses which are his native habitat. But always, against the diseased mutations of the human heart, which he uses both literally and metaphorically, he finds survival in a compassion which displaces self-pity.

The evidence, as Robert Lowell rightly points out, is in "April Inventory" and in the clinical symbolism of "The Operation." In these, and "Returned to Frisco," W. D. Snodgrass has come through both suffering and war. And in returning to what is "common in experience—uncommon in writing," he returns all of us to face our essential humanity.

In the apparently most pedestrian language, which gets sharpened to the force of street-corner metaphor, he both controls the progress of his poems and involves his reader in the complex conditions of human love. High-pitched as his poems sometimes are, they are infallibly saved by irony and self-effacing good humor.

"I'm replenishing verses of nobody else's world," he says.

Christian Science Monitor, 14 May 1959. Reprinted by permission from *The Christian Science Monitor*. Copyright © 1959 The Christian Science Publishing Society. All rights reserved. Mr. Booth begins with a review of Thom Gunn's *The Sense of Movement*.

But because he has risked himself so wholly, he's wrong (for once): these are poems for whoever will risk being human. And whoever, having been welcomed to that condition by these poems, must surely be thankful (with none of the irony which the poet intends in his already famous line) that "Snodgrass is walking through the universe."

WILLIAM DICKEY

Review of *Heart's Needle*

It seems a long time to have been waiting for W. D. Snodgrass's first book of poems, not only because a voice so clear, so honest and so moving deserves its proper recognition, but also because Snodgrass's poems have never seemed like isolated events, each produced by a different moment of the mind or surge of tempera-ment. They are parts of a consistent statement, and, seeing them together, it is possible for us to realize more completely what that statement is.

Snodgrass, as a poet, is like a man who has fallen among thieves and been robbed of watch fobs, seal rings, mandarin fingernail guards—of everything, in short, which is not strictly vital to the pursuit of his occupation. He cannot indulge in ele-gances of attitude, he has no opportunity to collect and exhibit fashionable *bijouterie*. He has been left standing in his shirt and, with no more protection than that, will have to learn what his body and mind can tell him about themselves and their relevance to the road he is standing on. No Snodgrass poem is occasional, save when the occasion strikes at these questions. Nor, though the tone may sometimes be deceptive, is any of his poems other than serious.

The effort these poems make is to determine as clearly as possible what and who the speaker is, to judge and set aside the answers of conventional oracles, to resist with a bitter stubborn-ness any effort of authority to impose definitions. The poems are engaged in that extraordinary and uneasy struggle: to get at the truth. And their assumption is that the truth of a person may be most understood in his private, not his public, actions. The popu-lation of the poems is, for this reason, a limited one. We encoun-ter mainly family relations, or those of lovers. To this intimate world the public world serves only as an apocalyptic chorus, a chant of disgusting overstuffed voices making unkind comments at the peripheries.

Epoch 9 (Spring 1959): 254–56. Copyright © 1959 *Epoch*. Reprinted with permission.

The belief in the personal over the public world is dangerous only if it supposes that simple antagonism to the public will justify any attitudes the personal wishes to display. Snodgrass is never guilty of this evasion. Much of our common world he dislikes, but it is excluded from his poems principally so that on the matters of first significance a more concentrated scrutiny can be brought to bear.

This scrutiny is by turns amused and terrified, exalted or moved to a loathing for the world so intense that it will, as it is brutally meant to do, leave the reader nauseated. It may seem too great a distance from the bemused insouciance with which "These Trees Stand" concludes ("Come, let us wipe our glasses on our shirts: / Snodgrass is walking through the universe.") to the catalog of horrors that paralyze and enact human hatred in one section of "Heart's Needle" ("I stand by the unborn, / by putty-colored children curled / in jars of alcohol . . ."). But, when we have determined to follow honesty, honesty demands the recognition that our rages are as true a part of us as are our civilized amusements, that one is as necessary of being understood as the other.

The honesty in the effort at understanding is served by language of great directness and force. Indeed, we might say of the language that it is serviceable, that it does not intrude, and also that it is accessible. It may be as blunt as this couplet: "In thirty years I may not get / Younger, shrewder, or out of debt." It may present a much more intricate description, as this, of Ixion: "That screaming half-beast, strapped at the hub, / Whom Juno's animal mist had known." Or, from the same poem, Orpheus' first sight of Eurydice in hell: "In one long avenue she was / Wandering toward me, vague, uncertain, / Limping a little still. . . ." It may be mockingly syncopated: "sing for the fly-boys, birdy, / in praise of their profession. . . ." It is flexible and various, but it is never permitted to indulge in meaningless pyrotechnics, and it is never obscure.

The long sequence of poems that gives the book its title, and that won the first Ingram Merrill Foundation award, requires some special comment. Here both the concern with the personal and the insistence that all the evidence experience provides shall be made available to the poem—that nothing shall be evaded—reach their full statement. The poem magnificently avoids the twin uglinesses of compulsive decorum and compulsive confession. It does not suppose that we should eat our meat and pretend the maggots of hatred and unpleasantness are not in it, but neither will it elevate unpleasantness to the position where to be unpleasant is to be sincere. "Heart's Needle" will prove an equally embarrassing poem for those who feel that detachment is all and those who feel it is nothing.

The poem, moreover, demonstrates Snodgrass's ability to handle complex structural problems in a way that his earlier poems, with their more limited possibilities, had not. Not only is seasonal chronology used as a reinforcing device, but the varying relation of the father and child who are separated is consistently presented through reference to the world of animals—live, caged, embalmed, as the occasion requires. Like most successful structural devices, this reference is not obtrusive, but it serves to enforce a conception of unity which underlies and connects the different, the extreme, emotional attitudes of the poem.

"Heart's Needle," in more ways than can be quickly stated, is an accomplishment of the first order. It is not a very quotable poem—each line, being serviceable, depends for its effect on its context. Reading an isolated sentence here and there, we might assume that the simplicity is forced, that this is the voice of the *faux naïf* speaking. But we cannot maintain that attitude long, not even after as slight a context as the opening stanza of the third section: "The child between them on the street / Comes to a puddle, lifts his feet / And hangs on their hands. They start / At the live weight and lurch together, / Recoil to swing him through the weather, / Stiffen and pull apart."

"Heart's Needle" is not a comfortable poem; it is not Snodgrass's quality to be comfortable. But in any period it may be the uncomfortable poets to whom we are likely to turn if we value an accurate knowledge of their, and our, perceptions. That uncomfortable single-minded determination to understand is rare enough, and the wholly consonant ability to express that understanding is something we must rejoice to encounter. *Heart's Needle* is a first book of poems so technically competent that we must wonder how its author had time to acquire anything other than competence, so wise that it must puzzle us that he had any leisure ever available for considerations of technique. We have been greatly concerned in recent years with identifying, elucidating, and admiring masks, or personae, we have seen innumerable puppets articulated, sometimes in life, but more often *in articulo mortis*. Perhaps it is time for the puppet-masters to put off their apparitions, dissolve the magical box, and show us what they look like. Certainly Snodgrass shows us this in *Heart's Needle,* and the success of his example might serve to indicate to us that, even though they abstract your purse of glittering alliterations, purloin your Greek references and give them to the poor, refuse you the sanctuary of your last guarded reticence, there may be worse poetic fates than to have fallen among thieves.

JOHN HOLLANDER

From "Poetry Chronicle"

W. D. Snodgrass may very well have written, in *Heart's Needle*, the strongest first book of poems in fifteen years. I set this date to the appearance of Robert Lowell's *Land of Unlikeness*; it is interesting, and perhaps characteristic of two rapidly shifting eras, that, while Lowell's book had found a unique and personal tone of voice which nobody else seemed then even faintly interested in reaching, Snodgrass has managed to be almost phenomenally successful in pitching his own range squarely in the middle of the tessitura in which so very many poets of this generation continually aspire to sing. Poems today can do many sorts of literary and speculative work. In some senses the long, reflective poem may be thought of as the only modern equivalent of the familiar or even the formal (noncritical) essay of the last century. Other modes of writing approach the secular religious meditation, the sermon, the familiar letter, and other genres whose received prose forms today usually constitute only degraded versions of what once they were. Mr. Snodgrass's poems represent the increasingly sought after effect of the journal entry, of the autobiographical report, not assembled from deep images in a kind of rhetorical patchwork, like so many of Dylan Thomas's reminiscences, for example, but written out of considered reflections, summoned up for judgment, whose preparatory motions would always have seemed to consist rather of pencil nibbling than of vocalizing. In such a form wit is seldom an end in itself but, instead, always serves to keep the open skepticism of the narrator's scrutiny clear of the attractions of abject sentimentality, on the one hand, and of self-conscious posturing, on the other. Poems like "April Inventory," "A Cardinal," and the title sequence, a group of poems for the poet's daughter (it takes its title from a phrase in a translation of an Old Irish story: "an only daughter is the needle of the heart"), all succeed in being openly

Partisan Review 26, no. 3 (Summer 1959): 503–6. Reprinted with permission of the author. Copyright © 1959 by John Hollander. Mr. Hollander also reviews *The Sense of Movement*, by Thom Gunn, and *Of the Festivity*, by William Dickey.

autobiographical, intense, and delicate at once, and never embarrassing. Philip Larkin can write of himself this way; Robert Lowell's most recent poems sometimes approach this (although they are much more, I feel, than the mere autobiographical sketches they purport to be), and an occasional magnificent poem like Anthony Hecht's "The Vow" attains the right temperament in its balance of tension and relaxation of diction. But this sort of self-examination seems to be peculiarly Mr. Snodgrass's forte. He can even redeem his tendency to fall into a half-self-critical, genial-but-*serious* E. B. White kind of tone with the corrective image, as in "April Inventory":

> The trees have more than I to spare.
> The sleek, expensive girls I teach,
> Younger and pinker every year,
> Bloom gradually out of reach.
> The pear tree lets its petals drop
> Like dandruff on a tabletop.

Later on in this same poem, which will probably stand for some time as the canonical utterance of the writer of unscholarly disposition doomed, in the 1950s, to an academic life in which he will always feel somewhat uncomfortable, Mr. Snodgrass can be frank in a much simpler way, without once giving the reader the feeling that he is being taken by the hand and forced to look, honestly, openly, at what is deeply moving and *real:*

> I taught myself to name my name,
> To bark back, loosen love and crying;
> To ease my woman so she came,
> To ease an old man who was dying.
> I have not learned how often I
> Can win, can love, but choose to die.
>
> I have not learned there is a lie
> Love shall be blonder, slimmer, younger;
> That my equivocating eye
> Loves only by my body's hunger . . .

It is not, however, that Mr. Snodgrass can only write within one narrow range. Some of the speculative passages in the "Heart's Needle" poems, no matter what the method of selection and organization by which they evolved (such an evolution was outlined by Mr. Snodgrass himself recently in this journal) move toward a more conventional editorial tone. But they are usually as effective as the reflections of the author, moving "among the enduring and resigned / stuffed animals,"

> where, through a century's
> caprice, displacement and
> known treachery between
> its wars, they hear some old command
> and in their peaceable kingdoms freeze
> to this still scene,
>
> *Nature Morte.* . . .

It is with a kind of inevitability, too, that, after hints of the poet's concern with his own name, we find ourselves confronting the opening lines of "These Trees Stand . . ." which conclude with the poem's resonant refrain:

> These trees stand very tall under the heavens.
> While *they* stand, if I walk, all stars traverse
> This steep celestial gulf their branches chart.
> Though lovers stand at sixes and at sevens
> While civilizations come down with the curse,
> Snodgrass is walking through the universe.

The only thing really disappointing about *Heart's Needle* is its relative brevity. It is not a question of the appalling slimness of the oeuvre of W. D. Snodgrass, but, aside from the sequence of ten lyrics, there are perhaps six or seven faultless pieces among what will perhaps be the less permanent ones (the easy grace of "Returned to Frisco, 1946" has strong affinities with that of some of Mr. Snodgrass's English contemporaries but doesn't seem to be his characteristic manner). All one can hope is that, in the future, his talent will not suffer dilution from an expansion of quantity or scope. At present it is most impressive.

LOUIS SIMPSON

From "In the Absence of Yeats"

I wish I could find a poem in Mr. O'Gorman's book to admire, but, as five judges have admired it, I will pass without anxiety to W. D. Snodgrass's *Heart's Needle*. This poet, it seems, has been exposed to as much education as Mr. O'Gorman, but his poetry is not compounded of literary and classical references and striking attitudes. He is original; his ideas and language are never worked up to impress the reader; he carries his feelings as far as they can go and no further. I think I could recognize a poem by Mr. Snodgrass anywhere, after reading only a few lines. He has managed to discover himself, and, though the self is not in the grand manner, it is pervasive. He works at the other extreme from rhetoric; if anything, his tone is a little too relaxed. Now and then, from the light-moving stanzas there flashes a comment that startles by its appropriateness, and the phrasing at such moments is naturally perfect. Mr. Snodgrass recognizes the main task of the poet: to tell the truth and avoid falsifying. He has put on no fine masks to which his features must hereafter conform; he is free to develop. The occasional thinness of his poetry may be corrected by increasing the qualities he already has.

The ending of "The Marsh" shows this poet's originality. The marsh he trudges through is a weedy, stinking place (here, as in other descriptions, Mr. Snodgrass reminds me of the author of "Peter Grimes"):

> You look up; while you walk
> the sun bobs and is snarled
> in the enclosing weir
> of trees, in their dead stalks.
> Stick in the mud, old heart,
> what are you doing here?

Reprinted by permission from *The Hudson Review*, Vol. 12, No. 2 (Summer 1959). Copyright © 1959 by The Hudson Review, Inc. *The Night of the Hammer*, by Ned O'Gorman, *Oddments Inklings Omens Moments*, by Alastair Reid, *Plays and Poems 1948–58*, by Elder Olson, *Fighting Terms*, by Thom Gunn, and *The Sense of Movement*, by Thom Gunn, are the other books reviewed.

The trick, of course, is in the last two lines; no amount of anything but talent could have invented that irrelevance. Or let us choose a stanza from "April Inventory." The argument is that the speaker, a teacher in a girls' school, is visibly decaying, while they are not; moreover, as he is not a scholar, he is falling behind his colleagues in the profession. He concludes:

> Though trees turn bare and girls turn wives,
> We shall afford our costly seasons;
> There is a gentleness survives
> That will outspeak and has its reasons.
> There is a loveliness exists,
> Preserves us, not for specialists.

The point is made lightly, yet it is vital, and it could scarcely be made more happily.

The sequence titled "Heart's Needle," on which the book is centered, recounts some emotional and practical difficulties entailed by the breakup of a marriage. Divorce may be to this century what the frontier was to the last; Mr. Snodgrass's poem is a sort of American epic. Here it all is: the ordeal of "visiting," the divided child, the staring reproachful toys, the nostalgia, the sticky trip to the zoo, and the necessary, useless expense of guilt. It may not be all poetry, but it seems terribly real and as moral as anyone could wish. The speaker ends at the zoo in front of the cages:

> If I loved you, they said, I'd leave
>   and find my own affairs.
> Well, once again this April, we've
>   come around to the bears;
>
> punished and cared for, behind bars,
>   the coons on bread and water
> stretch thin black fingers after ours.
>   And you are still my daughter.

Mr. Snodgrass's strength is in the language that is both ordinary and poetic, which Wordsworth recommended; in a time of much pedantry *Heart's Needle* seems doubly original.

JUDSON JEROME

From "Poets of the Sixties"

Wisdom and art combine like man and wife in the best poems of
W. D. Snodgrass, whose first volume, *Heart's Needle,* is clearly a
candidate for a National Book Award or Pulitzer Prize—or per-
haps just immortality. It is the only book I have read this year in
which the hard ribs of sincerity show through. Snodgrass wants
us to know what he has learned—with terrible earnestness—and
he shapes his poems, almost confessions, with painful beauty.
Some are the bright, hard sort done so well by Shapiro, Jarrell,
Ciardi, and other "mid-century" poets—"Ten Days Leave," "Re-
turned to Frisco, 1946," "The Operation," "The Campus on the
Hill." In the last of these, however, we hear the truly individual
voice—the sudden breaking of all posture into a heart-rending
plaint for honesty—which is peculiarly Snodgrass's contribution:

> What shall I say to the young on such a morning?—
> Mind is the one salvation?—also grammar?—
> No; my little ones lean not toward revolt. They
> Are the Whites, the vaguely furiously driven, who resist
> Their souls with such passivity
> As would make Quakers swear. All day, dear Lord, all day
> They wear their godhead lightly.

In this poem, as in all his best work, an awareness of the large
world ("Aged in wrong, the empires are declining, / And China
gathers, soundlessly, like evidence.") bears upon the difficult
personal moment; as he puts it in "These Trees Stand . . .":

> While civilizations come down with the curse,
> Snodgrass is walking through the universe.

I keep hearing him ask, Who are we kidding? Beneath "the gold and silver in my teeth" I am (he might say) pathetically inadequate to endure the world or celebrate its beauties—but, damn it, if I wipe my glasses on my shirt and look as clearly as I can, something endures, values (like gentleness, loveliness) persist, there is more in me than I thought. So long as I don't delude myself. "April Inventory," an amusing rejuvenation from scholarly fatigue, summarizes most of this.

I want to comment and quote poem after poem but will have to settle for "A Cardinal," a pastoral narrative about the poet's encounter with a noisy bird. He tromps off to the woods from his "refurbished quonset / where they let me live," searching for a natural horizon, a place to write: "I carry a sacred silence / with me like my smell," but the civilized squeals and roars, the cadence of cadets marching, penetrate the woods:

> the ground bass of our credo—
>
> faith in free enterprise
> and our unselfish forces
> who chant to advertise
> the ancient pulse of violence.
> Meantime, I fuss with phrases
> or clamp my jaws in silence.

Then he is distracted by an "Old sleek satanic cardinal . . . natural Jesuit" singing a "Hosannah to Appetite": the poet tells the bird,

> sing for the flyboys, birdy,
> in praise of their profession;
> sing for the choirs of pretty
> slogans and catch-phrases
> that rule us by obsession;
> praise what it pays to praise:
>
> praise soap and garbage cans,
> join with the majority
> in praising man-eat-man,
> or praise the young who sell
> their minds to retire at forty.
> With honor.
> Go to hell!

But then the poet recognizes that he has been absurd—"as if I'd ask a bird / to mortify his body." He hears the bird singing from the next ravine and recognizes a truer song, an honest request for "my meals and loving":

> "The world's not done to me;
> it is what I do;
> whom I speak shall be;
> I music out my name
> and what I tell is who
> in all the world I am."

There is courage in being "selfish, unorthodox," in recognizing that it's "nobody else's world." Assert, assert, and music out your name.

"Heart's Needle" is the title of a sequence addressed to a daughter by an earlier marriage: built on the poignant moments of infrequent reunion, the memories, the awkward visits to zoos and museums, the torture of necessary discipline, the little-hand, big-hand love, so one-sided in understanding, so impossible to protect, so difficult to assert against the world. "I don't know the answers," "I cannot fight / or let you go."

> If I loved you, they said, I'd leave
> and find my own affairs.
> Well, once again this April, we've
> come around to the bears;
>
> punished and cared for, behind bars,
> the coons on bread and water
> stretch thin black fingers after ours.
> And you are still my daughter.

Snodgrass has a remarkable way of rolling natural details into a gentle symbolism, to restate, on the level of bears and bars and coon fingers, the underlying emotion of the actual relationship:

> I lift you on your swing and must
> shove you away,
> see you return again,
> drive you off again, then
>
> stand quiet till you come.

He never affronts us with ingenuity, invariably shares his wisdom simply, as, indeed, for a daughter who won't, at best, quite understand or be impressed.

A half-dozen poems (e.g., "Orpheus") don't work for me; sometimes he tries a kind of poem which demands, I think, someone else's voice—and gets tangled. (E.g., in "Papageno" an elaborate simile of caging birds gets twisted unaccountably in the last lines, the cager becoming the caged. I find it merely confusing.) But his own voice is clear, personal, and compelling when he discovers it, holds it. I hope it is an influential voice in the 1960s.

M. L. ROSENTHAL

From "Notes from the Future:
Two Poets"

"Snodgrass," I recently heard a distinguished older poet say, "is frankly bourgeois. The rest of us try to hide our bourgeois nature from ourselves, but he is plainly and openly what he is." I suppose his calling Snodgrass bourgeois had something to do with this young writer's acceptance of simple, normal marital and domestic relationships as possible, and desirable, in themselves. In this sense he is uncritically "bourgeois"; he apparently has no bohemian suspicion that a good marriage in which husband, wife, and children are both affectionate and responsible to one another is necessarily death to the free, creative life.

Not that these are happy poems, as the pieces in John Ciardi's *I Marry You* are. In point of fact the long title sequence presents the poet in a state of deep soul-sickness because of his divorce and because of the dangers that a new marriage presents to his relationship with his baby daughter. Snodgrass, though much less violent, is a confessional poet like Robert Lowell, and he is writing about a stubborn if almost abject father-love hanging onto its object with animal persistence. The quietly satisfying bourgeois family is for him an ideal as genuine peace is an ideal for a world ravaged by actual and by cold war. The figure is one on which he depends repeatedly:

> Child of my winter, born
> When the new fallen soldiers froze
> In Asia's steep ravines and fouled the snows,
> When I was torn
>
> By love I could not still,
> By fear that silenced my cramped mind

Nation, 24 October 1959. Reprinted by permission of the author. Copyright © 1959 by M. L. Rosenthal. The other poet is Robert Duncan. Mr. Rosenthal reviews two books by Duncan, *Selected Poems* and *Letters*.

> To that cold war where, lost, I could not find
> My peace in my will . . .

The ten-part sequence takes us from the child's birth to the divorce, the second marriage, and the muted triumph that a second winter of separation should have been survived—"and you are still my daughter." Snodgrass has built a moving poem out of something we treat far too casually: early divorce, in which it is the love between children and their parents that receives the deepest wounds. The undramatic misery of the troubled father anxious to create common memories—pushing his child on a playground swing, learning to make omelettes and pancakes so he can feed her at home when she visits him, and so on—has great authority. Snodgrass gains it through a gift of understatement that is yet saturated with feeling:

> The window's turning white.
> The world moves like a diseased heart
> packed with ice and snow.
> Three months now we have been apart
> less than a mile. I cannot fight
> or let you go.

Perhaps another "bourgeois" aspect of this poet's work lies in the kind of psychological problems he admits to having generally. In "April Inventory" he recites some of the lessons he has learned—that is, has *had* to learn—over the past year:

> I taught myself to name my name,
> To bark back, loosen love and crying;
> To ease my woman so she came,
> To ease an old man who was dying.
> I have learned how often I
> Can win, can love, but choose to die.

Earlier in this same poem he mentions "my analyst," and perhaps that phrase too is peculiar to one kind of bourgeois life adjustment. But I think the older poet's real objection (I'm somehow sure it was really an objection, though it has a certain admiration in it too) was the absence of hatred in the poems of *Heart's Needle*. Snodgrass pays token service to the usual creed of sophisticated aversion to Philistinism and commercialism, sounding something like a paler Cummings. But he accepts, always. The explosive anger of Lowell is nowhere to be found, and the truly striking notes are of a winning sensitivity and candor, and an ability to endure the rigors of experience with pathetic courage and a nostalgia paid in advance. These observations are not meant as moral judgments, but as a definition of the kind of energy his poems possess. I should add that he has a disciplined skill that is pure delight in the delicately modulated "The Operation," a poem detailing with the most vivid impressionism the successive physical sensations and shifts of awareness before and after surgery, and in the restrained sexuality of "Winter Bouquet"—two examples among several outstanding pieces. He is able to use description and imagery so suggestively that he can postpone explicit statement of feeling, when it is needed at all, to brief, strategic moments, usually at the very end of a poem. He uses this ability so tactfully in the "Heart's Needle" sequence that he sustains, without faltering, a theme that otherwise, over so long a haul, must have bogged him down in sentimentality. The poem remains true to its germinating feeling of quiet suffering and to its author's special talents.

From "Three Poets"

It isn't surprising that Miss Deutsch's book, an offering of new poems and selected old ones, contains some failures, but it contains some successes too, notable specimens that will bring pleasure to any reader of poetry. The case of W. D. Snodgrass is rather different. Miss Deutsch is well known to us; Snodgrass is a newcomer whose work we are seeing for the first time. Moreover, although Snodgrass's talent for descriptive writing is clearly the equal of Miss Deutsch's or anyone else's, his poems reach beyond and are chiefly lyrical and sophisticated in tone, meditative and moral in import. In short, he is an academic poet in the School of Ransom, but let me make haste to dispel the stigma of typicality by saying that, unlike the dozens of other poets of his generation to whom this identification can quite justly be applied, Snodgrass offers us, first, a genuine subject imbued with genuine feeling and, second, a voice that is, at least much of the time, personal and distinct. One naturally hesitates to risk judging a poet who makes such a slim showing—this book, his first, contains only twenty poems, although the one from which the volume takes its title, *Heart's Needle,* is really a sequence of ten individual lyrics—but nevertheless I think it is only fair to say that Snodgrass seems to me by far the best poet to have appeared so far in this decade and probably one of the best of any age now practicing in America. The finest poems of his twenty are too long to be reprinted in a review, but a couple of shorter examples will do nicely:

WINTER BOUQUET

Her hands established, last time she left my room,
this dark arrangement for a winter bouquet:
collected bittersweet, brittle stemmed Scotch broom,

From *Poetry* 95, no. 2 (November 1959): 118–21. Reprinted with permission of the editor of *Poetry*. Copyright © 1959 by The Modern Poetry Association. The other two poets are Babette Deutsch and Mary Phelps. Mr. Carruth reviews Deutsch's *Coming of Age: New and Selected Poems* and Phelps's *A Bed of Strawberries.*

perennial straw-flowers, grasses gone to seed,
lastly, the dry vaginal pods of milkweed.
These relics stay here for her when she's away.

Bulging like a coin purse fallen on the ground
of damp woods, overgrained with moss, mould and frost,
their husks are horned like the Venus'-combs I found
on Garipan. Those war years, many a wife
wandered the fields after such pods to fill life
preservers so another man might not be lost.

Now she's home. Today I lifted them, like charms
in the March sunshine to part the pods and blow
white bursts of quilly weedseed for the wide arms
and eyes of the children squealing where they drift
across the neighbors' cropped lawns like an airlift
of satyrs or a conservative, warm snow.

RIDDLE

So small it is, there must be at least two
Helping each other see it. If each stands
Close enough he may come to be foureyed
And make their sight bifocal, looking through
Each other. If they act as a microscope
Of mounted powers it shall be magnified
Like an airy globe or beach ball that expands
Between them so vast they could never hope
To grasp it without all four of their hands
        Opened wide.

It lengthens, outstretched like a playing field
Where they stand as the two opposing goals
That can't be reached. Or it's a field of force,
Ethereal continuum, whereby they wield
Influence through matter, time and space
(Of all which it's the grave and radiant source),
Yet where attraction drives out their like souls
Across the expansive universe they've built as the poles
That only in circumference embrace
        And by divorce.

You have the damnedest friends and seem to think
You have some right to think. You have kept keen
Our arguments and souls so we have grown

Closely together where most people shrink.
You sleep tonight with threatening relations
In El Dorado; I am here alone
To tell you, *"Vive la difference!"* We have seen
The energetic first stuff of creation
So that today, if there's a world between
      Us, it's our own.

With these should be placed "The Operation," "A Cardinal," "The Campus on the Hill," and "April Inventory" at least; they are all superb poems.

The long poem, "Heart's Needle," has for its theme the relationship between a father and his small daughter whom he has lost in a divorce. Of it Robert Lowell says on the dust jacket: ". . . it's the best parts of the sequence entitled "Heart's Needle" that I want to go all out for. They are . . . a break-through for modern poetry. Their harrowing pathos will seem as permanent a hundred years from now as it does now." Yes, these poems will tear your heart, anyway mine. And they are brilliantly written. Yet there is something wrong with this pathos, and we remember that the Greeks reserved pathos for their heroes, while even Mr. Ransom's little girls, John Whiteside's daughter and Janet, are heroic figures inverted: they were legendary the moment they were created. But the little girl in the poems of Snodgrass is so patently, so painfully, the daughter of the man himself, the poems contain references so clearly meaningless to anyone but the people who occur in them, that in my mind the question raises itself whether or not the poems should ever have been published at all. This is not simply a matter of propriety, but of the warping sentimentality that is engendered in the recording of experience so little transmuted from private specificity. This transmuting, which is, of course, the really central problem, operationally considered, of postromantic poetry, is a process upon which I am no better qualified than anyone else to give advice; but I will say, if I may do so very humbly and without presumption, that I think it is something for the poet to think about as he goes on.

Otherwise, there is not much to add except bravo! Here and there obscurities are detectable at the merely verbal level, but very likely these will disappear as Snodgrass works, on one hand, more securely into his personal idiom and, on the other, more broadly out of his personal susceptibility. Mainly one hopes that he will write more poems, lots of them, without paying any more than manageable heed to the consciences of reviewers.

W. W. ROBSON

From "True Voice of Feeling"

Some very good American poetry is being written nowadays, even if no living American poet is as great as Whitman, and part of the pleasure an English reader gets from a poet like Mr. Robert Lowell comes from the feeling that American English is not, after all, a different language. So that when a new American poet appears enthusiastically sponsored by Mr. Lowell English readers of poetry should be all attention. And Mr. Snodgrass's work should not disappoint them.

He is indeed a discovery. It is true that at a first reading he seems disturbingly easy to place. Much of what he has published in *Heart's Needle* is confessional poetry, and the character he confesses to—the middle-aged teacher at an American girls' college, beginning to feel his age when he has to "nudge himself to stare" at the "sleek expensive girls" who seem to get younger every year—is rather like the character we have met over here in Mr. Philip Larkin's work or, without the academic slant, in Mr. Betjeman's. There is a similar self-deprecating, consciously "minor" pose, a similar use of protective irony, a similar wryness, to which Mr. Snodgrass adds a certain winsome quality that seems to derive from Robert Frost:

> It should be recognized
> I have not come sneaking
> and look for no surprises.
> Lives are saved this way.
> Each trade has its way of speaking,
> each bird its name to say.

There is the obvious debt to William Empson which is so common in this kind of poetry:

The Observer, 12 March 1961. Copyright © 1961 by *The Observer*, London. Reprinted by permission. One other book is reviewed here—*Poems*, by A. D. Hope.

She can't make up your mind. Soon as you know it,
Your firmament grows touchable and firm.

What is more disquieting is that all this is very self-conscious; the
poetry itself seems to be inviting this kind of placing, anticipat-
ing the sympathetic or patronizing reviewer with his gratified
sense of the familiar.

But in the best of the poems, in things like "April Inventory"
and, above all, in the sequence which gives the book its title, we
are aware of a truer and steadier voice of feeling, of a greater
poetic maturity. Mr. Lowell was right to be enthusiastic, though
some of what he says about the poems is rather odd; I see no
"shrill authoritative eloquence" in the poems we are given
here—Mr. Snodgrass's voice, though distinctive, is quiet and
"tremendous accomplishments" seems rather strong even for
good, accurate, and truthful poems like "The Operation," to
which Mr. Lowell refers.

But in stressing Mr. Snodgrass's "content"—that is, not his
contentedness but what the poetry contains—Mr. Lowell is surely
right. There is a human value in the "Heart's Needle" sequence
that makes most of the current output look like literary flaunting.
These poems, with their obviously confessional quality, do some-
thing delicate and difficult—their background is a painful divorce
and the experience of being mother-and-father to his young
child. The risk of what in our cruel and nervous age is called
sentimentality is boldly met here, and the meeting of it is what
gives the poetry its characteristic tone, in its quiet evocation of
hope and tenderness in a grown man for whom recent pain and
suffering are still alive. Perhaps a short quotation will suggest this
quality:

Outside the thick snow swarms
Into my prints

And swirls out by warehouses, sealed,
Dark cowbarns, huddled, still,
Beyond to the blank field,
The fox's hill

Where he backtracks and sees the paw,
Gnawed off, he cannot feel;
Conceded to the jaw
Of toothed, blue steel.

DONALD DAVIE

From "Australians and Others"

I am probably wrong about W. D. Snodgrass. All my friends
think him a very good thing, but I can't get on with him at all.
Just as I'm getting him into focus as a poet (and a very accom-
plished one), there he is at my elbow, smiling his warm, bril-
liant, sad, understanding smile, pleading, "Judge me not as poet
but as person. Am I or am I not the nicest, kindest, dearest
fellow you ever met? Wasn't I the most devoted of Daddies, the
most understanding of teachers?" And, of course, he's confident
of my answer; though, in fact, if the much anthologized "April
Inventory" is anything to go by (and it's singled out by Lowell in
an exceptionally fulsome blurb), I'm puzzled and a little shocked
at what goes on in Snodgrass's classroom, where he can't remem-
ber dates but on the other hand

> . . . showed one child the colors of
> A luna moth and how to love.

No, confound it, it's my friends who are wrong: self-pity, self-
esteem, all sorts of self-regard, are fatal to poetry—and most of
the poems in *Heart's Needle* are self-regarding. A poem is not the
public parade of a private emotion; however smoothly executed,
such paradings belong elsewhere than in the blessedly imper-
sonal art of poetry.

The Spectator (London), 24 March 1961, 416. Copyright © 1961 by *The Spectator*.
Reprinted by permission. The other books reviewed by Mr. Davie are *Poems* by
A. D. Hope and *Once Bitten, Twice Bitten,* by Peter Porter. Mr. Davie also
reviews a recording: *William Empson Reading Selected Poems.*

GILBERT SORRENTINO

Review of *Life Studies*, by Robert Lowell, and *Heart's Needle*, by W. D. Snodgrass

Reading these books, I was reminded of the old academic arguments I used to have when I was a younger man, arguments which can be phrased something like: "If a poem is written in an outworn form, if the content takes shape in a ready-made receptacle—and if that poem be perfectly executed—is it valid for the poet to present it as 'a work of art'?" A number of years and poems have got in between that old phraseology and the present, and I don't remember when it was that I forgot it or, at any rate, no longer thought about it: that half-arrogant, half-sentimental old argument re: aesthetics that we got stoned over, shouted ourselves hoarse over, and thought that we were pretty damned bright, serious. Not that I want to lay the "maturity" business on you; what I drive upon is that at some time between then and now this argument ceased to have meaning, for me. It was no longer pertinent. It is the kind of argument that people who are not involved in writing revel in. Not pertinent, but you can sound like someone out of *Point Counter Point*.

Lowell and Snodgrass. I imagine them having this argument with themselves as they wrote these poems. The books are sad and hopeful at the same time, the hope lying in the fact that they, for sure, have ended the deluge of naive sophistication, or sophisticated naïveté given its momentum by Auden. After the Snodgrass book no more can be done along this line. Praise God. I thought at one time that Empson had taken the old horse to the edge of the pasture, but Snodgrass has broken down the final fence and walked out into the woods beyond. Lowell, well, that is something else again. The man with the perfect ear for closed verse has opened his line and written—prose. Too bad.

Yugen 7 (1961). Copyright © 1961 by Gilbert Sorrentino. Reprinted by permission. As Mr. Sorrentino interweaves his reviews of *Life Studies* and *Heart's Needle,* I have included his treatment of both Lowell and Snodgrass.

        his illegal home-made claret
        was as sugary as grape jelly
        in a tumbler capped with paraffin.

This Sandburgian bathos: from the man who wrote *Lord Weary's Castle*. It's as if Lowell had suddenly looked around him and saw where on earth he stood, opened the end of his line—and fell off into the cold spaces surrounding. Because to kick out the iambic fence that safely closes the line in, one should have compass without: Pound and Williams, at the very least. What Lowell gives us here is free verse. But good, in that Lowell has done it, writes lines as hopeless as the above and lets it go through. Why not? Everybody gets started sometime. Olson impinging on Lowell and that morocco-covered world of his: Who can tell what would occur?

Snodgrass, on the other hand: the left hand. The stuff is the epitome of the "I" divorced from all things, the cute "public" poetry of an American MacNiece, for all the self-humbling attitude, etc., etc., snobbism of the most pathetic sort, a kind of pride in the deadly middle class out of which all these attitudes come. They have certainly found their poet, all the trappings there, the midwestern chair and pencil and paper, the half-bitter complaints that he is a poet and not a businessman, as if that still had pertinence today. That someone can mock his own vocation because of the "neighbors," etc., etc. I AM A POET, the works, the whole compulsive attitude of writing poems against the group that will fold *Heart's Needle* to its bosom. The whole damn tone is wrong, wrong, self-conscious attitudinizing via Auden of "September 1, 1939": "I am the only one who can feel the world giving way beneath my feet, while you drink and carouse, with nary a thought for the morrow, I (THE POET) can see how pathetic we all are." This is the tone of the book, expressed perfectly in "Home Town":

                I go out like a ghost,
                nights, to walk the streets
                I walked fifteen years younger—
                seeking my old defeats,
                devoured by the old hunger . . .

Lazy and banal. The whole book, technically perfect in that classroom sense, like you can give the poems marks, A, B plus, C minus, etc., the whole book like this, and none of it mattering

in the least. They are to *Sour Grapes* and *Cantos* I–XXX, and all
the work between, what Abbott and Costello are to the Marx
Bros. of *Duck Soup, A Night at the Opera:* a vague gesture in the
general direction of that excellence, but only vague. Like Snod-
grass *did* hear of WCW [William Carlos Williams]. And is his
parodist, certainly, wife, child, garden, and the rest, but with
what a difference. WHAT a difference. He's taken it out as far as it
can get without its becoming ludicrous, and I'm not even sure of
that,

Observe the cautious toadstools

there have been worse lines written, I guess.

So. What have we got? We have a man who has broken out of
what he knows how to do into a conception of verse which
Eberhart did better twenty years ago. And another, much youn-
ger man, writing carefully balanced caricatures of Auden and
Spender and MacNiece, picking up the one thing that Williams
does, which no one but Williams can use. The private man in his
backyard, etc. We get into Delmore Schwartz a little, see:

Up the reputable walks of old established trees
They stalk, children of the *nouveaux riches;* chimes
Of the tall Clock Tower drench their heads in blessing . . .

God! That corny kind of bitter pose: "reputable" walks, "estab-
lished" trees, etc. Who cares, except those who are convinced
that these things are unique to a poet. They are old, old, any
rotten movie tells you more about this area than Snodgrass. I'd
like to care, but I'm afraid that this kind of stance is something
that left me with my leaving college, or thereabouts.

What is worst is that both of these men indicate no attempt to
get hold of the validities of American poetry, as defined by
Pound, Williams, Olson, and the others. Hart Crane could have
told them all that they are still bitter about, and even Eliot was
more American than they are. They stand in the middle class;
they are concerned with the car in the driveway; they are wild
over the fact that their parents were not "accepted" or slightly
futile. Out of it they make what is at best a footnote to Scott
Fitzgerald and the early O'Hara.

Well, let's hope that Lowell will make it; he's still young. And
let's hope that Snodgrass will get to the point, in the next ten
years, at which Lowell now stands. It's all really a hell of a waste.

PART TWO   *Reviews and One Notice,*
            1962–71: After
            Experience *and* Remains

GEORGE MONTEIRO

Snodgrass Peoples His Universe

In *New Poets of England and America: Second Selection* (first print-ing June 1962),[1] its editors Donald Hall and Robert Pack seem either to have been the victims of a fairly obvious but harmless hoax or, more reasonably, to have abetted that of another. The editors promise sixty-two poets and deliver sixty-two names, but only sixty-one individuals.

Among those American poets represented is W. D. Snodgrass as the author of *Heart's Needle* (1959) and Snodgrass as the pseud-onymous S. S. Gardons, a simple anagram. The consequence is that S. S. Gardons is given as the author of two poems, "The Mother" and "To a Child," while Snodgrass appears, one hun-dred and thirty-eight pages later, with three poems, "A Flat One," "Mementos, i," and "Mementos, ii."

One could complain about this double appearance simply on the basis of the usurpation of limited space in such a venture as this, especially if one were a poet (which I am not) under forty (which I am). None of this is particularly striking, but the matter becomes a bit suspect when we notice that not only are we not told that Snodgrass and S. S. Gardons are one, nor that the poem "The Mother," published here as the work of Gardons, appeared originally in the *Hudson Review* under the name of Snodgrass,[2] but that the editors of *New Poets* have in fact supplied separate biographical notes for Snodgrass and Gardons.

W. D. Snodgrass: born in Wilkinsburg, Pennsylvania, 1926. He has published a book of poems, *Heart's Needle,* and his poems have appeared in a number of magazines. He teaches at Wayne State University. (383)

S. S. Gardons: born in Red Creek, Texas, 1929. Works as a gas station attendant in Fort Worth. He has published in *Hudson Review.* (378)

Papers of the Bibliographical Society of America 56, no. 4 (1962). Copyright © 1962 by George Monteiro. Reprinted by permission.

With these quite different sets of biographical details, compare the less disingenuous contributor's note in *Hudson Review* a few years ago on the occasion of the publication of some of Gardons's other poetry: "S. S. Gardons is the pseudonym of a former Hudson Review Fellow in Poetry who now teaches at Wayne State University."[3]

More interesting, though, is the possibility opened up by the fact that, while Snodgrass's birthdate is given as 1926, Gardons's is given as 1929. The editors of *New Poets* write in their preface: "Poets included in the earlier volume who are now over forty have been omitted. . . . We have retained the age limit in order to continue an emphasis on the new and relatively unknown poets" (15). For the purposes of any future *Selection* of poetry by the younger American poets and given the continuation of this policy of selection, Gardons's youth by three years may come in handy for the poems of Snodgrass. Separate and equal appearance in the *New Poets of England and America: Second Selection* has already helped to launch S. S. Gardons.

NOTES

1. (Cleveland and New York: Meridian Books, World Publishing Company, 1962.)

2. *Hudson Review* 11 (Autumn 1958): 368–69. In the version that appears in *New Poets* Snodgrass, besides making a number of stylistic changes, primarily in diction and punctuation, omits the explanatory note "from the Russian of Kozma Petrovich Prutkov." But the other poem "To a Child," again with some changes, did appear originally under the imprint of S. S. Gardons (*Hudson Review* 13 [Winter 1960–61]: 512–14).

3. *Hudson Review* 12 (Winter 1959–60): 592.

DENIS DONOGHUE

From "That Old Eloquence"

Mr. Snodgrass has already consoled us [in writing poetry "certified by the propriety of the voice"], notably in the famous title sequence of *Heart's Needle* (1959). It is usual to say that those were divorce poems as other poems are love poems or death poems. But it is more relevant to say that they were Orphic poems. Near the beginning of *Heart's Needle* Mr. Snodgrass gave this idiom in the poem "Orpheus": "All ruin I could sound was there." Again: "And I went on / Rich in the loss of all I sing / To the threshold of waking light. . . ." The next poem, "Papageno," ends: "In that deft cage, he might sing true." This is the Orphic role, turning grief into song. In a longer poem, "A Cardinal," the bird is Orphic, commanding the universe:

> "The world's not done to me;
> it is what I do;
> whom I speak shall be . . ."

So the poet walked through the universe, sorrowing, singing, commanding trees and rocks: "we need the landscape to repeat us."

After Experience, a remarkable book, is true to this idiom, to the sense of a poetic fate which is at the same time a poetic vocation. In "What We Said" the landscape repeats every human grief. The leaves are inflamed, "sick as words": a hole in the ground closes up "like a wound." In "Partial Eclipse," the eclipse seems to be total because of light mists and low clouds; on earth the lover knows that his eclipse is indeed total: "Next morning you had gone." In "Autumn Scene" "the elms repeat some shocking / News of what's to come." So the new poems recite "old affections," officially denied but deviously retained in the pain of

From the *New York Review of Books,* 25 April 1968. Reprinted with permission from the *New York Review of Books.* Copyright © 1968 Nyrev, Inc. Two other books are reviewed here: *Not This Pig,* by Philip Levine, and *A-12,* by Louis Zukofsky.

the denial, like an old photograph in the poem "Mementos." The book is full of care for things by which life is preserved, if it is preserved; as two lovers try to send a kite aloft, "to keep in touch with the thing." And many poems imply a life long ago, far away, which man and wife lived and shared. Now the objects of that life are gone, but mortally active, too, as reminders, mementos.

The Orphic poet turns grief into song by turning life into ritual, then into play, as a father plays with his lost child. Mr. Snodgrass tells himself, as if to justify the cost, that something like this has been going on, in art and thought, for a century: the destruction of matter for the energy released by the destruction. In the new book he invokes this pattern to celebrate Matisse's painting, "The Red Studio," where everything, fractured, is transformed to energy, "crude, definitive and gay." Elsewhere Mr. Snodgrass has spoken of Freud, breaking the solid forms of personality to release energy otherwise constrained. In a poem on Monet's "Les Nymphéas" the painter is determined to feel nothing on public authority but everything on his own authority, his will, at his own risk, with his own care:

> These things have taken me as the mouth an orange—
> That acrid sweet juice entering every cell;
> And I am shared out. I become these things:
> These lilies, if these things are water lilies
> Which are dancers growing dim across no floor;

Mr. Snodgrass's new poems may be received in this setting, attempts to read the fracture of his personal life as an act of destruction, a necessary act if new energy is to be released. It may be remarked at once that none of the resultant poems is as demanding, as harrowing, as the divorce sequence in *Heart's Needle,* but to such memorable poems as "Home Town," "The Operation," "The Campus on the Hill," and "April Inventory" the new book adds several poems, especially "Autumn Scene," "The Platform Man," "Vampire Aubade," "Monet: 'Les Nymphéas'," and "Regraduating the Lute."

It could be argued, incidentally, that in *After Experience* the center of gravity has shifted from the confessional poems to a group of translations, which come at the end. Three of these poems seem to me to bear a particular weight of feeling. The first is Gerard de Nerval's "El Desdichado," especially significant because it may be taken to resume all the occasions of grief, including those represented in *Heart's Needle:*

> Je suis le Ténébreux,—le Veuf,—l'Inconsolé,
> Le Prince d'Aquitaine à la Teur abolie:
> Ma seule Etoile est morte,—et mon luth constellé
> Porte le Soleil noir de la Mélancolie.

Then "Suis-je Amour ou Phoebus?" Nerval asks. The next line acknowledges the perpetuity of absent love as if to concentrate in one sentence the longing of Aurelia and Sylvie: "Mon front est rouge encor du baiser de la Reine"; in Mr. Snodgrass's lovely cadence, "On my forehead, still, the queen's kiss holds its fire." The poem ends with an Orphic assertion:

> Et j'ai deux fois vainqueur traversé l'Achéron
>
> Modulant tour à tour sur la lyre d'Orphée
> Les soupirs de la Sainte et les cris de la Fée . . .

—in Mr. Snodgrass's version:

> I have crossed over Acheron, triumphant, twice.
> And modulated, one by one, on Orpheus' lyre
> Sighs of the saints and the damned spirits' cries.

Still everything speaks of loss. In "Regraduating the Lute" one face speaks of another:

> Keeping the strings
> Tuned and under tension, we gradually
> Pare away, while playing constantly,
> All excess from behind the tempered face.
> The way a long grief hollows the cheeks away.

The second crucial poem, I would say, is Nerval's "Vers Dores," with its assertion of spirit in matter, voice in body. Strangely, Mr. Snodgrass does not give the Pythagorean epigraph, "Eh quoi! tout est sensible!" perhaps because he meets it again in the body of the poem itself: "Tout est sensible;—Et tout sur ton être est puissant!" The poem is resolutely Orphic, admonishing man to attend the universe and its voice: "A la matière même un verbe est attaché. . . ." If this feeling is not the source of

Mr. Snodgrass's new poems, it is their attendant spirit, moving him toward play, natural piety, and love—Mr. Zukofsky's "pleasure that dwells on its cause." Resistance to the Orphic invitation is given in "A Friend" and other poems, where the feeling is corrosive; of their poet it is permissible to say, as Mr. Snodgrass writes of someone else in "A Character": "He thinks the world is his scab and picks at it." But this resistance is occasional.

Many of the recent poems try to speak the *verbe* of Nature by listening to it and trusting it to sound in the human words. Nerval says of that voice, giving the motto, "Ne la fais pas servir à quelque usage impie"; and to enforce the care, "Souvent dans l'être obscur habite un Dieu caché." So the poet takes the world into his councils, the world "où la vie éclate en toute chose": anything but self and its doomed resentment:

> Respecte dans la bête un esprit agissant . . .
> Chaque fleur est une âme à la Nature éclose;

—as Mr. Snodgrass translates:

> Revere that restless spirit stirring in the beasts;
> That soul, opening to Nature, which is each flower.

The connection between these two poems, in Mr. Snodgrass's context, is that phase of the story in which Orpheus, dismembered, passes into all natural things, which then become alive and eloquent. *Heart's Needle* stopped with dismemberment: *After Experience* has similar moments, but it goes beyond them into the natural world, listening to the voice, miming the word. Nature is not asked to be a function of self. The story is wonderfully complicated by the fact that Mr. Snodgrass also translates several of Rilke's *Sonnets to Orpheus,* including those first poems in the sequence which tell of "new origins, beckonings, and change": "Doch selbst in der Verschweigung / ging neuer Anfang, Wink und Wandlung vor." But a third poem, here translated, points even more resolutely to change. In Rilke's "Archaic Torso of Apollo" the stone glistens, shining like a star. The confrontation of torso and the beholder's eye is so demanding that every part of the stone engages in the encounter: "denn da ist keine Stelle, / die dich nicht sieht." The last words of the poem are extraordinary: "Du musst dein Leben ändern," as if to demand that the beholder, to be worthy of the experience, must become, like the mutilated torso against all the evidence, whole, complete, shining. "What you look hard at seems to look hard at you," Hopkins noted. Mr. Snodgrass's new poems accept the challenge of that look; this is their significance. The evidence is a new note in these poems. The rhetorical finesse of "Monet: 'Les Nymphéas'," for instance, is a new achievement in Mr. Snodgrass's style, a sostenuto language which, taking *Heart's Needle* for granted, goes beyond it. To mark the direction the feeling takes, it is enough to point to the translated *Sonnets to Orpheus* (1, 9, and 10) where the Orphic spirit comes back from the dead and the poet invokes "the dual kingdom" as the source of calmest speech; welcoming from death, as Mr. Snodgrass translates the phrases, "the once more opening mouths / That knew already what the silence meant." This is a classic moment in the new book. Indeed, it is already clear that the translations at the end of *After Experience* represent a new movement of feeling toward "inclusiveness," to use Mr. Zukofsky's word and some of his meaning. The characteristic danger of *Heart's Needle* was sentimentality, feeling in excess of its occasion, however poignant the occasion. But the new translations have the effect of calming the style, hiding the self, silently, among its materials. The old eloquence persists, but it is richer now because it listens to other voices and knows something of what silence means.

JUDSON JEROME

From "Uncommitted Voices"

With a sigh we leave the brawling playground for the cool library as we turn to the more respectable poetic offerings of the season. I imagine W. D. Snodgrass is as reluctant as I am to make the change. His first book, *Heart's Needle* (Pulitzer Prize, 1960), told us about his abandonment of the Ph.D. route when he realized that in a year he had not "read one book about / A book." And his new volume, *After Experience,* contains a powerful indictment of academia, "The Examination." But something about the book suggests a dissertation. Nearly half of it consists of translations (Hugo, Nerval, Rimbaud, Bonnefoy, Govoni, Mörike, Eichendorff, Rilke) and poems about painters (Matisse, Vuillard, Manet, Monet, Van Gogh). The poetry is elegant, as we expect from Snodgrass, but held at arm's length. In the 1950s and 1960s we have had a lot of such art about art. Perhaps with these academic credentials out of the way Snodgrass can return his attention to life.

That title, though—*After Experience*—is not reassuring. We have awaited this second volume eagerly for several years because the first one so clearly established Snodgrass as the one poet younger than Lowell who might lead the way between the Scylla of precious formality and the Charybdis of pure expression that have threatened poetry in the last decade. In *Heart's Needle* he established an easy, familiar tone, a poignancy, an excruciating honesty, a tight formal control, and an almost cocky insistence on personal identity. I suppose we should be grateful to get more of the same in *After Experience,* but it seems curiously weary and dated in 1968:

> Next year we'll hardly know you;
> Still, all the blame endures.

Saturday Review, 1 June 1968. Reprinted by permission. The other books reviewed are as follows: *The Pearl Is a Hardened Sinner: Notes from Kindegarten,* by Stanley Kiesel, *Not This Pig,* by Philip Levine, *So Long at the Fair,* by Miller Williams, *Body Rags,* by Galway Kinnell, *Touch,* by Thom Gunn, and *Coming Close and Other Poems,* by Helen Chasin.

This year you will live at our expense;
We have a life at yours,

Now I can earn a living
By turning out elegant strophes.
Your six-year teeth lie on my desk
Like a soldier's trophies.

Ah, yes—the divorce, the painfully tender father-daughter relationship, the neat stanzas, the sadly ironic juxtapositions, the faint self-satire—we have them all again. But have they become merely manner? Is there a response to the immediate world? Is experience really all over?

There are some new areas of experience opened up here—for example, adultery. A sequence of bold poems explores the pain of sitting before the "boob-tube" with the lady and her husband (that "squat toad"), of recognizing the ephemeral and futile nature of clandestine love, of beholding a mistress as she is reabsorbed into her own life:

So he has taken you, as trolls
    Snatch back their lovely own;
As if, with the twilight failing,
    Some sluggish majesty
Rose from the sour lagoon to snag you,
    Rapt as a memory, behind
The green, grained mirror. Silence;
    The unblinking pond goes blind.

Again and again I gasp, as I do here, at the sheer splendor of the writing: the accuracy, the clarity, the perfect symbols for loss, bitterness, and indifference. I relish, too, the realism: lovers leaving a motel are careful not to take the matches or leave identifying objects, but they put aspirin in the vase of lilacs they have gathered so that the life of the flowers, at least, may continue briefly.

Accuracy, clarity, realism—these are qualities of classicism, as is impersonality. In this book, as opposed to his first, the poet increasingly removes himself from the scene, seeking the symbolic, external experience that can stand for universal truth. A village after a flash flood is described with Swiftian objectivity and irony: disaster gave individuals significance and neighbors a reason for talking to one another. A lobster in a restaurant win-

dow emerges momentarily "From the deep chill of his sleep //
As if, in a glacial thaw, / Some ancient thing might wake . . ."—
a powerful symbol of primordial life dredged from the dark
depths.

Snodgrass is undoubtedly one of the handful of best poets
today, and his second book is solid, expert, and occasionally
moving. But I cannot testify that it renewed the excitement I felt
on first reading *Heart's Needle;* there are too many formulas,
exhausted veins, and ironies gone flat.

STANLEY MOSS

To the Dispossessed

After Experience, continuing W. D. Snodgrass's first book, *Heart's Needle,* is a work of musical splendor. Snodgrass is a tragic poet who has fashioned some kind of beast, alive and festered, not just a book. He seems most himself when he is satanic. No God hunter, he does not hope to call God out by reverse conjuring or by cursing him. But in half a dozen poems he upsets, and means to, with cruelty after cruelty, with princely evil he attacks himself, the reader, the world, eliminating everything but a new "outlawed Good."

> And you, whiner, who wastes your time
> Dawdling over the remorseless earth,
> What evil, what unspeakable crime
> Have you made your life worth?

If the passage reminds us of Baudelaire and Rimbaud's demanding "a crime quick" and Dostoevsky's crime "to provoke God to declare himself," it is because Snodgrass continues that work.

T. S. Eliot observed that Baudelaire's satanism, insofar as it was not an affectation, was an attempt to enter Christianity "by the back door." Inevitably, a poem entitled "The Men's Room in the College Chapel" is the only one in *After Experience* which is given a religious setting. It is a helpful but minor piece, a slip of the tongue beside some of the important poems.

Although he intends a secular and worldly poetry, Snodgrass has driven into his temple characters usually outcast and unforgiven. He has found place for emotions felt but previously left without words and out of consciousness. He has identified himself with exquisite suffering and guilt and with all those who barely manage to exist on the edge of life. (He even plays a grotesque love scene with Eichmann.) Read in this light, he is a

New Republic, 15 June 1968. Copyright © 1968 by the *New Republic.* Reprinted by permission.

religious poet. But, like the apple in the garden, some of Snod-grass's initiations leave us with a bad taste in the mouth.

"The Platform Man," a poem concerned with a legless man on a dolly in front of a five-and-ten-cent store, straddles the book. It is the one poem in *After Experience* in which the world's tragedy and Snodgrass's own are made one. After examining the crippled man—

> His stare level with my
> Stare, when I was a child.

—the poet walls in the cripple with those who speak from other platforms and lecterns offering their "spectacular handicaps." Snodgrass finishes the great poem with a pun lodged soundly in a passage hard as marble:

> I'd travel light: take nothing
> Free and give no quarter.
> The curse is far from done
> When they've taken your daughter;
> They can take your son.

Snodgrass's justly celebrated poem, "The Operation," from his first book, has already, for better or worse, established a genre. "The Flat One," which I saw in an earlier version in the old *New World Writing,* introduced the long-dying patient; here are all the clamps, gadgets, and emotions with which we hold onto him and push him away.

In an essay on *Crime and Punishment* published about the time he began work on this poem, Snodgrass pointed out that "to Dosto-evsky those characters who are sick and handicapped . . . seem to be specially Godly and blessed. The crushing hand of God has already been laid upon them; they have received His attention, accepted suffering . . . in advance . . . and so are blessed!"

Snodgrass is often drawn to creatures and objects on the furthest margins of their world: dying, mutilated beggars, lobsters on ice in a restaurant window, a first leaf. Similarly, he likes to move to the far borders of meaning and syntax. Part of the excitement and strain of reading him comes from his efforts to get out of the poem. He changes his mind, tries to get into the world as it is, out of the metaphysical, symbolist poem in which he is trapped by his temperament and the tradition of which he is part. Addressing himself to the dying man, not worth his haddock or his grilled tomato, suffering prolonged torture, he says:

> Men starve. How many young men did we rob
> To keep you hanging on?

No poet now writing looks at the "sad hospital" of the world with such a continuous stare. Occasionally, Snodgrass chooses to travel into the world through the tunnel of art. There is a group of poems on life seen in much reproduced French paintings: Matisse's "The Red Studio," Van Gogh's "Starry Night," Manet's "Execution of Maximilian." These poems on painting, except for that on Monet's "Les Nymphéas," are poetic descriptions, sometimes dramatic, but essentially tiring virtuoso performances. "Monet: 'Les Nymphéas' " describes the water lilies—what is almost not there—a fine, abstract, Debussy-like piece. Another beautifully composed poem on a plaster replica of the Aphrodite of Melos almost finds joy.

The book is haunted by poems on the division of families, the loss of a daughter in divorce, the shoddiness of love, the mementoes of his own true-to-life love story. There is a little Anna Karenina in every man. Snodgrass has found the proper forms for Strindbergian warfare and armistice. He can handle material in poetry usually reserved for the novel or the film. Should what is better said in poetry be left to film, even a very good one? To my mind, Snodgrass's twenty-eight-line poem, "A Friend," on the pangs of a divorced father's visiting rights, outweighs a dozen new-wave films. And Snodgrass works on such a low budget. Here are fourteen cinematographic lines:

> Once they're in bed, he calls you "dear."
> The boob-tube shows some hokum on
> Adultery and loss; we yawn
> Over a stale joke book and beer
> Till it's your bedtime. I must leave.
> I watch that squat toad pluck your sleeve.
> As always, you stand shining near
>
> Your window. I stand, Prince of Lies
> Who's seen bliss; now I can drive back
> Home past wreck and car lot, past shack
> Slum and steelmill reddening the skies,

> Past drive-ins, the hot pits where our teens
> Fingerfuck and that huge screen's
> Images fill their vacant eyes.

The book concludes with some splendid translations from Rilke, Nerval, Hugo, and Rimbaud, among others. Snodgrass often manages to find poems to translate with themes that parallel his own. In the translations he finds a calmer, almost neoclassical voice.

I have not mentioned an uncanny poem, "A Character," in which Snodgrass gives us a portrait "in hospital whites" of an immaculate narcissist who makes his all-white "haven some small fortress against manifest vulgarity and worldliness." The poem is an eerie parody, an exaggerated prophecy of Snodgrass's self-preoccupation—"he thinks the world is his scab and he picks it."

Hardly squinting at history, past or present, he is a poet of the "uncommitted regions." Passing lobsters he thought dead in a restaurant window then seen "Struggling to raise one claw / like a defiant fist," Snodgrass greets the still-living creature with sympathy,

> I should wave back, I guess.
> But still in his permanent clench
> He's fallen back with the mass
> Heaped in their common trench
> Who stir, but do not look out
> Through the rainstreaking glass,
> Hear what the newsboys shout,
> Or see the raincoats pass.

After Experience is a mysterious song of the dispossessed.

JOSEPHINE JACOBSEN

Review of *After Experience*

What doubles the interest of W. D. Snodgrass's interesting po-
etry is that it shows us a sort of quintessence of a predicament
now overwhelming most of America's reasonably perceptive
writers. The credibility gap has reached its final location: be-
tween a man and himself. A strikingly germane writer in fiction,
John Cheever, has been able to brand on the reader's conscious-
ness the sobering recognition that the gods were fake, and that
their debilitating service has endured so thoroughly that the
server's ability to serve any others is gone the way of his faith in
those he served. But between prose and poetry there takes place
a sea change into something more poor and familiar. Part of the
problem is that prose can sustain, uninjured, more diagnosis and
less passion, than can poetry; part, that Mr. Cheever never settles
for the wry self-pity that is the booby-trap of the perceptive and
unhopeful poet.

Mr. Snodgrass's book is a very good book, his best to date.
These poems are lucid, original, controlled, even formal; com-
pact of irony, intelligence, and the true gift for metaphor. In the
book's third poem, "Reconstructions," the psychological posi-
tion, never to be shaken, is defined. After a sharp and touching
series of incidents illustrating damage to a relationship with a
child: "We are like patients who rehearse / Old unbearable scenes
/ Day after day after day. / I memorize you, bit by bit, / And
must restore you in my verses / To sell to magazines." A line
might read as the book's epigraph: We take things as they are.

But it would be a tricky conclusion. This is no make-the-best-
of-a-bad-job stoicism; it is, on the contrary, the ironic expression
of the poet's sense of the intolerable, which will yet be tolerated.
Moving all the way up to its most acute expression, "A Visita-
tion," a poem about the-Eichmann-in-us-all, Mr. Snodgrass pa-
tiently and brilliantly repeats, "you poor slob, pull up your socks

Commonweal 88 (21 June 1968): 417–18. Copyright © Commonweal Foundation.
Reprinted by permission. *The Harvester's Vase*, by Ned O'Gorman, and *Figure in
the Door*, by Arthur Gregor, are the other books reviewed.

and get on, without kidding yourself . . ."—get on, that is, with a wry, sincere self-pity which includes others in one's own lot. It isn't whine self-pity. It is deepened and universalized, and its witchbroth of disenchantment simmers over a continually renewed heat of resentment against the actual composition of the human mind and heart. The picture of men and women, now, here, is so eye-to-eye with John Cheever as to be striking, yet, in distinction from Mr. Cheever's astringent but steady-eyed stories, *After Experience* implies less a wrong route chosen than a distastefully irremediable necessity. This deadens the resonance a bit; it limits the sense of vitality and the unpredictable.

Yet the best poems are so awfully good. "Lobsters in the Window" and "The Men's Room in the College Chapel" show what Mr. Snodgrass can do when he shakes loose from the "mea culpa, but, so?" syndrome. The lobster on ice raises its claw. "I should wave back, I guess. / But . . ." If and when Mr. Snodgrass waves back, it should be quite a book.

All the translations are good; the Bonnefoy and Rilke translations are outstanding.

CLIVE JAMES

Sniper-Style

A poet in a country where anything can be turned in for a new one, W. D. Snodgrass stays loyal to his unpoetic surname, and the essential claim his poetry makes is that it is necessary to write beautifully in spite of circumstances. Reading his list of acknowledgments in *After Experience* (they have already been quoted by British reviewers, to whom names like the Corporation of Yaddo will always sound as if a homeward-bound Dickens is contemptuously pronouncing them) and remembering earlier awards and fellowships from the Ingram Merrill Foundation and the *Hudson Review,* the reader is more than mildly put off, as by the abstractly unimpressive multiple rows of fruit salad on the chests of American generals. But the crucial point is that all this information is available: Snodgrass does not cover up. It is nowadays very difficult for an American poet of manifest talent to be put out of business by want or by neglect. Snodgrass does not pretend otherwise. Hemmed in by endpapers and wrappers proclaiming his jobs, honors and awards (naturally the foundation will bear your expenses), his poetry steers clear of the poet's condition, which is obviously in A1 shape, and concentrates on the personal condition, which seems to be in a fruitful state of permanent confusion.

If "confessional" poetry exists at all (and, if it does, Snodgrass and Lowell are still the two best Americans writing it), its basic assumption is that the time-honored separation of the private man and the public artist can now be closed: the pose is over, and all the masks can be put away. The trick is worked, when it works, not by lowering the universal to the level of personality, but by elevating the vicissitudes of private life to the level of the universal. Insofar as the poet succeeds in convincing the reader that his personal suffering has an impersonal resonance, his work will chime: insofar as he does not, it will grate. Snodgrass grated

The Times Literary Supplement (London), 2 January 1969. Reprinted by permission. The review was reprinted earlier in Clive James, *The Metropolitan Critic* (London: Faber & Faber, 1974).

badly in passages like this from the title poem of his first book, *Heart's Needle:*

> In their smooth covering, white
> As quilts to warm the resting bed
> Of birth or pain, spotless as paper spread
> For me to write,

Or this, from the same poem:

> Like nerves caught in a graph,
> the morning-glory vines
> frost has erased by half
> still scrawl across their rigid twines.
> Like broken lines
>
> of verses I can't make.

Years later, in the work collected in *After Experience,* the same slate is scratched:

> Now I can earn a living
> By turning out elegant strophes.

The reader's first and sound reaction is that he does not want to hear this: just read the news, please. The reaction is sound because this new habit of calling attention to the practical business of putting words on paper is the trivialization of what for some centuries has correctly been regarded as a divine act, an act which no decent practitioner should regard as his own preserve. The effect is childish, even in a poet of Snodgrass's abilities: he is joined in this to those academically environed hordes of giftless poets who utterly fail to realize that man is not the measure of art. But before we come to that general point, it can be put beyond doubt that Snodgrass is a poet capable of extraordinary effects. His acute, sparely employed (in fact, underindulged) metaphorical sense can put an era into an image:

> This moth caught in the room tonight
> Squirmed up, sniper-style, between
> The rusty edges of the screen;

Faster and neater than that you don't get: a whole background comes over in a flash. The well-known virtuoso effort "The Examination" (once "the Phi Beta Kappa ceremonial poem at Columbia University," save the mark), detailing the ghastly victimization of a generalized Otherness and recalling the eerie dismemberment of angels in the film by Borowczik, has an exquisitely schooled timing in its local effects that creates for the reader a nightmare he cannot stop.

> Meantime, one of them has set blinders to the eyes,
> Inserted light packing beneath each of the ears
> And calked the nostrils in. One, with thin twine, ties
> The genitals off. With long wooden-handled shears,
>
> Another chops pinions out of the scarlet wings.

You can see how each line of the stanza infallibly brings something worse to life, and how, after the qualification "wooden-handled," has placed your own garden shears in your hands, the jump across the gap to the next stanza tells you that the next thing is the worst of the lot. In an age of fake rough stuff turned out by those youngish poets who seem fascinated by greased hair and high boots this poem, and another called "A Flat One" about an old man dying, are evidence that Snodgrass is capable of genuine tragic power—a power that the fashionable preoccupation with violence tends to dissipate. And it is not accidental that in these two instances the viewpoint is impersonal: the crippling assumption that one man can be a world is not in evidence.

Of those poems referring to a life meant to sound like his own the best are those in which the experience has a general applicability to a time, to a culture. "What We Said," a gently singing reminiscence of estrangement, is a good example. When he tries extra hard to supply the specific detail which will give the sense of a particular life (this is really *me* talking) he tends to be in the first place flimsy ("Mementos I" fades right out beside Larkin's poem using the same properties, "Lines on a Young Lady's Photograph Album") and in the second place dishonorable, since the theme, reduced to the loss of happiness, seems to assume a *right* to happiness—which for sound reasons has never been counted among an artist's legitimate expectations. Betraying themselves technically by a prevalence of shakily cantilevered rhymes (bringing the reader as near as he will ever get to groaning at poetry of this accomplishment), such poems demonstrate that a necessary consequence of abolishing the distinction between private life and public life is that ordinary privacy ceases to exist as a concept: characterized with a ruthless hand and unable to answer back, the true sufferers in "confessional" poetry are the poets' wives.

The contradiction inherent in confessional poetry which goes beyond its scope is damagingly evident in Snodgrass's attempt at a poem about Eichmann, "A Visitation." Technically very interesting, it creates an effect of jammed dialogue by interlacing two monologues, one by Eichmann, the other by the poet. (This exceedingly difficult trick of stereo voicing is used by Snodgrass elsewhere in "After Experience Taught Me . . ." and he may be said by now to hold the copyright on it.) But examined close to, the poem reveals itself to be dependent on all the usual weary banalities that would trace the phenomena of mass-murder to tendencies in the artist's own soul, provide the illusion of debate, and flatter the pretensions of the liberal spirit toward a forgiving generosity. In view of this it is particularly unfortunate that the poem should carry as an epigraph a quotation from Hannah Arendt, who has certainly declared (in the very book from which Snodgrass quotes) that these events can be understood in the long run only by the poets, but who equally certainly, and as long ago as the appearance of her monumental *The Origins of Totalitarianism,* made her views known about those who thought "that inner experience could be given historical significance, that one's own self had become the battlefield of history."

Confessional poetry has taken a small, previously neglected field among all the possible fields of poetry and within that field pushed on to a new adventure. It becomes absurd when it usurps the impersonal fields with the language of the personal—when it fails to recognize its limitations. Eichmann's crimes, for example, were in the public realm; they are not to be traced to the sadistic impulse which is in all of us or to any other impulse which is in all of us; they can be understood only in history. When the poet pretends to contain, mirror, or model history within his own suffering, his talent gives out for just as long as the folly lasts; the better he is, the worse the work he does; and even a first-rate talent like Snodgrass's produces the smoothly "distinguished" work which is the bane of our lives and to which we do not normally expect a man of his powers to contribute.

ROBERT BOYERS

From "Mixed Bag"

The title of W. D. Snodgrass's new volume, his first in eight years, would seem to point to a cooling of those intensely personal concerns he developed with such great care and skill in the earlier *Heart's Needle*. In fact, and here one does not know whether or not to include "alas," the concerns remain, as urgent as ever; the voice persists, no less whimsical and pathetic than it was; the landscape has not improved. The poems in *After Experience* are different, though, more depressing, if that seems possible. The poet's experience has structured perception in such a way that what once in the poems seemed peculiar to Snodgrass, if nonetheless mundane and familiar, no longer seems merely a personal problem at all. Snodgrass's more recent poems reverberate with irony and dismay at the downward drift of an entire culture, and we attend as much to patterns of hopelessness and betrayal as we once did to the particularities of obstructed intimacy.

Of course, it is not the context in which Snodgrass thinks and feels that concerns us very much, but the degree to which he can artfully embody his concerns in language that makes them somehow meaningful for us. Largely he has succeeded, in spite of the grave risks he has incurred in the preparation of his new volume. A great many of the poems he has collected here are dangerously close to being set pieces, rather stagy, and so judiciously molded that they seem almost too nice, too clean and transparent and predictable to be true. A poem like "Leaving the Motel" is perfect in its way, perhaps on first acquaintance even a little too perfect, inevitable in the particulars of its unfolding, the rhymes so evenly modulated as in these times to call attention to themselves.

> Outside, the last kids holler
> Near the pool: they'll stay the night.

Partisan Review 36, no. 2 (1969): 306–9. Copyright © 1969 by Robert Boyers. Reprinted by permission. "Mixed Bag" also includes reviews of *Firstborn*, by Louise Gluck, *The Back Country*, by Gary Snyder, and *The Ribs of Death*, by Paul Zimmer.

Pick up the towels; fold your collar
Out of sight.

Check: is the second bed
Unrumpled, as agreed?
Landlords have to think ahead
In case of need,

Too. Keep things straight: don't take
The matches, the wrong keyrings—
We've nowhere we could keep a keepsake—
Ashtrays, combs, things

That sooner or later others
Would accidentally find.
Check: take nothing of one another's
And leave behind

Your license number only,
Which they won't care to trace;
We've paid. Still, should such things get lonely,
Leave in their vase

An aspirin to preserve
Our lilacs, the wayside flowers
We've gathered and must leave to serve
A few more hours;

That's all. We can't tell when
We'll come back, can't press claims;
We would no doubt have other rooms then,
Or other names.

Why, then, does the poem work as well as it obviously does?
Perhaps because the poet has been so very relentless in the cata-
loging of those *things* that in essence constitute the reality of his
experience, an experience so fragile, so impermanent as to have
left no other marks on the poet's psyche. Precisely what is en-
forced in Snodgrass's poem is the anonymity of experience in the
modern world, a radical skepticism about the communicability
of emotions within contexts that are socially conditioned or im-
posed. No sense of persons, of personalities, emerges from the
poem. Even the authority that lurks somewhere beyond the

scene is faceless, perhaps more a product of the imagination than anything substantial. The specter of the haunted self locked within itself, yet in fitful combat with the world, is wonderfully suggested by the poet's use of words like *others* and *they*. Who these others are we cannot be expected to say, nor would the poet be likely to identify them with precision. And yet, mysteriously, all of us know, beyond saying, for we trust Snodgrass as a guide in these matters.

There have been a number of complaints already that Snodgrass's "despairing voice is half-heartedly one-toned," as one reviewer put it. I should speak instead of control, the poet's unyielding stranglehold on the ordering of events in his poems, events which otherwise might threaten to tear to shreds the fabric of the poet's sanity. I don't know that singleness of tone need be a liability, at least not insofar as the poet is the maker of individual poems, complete unto themselves, rather than the maker of a whole range of poems that together constitute his opus. It is certainly too early to speak of Snodgrass as a major figure in the poetry of our time, precisely because he has not written enough for us to make such judgments, and because there is relatively little variety in his approach to his craft. What we can say is that he has written a number of exquisite poems that seem destined to be remembered as part of the finest lyric poetry of our time. Certainly he has succeeded the late Randall Jarrell as our most heart-breaking poet, this being a title originally ascribed to Jarrell by his friend Robert Lowell. In fact, Snodgrass's poetry has consistently evoked from readers a degree of pity and sympathy that has made it all but impossible to consider the poems with any kind of detachment. The voice has been so honest, so very familiar in its way, that we have experienced it almost as a revelation of our own imminent possibilities.

It would be foolish, of course, to recommend Snodgrass's new volume unequivocally. In a number of poems the versification works against the emotional content, as in "The Platform Man," where the imperatives of a particular form impose the poet's resort to crude devices. In other cases, as in the pathetic "A Friend," the connections between domestic despair and cultural wasteland are hinted at, but never really demonstrated. In such a poem we have the wish for a connection, but no real linkage. A visit to the ex-wife to see the children is saturated in disgust over the banal evocations of "adultery and loss" reflected on the TV screen, in front of which the family sprawls together. The poem concludes: "As always, you stand shining near //

Your window. I stand, Prince of Lies / Who's seen bliss; now I can drive back / Home past wreck and car lot, past shack / Slum and steelmill reddening the skies, / Past drive-ins, the hot pits where our teens / Fingerfuck and that huge screen's / Images fill their vacant eyes." The poet's attempt here to relate levels of experience lacks coherence. One is tempted to attribute personal problems to the influence of the cultural milieu, but one is not certain this can always be securely managed. Is marital discord and misery of separation from one's children somehow concomitant with or derivative from teenage fingerfucking and the banal manifestations of popular culture? Is a poet of Snodgrass's sophistication, wit, and skill a product of drive-in movies and "stale joke-books"? Must the inevitable institutions and cultural detritus of our time overwhelm poets as they do others? Of such things it is difficult to speak confidently, but we must require of the poet like Snodgrass that he address himself to them in terms of their necessity rather than as random elements in a playing off of observations.

WILLIAM HEYEN

A Note on S. S. Gardons

S. S. Gardons. All right. There are reasons for his existence and now, we are told, his disappearance, and there are reasons that, to some, he should not be known. To say that the voice in the Gardons poems is too close to the voice of the author's other work and does not justify or necessitate a pseudonym, as one critic insists, is to miss the whole point. The familial love-hate relationships here bear too close a resemblance to persons living and dead, and the poet's vision is inexorable. Could your parents possibly understand how you could describe the "eyeshadow like a whore" on your dead sister's face? How could you say that? How could you remember her in that way?

The world of this sequence is a spider web which "The Mother" has woven and on which "her mates, her sapless young" are black shapes that hang precariously "where she moves by habit, hungering and blind." The father is here, too, a diplomat who will not take sides. His mission is to remain "a balance / of power in the family, the firm, the whole world through" ("Diplomacy: The Father"). The atmosphere is poisonous and complex. Gardons's feelings in some of these poems are so multiple and elusive that it is good and even surprising that he survived, escaped, remained negatively capable. We need only compare "Fourth of July" here with remarks the poet made about his dead sister in the spring 1959 *Partisan Review:* "To die on Independence Day seemed an act of terrible and destructive blamefulness, yet this may have been, in its way, the easiest solution of her dilemma. . . ." Looking back, he doesn't know whether to blame her for refusing to live or to whisper a fond farewell to her and to forgive her passivity and weakness. "Fourth of July" is just as much of a matrix of emotion and

Western Humanities Review, Summer 1971. Copyright © 1971 by William Heyen. Reprinted by permission. Only two reviews of *Remains* were published, this one and one by Robert Phillips, in *Poet Lore,* Spring 1973. Mr. Phillips largely incorporates his review of *Remains* into "W. D. Snodgrass and the Sad Hospital of the World," an essay included later in this volume.

indecision: "I keep my seat and wonder where, / Into what ingrown nation has she gone / Among a people silent and withdrawn." This poem's ending tells us just how much the poet had to live through (the "she" is the asthmatic sister):

> We tramp home through the sulfurous smoke
> That is my father's world. Now we must
> Enter my mother's house of lint and dust
> She could not breathe; I wheeze and choke.
>
> It is an evil, stupid joke:
> My wife is pregnant; my sister's in her grave.
> We live in the home of the free and of the brave.
> No one would hear me, even if I spoke.

Again, as in the famous earlier sequence, the potential for bathos is certainly here, but the metrical control and hard rhymes, because the employment of conscious technique always implies the poet is attempting to control highly emotional matter by mind, stop the voice from breaking, stave off the purely melodramatic. And there is, again, an undercurrent of rage here and throughout *Remains,* the hate and fury of a disciplined athlete. Many a game has been won that hate started and control finished.

The eight poems that make up this sequence ("The Mother," "Diplomacy: The Father," "The Mouse," "Viewing the Body," "Disposal," "Fourth of July," "The Survivors," "To a Child") bring us in to witness the residues of experience, the artifacts built on memories that will not subside. Returning home out of a morbid curiosity rather than out of any love or devotion for his parents, the poet finds, in "The Survivors," that nothing has changed in the year since his sister died. His parents have survived. He has survived. But when are the living, in any true sense, no more alive than the dead?—this is the question posed by several of these poems. In "The Survivors," as their property runs down around them, members of the family pass one another like zombies, unable to acknowledge their own existence: "At any time they come / To pass, they drop their eyes." The idea of Family now has no more meaning than does the lottery to the inhabitants of Shirley Jackson's village. Even evening togetherness and entertainment is rote and deadly:

> Only at night they meet.
> By voiceless summoning

> They come to the living room; each repeats
> Some words he has memorized; each takes his seat
> In the hushed, expectant ring
>
> By the television set.
> No one can draw his eyes
> From that unnatural, cold light. They wait.
> The screen goes dim and they hunch closer yet,
> As the image dies.

The images here (the ring and the light, for example) are so inevitable that paraphrase at once falls far short and is unnecessary. The poem continues: "In the cellar where the sewers / Rise, unseen, the pale white / Ants grow in decaying stacks of old newspapers." It is right that these ants are brought in, psychologically true to the poem's invention that the poet's mind turn to the cellar, turn to the base, the lower structure, to memory, to understand where he now stands. The image of the white ants flourishing in old newspapers is striking and true, but beyond the cliché of any rational explication. The ring, the unnatural light, the white ants—these images are not ornament. They are deep and true, so true that they don't need other words. They are right as they are.

And take the gruesome joke that surfaces earlier in the same poem. Though addressing his stanzas to his dead sister, the poet is not afraid to draw an ironic parallel—if the poem does not make this explicit, it is impossible to avoid hearing this— between his sister and an unwanted but protected fruit:

> On the tree they still protect
> From the ungoverned gang
> Of neighbor boys—eaten with worms, bird-pecked,
> But otherwise uncared-for and unpicked,
> The bitter cherries hang,
>
> Brown and soft and botched.
> The ground is thick with flies.

Decorum and good taste are not in question here. We must, at least, talk honestly to the dead. And there is no avoiding the fact that what remains, after experience, is a need for expression as urgent as air or food.

And the remains are splendiferous. Physically, this is a beautiful book—handset in Palatino, printed on "Shadwell paper made especially for this book over last Thanksgiving," hand-bound in leather and marbled papers. Mary and Walter Hamady have loved and labored at their Perishable Press, have made this book a work of art. For these poems, and this is the most important thing, the luxurious apparel is perfectly appropriate. The remains, as in "Viewing the Body," are dressed up, and when we view them we need, for the full shock of romantic agony, pages gray as shrouds and thick as plush carpets, a book as sensual as a funeral parlor, solid and gaudy as a gold coffin.

> Flowers like a gangster's funeral;
> Eyeshadow like a whore.
> They all say isn't she beautiful.
> She, who never wore

> Lipstick or such a dress,
> Never got taken out,
> Was scarcely looked at, much less
> Wanted or talked about.

The sister, plain and hidden, "gray as a mouse," asthmatic, "slept / Alone in the dim bedcovers." She is dull and dim and gray until she dies, "Till the obscene red folds / Of satin close down on her." Only when dead does she become the center of all eyes. And this red that folds down on her is lurid, bizarre. In "Disposal" she "lies boxed in satins // Like a pair of party shoes / That seemed to never find a taker." I don't know which way to twist my face. No one else is as good at these macabre effects as Gardons. W. D. Snodgrass, in "Heart's Needle," wrote a slightly longer sequence with the same grace and control exhibited in *Remains,* but Gardons touches nerves that are more exposed, probes a subject matter (parents and dead sister as opposed to wife and child) somehow deeper, more explosive, less public.

If we suppose, as I suspect we may, that the "Prefatory Note on the Author" was written by the author himself, then we can suppose that the deadly serious businesses of sublimation, exhumation, and exorcism going on in *Remains* have been, at least for now, transcended, that the poems helped the poet maintain his balance, and that now that all or most of the poems about it have been written, he can even laugh at his grotesque past. The author invented Gardons because Gardons could be made to appear when needed and disappear when not. The first biographical notes on him in periodicals and anthologies were briefer, perhaps plausible. He may first have been an alter ego, a wish-fulfilling second half, a member of the author's SS, *Schutz staffel,* protective echelon, who left academia. But now, to complete a process of separation, he has become a sort of redneck–hippie–James Dean–mechanic-musician-dropout, someone who couldn't possibly have written these poems.

> S. S. Gardons lived most of his life in and near Red Creek, Texas. For years he worked as a gas station attendant, although he took a few university classes in Houston, and later became an owner of a cycle shop. Also a musician, he played lead guitar in the well-known rock group, Chicken Gumbo. This sequence of poems was collected by his friends after his disappearance on a hunting trip in the mountains. From the condition of his abandoned motorcycle, it was impossible to determine whether he suffered foul play, was attacked by animals, merely became confused and lost, or perhaps fell victim to amnesia. At present, the case is listed as unsolved.

This is good. The poet's struggle has been, although his experience has taught him that love is at least as destructive as it is creative, to endure and hope. In "To a Child" he says that "Without love we die; / With love we kill each other." But the poem ends: "I tell you love is possible. / We have to try." It is good that Gardons himself can be put to rest now, at least for a time. God knows the life was maddening.

It seems to me that this sequence is at least as fine as Snodgrass's "Heart's Needle" and, as such, deserves high praise indeed. It may be, in fact, that its effect is even stronger. And it is fine that now, for a time, the poet can comically dismiss Gardons. I'm reminded here of John Berryman's Henry as he leaves us in "Dream Song 77": "it is a wonder that, with in each hand / one of his own mad books and all, / ancient fires for eyes, his head full / & his heart full, he's making ready to move on." Gardons may never, as did Henry, come back from the dead, but then he may not have to come that far. His case is unsolved, and I have a hunch that if he is needed—and there are some gaps in the sequence, certainly, that could be filled in with poems—he will show up again, maybe even change his name.

PART THREE   *Essays: The First
Three Books*

RICHARD HOWARD

W. D. Snodgrass
"There's Something Beats the Same in Opposed Hearts"

The times divide us against ourselves, so that we propitiate what
we would save of personality by savaging what falls from us, what
vanishes; there is a dialectical impulse we all endure, I think, a
vexed energy forever urging the meaning of our loves by means
of our hates, the justification of gardens, say, by the weeds we
guard them from, the hope of selfhood to be found by expelling
the foreign self rather than frequenting it. As if we remembered
that *divorce* and *diversion* share the one root, we project upon the
world the forking members of our will, casting about for duali-
ties, oppositions, enemies—indeed *casting* (in both the thrusting
and the immobilizing sense) into dichotomous roles men who
would be astonished to find themselves so encamped in contro-
version. And women too; think, as this poet has thought, of the
dissociation of the Naughty Mommy, the witch, the vampire
("Why so drawn, so worn, my dearest," Snodgrass's vampire
asks, in the cadence of Sir John Suckling—of course—"When I
do need looking after / and there's so much to be done, / Dear, it
surely isn't fair / so to hang on everyone. / Or don't you care?"),
from that aspect of our mothers which ranges quite as delusively
from Miss America to the Madonna. "She stands in the dead
center," the poet has written in a poem called "The Mother," and
he glosses the line by this remark in an essay: "woman and death
are one; [it is] our common tendency to see death as a mother, the
grave as a womb." And there is the other, equally common
tendency which the poet accounts for in a late, rich poem (wittily
titled "Leaving Ithaca": it is Ulysses setting out from Cornell,
leaving "the old house rough-hewn as we found it . . . / no

doubt it would have spoiled us to remain"), the tendency to see life itself as a loved woman, invagination as voyaging. The poem is dedicated "to my plaster replica of the Aphrodite of Melos" and thus liminally, thus intimately, the characteristic Snodgrass note is struck, the goddess invoked, the Real Presence affirmed— but in plaster; and rightly enough, Love's Lady in this poem comes, like death, from the poet's mother, "who mailed you, packed in towels, when I first married." The complications of Snodgrass's response to Eros are articulated by the transient households, the odyssey of faculty decorums, made evident in the neat facture of the encapsulating quatrains, the exasperated diction of all English teachers who must make do, and in this case make don't, with replica love-goddesses:

>   . . . Oh everloving Lady,
> You had been ruined quite enough already;
> Now the children have chipped off half your nose.
>
> My first wife tried to keep you in the attic;
> Some thought your breasts just so-so and your waist,
> Thick with childbearing, not for modern taste.
> My father thought you lewd and flicked your buttocks.
>
> One giddy night, blonde Susan tipped your stand—
> You, true to your best style, lost your head.
> You just won't learn how much smart girls will shed
> This year. Well, we must both look secondhand.
>
> Lady, we've cost each other . . .

Expenses of the flesh, though, can be accounted for with a certain grim and grainy efficiency which keeps the early poetry of Snodgrass cool. The first pieces in his first book, *Heart's Needle* (published in 1959, awarded the 1960 Pulitzer Prize), are poems of homecoming, the squalor and spookiness of repatriation (as a soldier, a son, a citizen, a lover . . .) bringing home indeed a fatal division from the self:

>   . . . you never
> Escape the sense in everything you do,
> "We've done this all once. Have I been here, ever?"

And it is precisely by this dividing, this sundering of self from the data which generally reassure, and by peering for a significant glimpse of "the shore of our first life," that Snodgrass, with what Robert Lowell calls "a shrill authoritative eloquence" in this first book, pairs himself off in order to arrive at identity, "to kneel by my old face and know my name."

This goal, the destination of all divided passages, is announced at once, in the next group of poems, which are an inspection of childhood (*Heart's Needle*, it should be said, is arranged in clumps of poems along the choked watercourse of the poet's biography: return from war, stock-taking of self and surround which includes the body and the body's history, then teaching, and marriage, fatherhood and divorce), and though such completion is not here to be achieved in terms of what Macbeth calls "understood relations" that bring forth the "secretest man of blood," the goal is nevertheless sighted, sensed as a poet will sense such things, in terms of the senses. For in—or out of—the welter of our experience, we look for the *sign* of that experience, the emblem to mediate it, as T. S. Eliot distinguishes between the experience and its meaning when he says that a man may have the one and yet miss the other. It is in the earlier poetry of Snodgrass that we have the experience presented but divided somehow from its meaning, and in his later poetry that we have the meaning too, the sign not merely stated, named, but enacted. Here in *Heart's Needle*, then, sensory images will be the *materia melica*, even in compositional stresses, so that the four little strophes ("Now I can earn a living," Snodgrass crows in his second book, "by turning out elegant strophes") of "At the Park Dance" have the gritty concreteness of stones, conglomerates, *made things*, poems:

> As the melting park
> darkens, the firefly winks
> to signal loving strangers
> from their pavilion
> lined with Easter colored
> lights, fading out together
>
> until they merge with
> weathered huge trees and join
> the small frogs, those warm singers;
> and they have achieved

love's vanishing point
where all perspectives mingle,

where even the most
close things are indistinct
or lost, where bright worlds shrink,
they will grope to find
blind eyes make all one world;
their unseen arms, horizons.

Beyond, jagged stars
are glinting like jacks hurled
farther than eyes can gather;
on the dancefloor, girls
turn, vague as milkweed floats
bobbing from childish fingers.

The formal organization of this bleak lyric, along with the imagery and the action of it, deserves inspection, for it is cunning in the rehearsal and incarnation of its theme ("William Empson was my first love," says Snodgrass, who has loved many times since), that elusive and perhaps illusory fusion of separates achieved at "love's vanishing point where all perspectives mingle." Though the poem, glanced at on the page, appears not to rhyme, when it is read aloud certain harmonies inhere, inhabit the reading voice, and enhance the effect of a fugitive unison which is the poem's burden: we notice almost simultaneously that the first syllable of each second and fifth line rhymes or assonates with the final syllable of each first and fourth line; and that the stanzas are in fact constructed in paired crescendos of five, six and seven syllables thus bonded by the edge-rhymes, the five- and six-syllable lines ending in an accented syllable, the longer seven-syllable lines ending in an unaccented one, with a single exception (the third line of the third stanza, where the final accented syllable *shrink* seems to withdraw from the missing seventh syllable). Yes, and then we see that there are terminal rhymes too, but separated by apparently irregular groups of lines: *strangers* in the third line of the first strophe, *singers* and *mingle* in the third and sixth lines of the second strophe, *fingers* in the sixth line of the last strophe; then are the intervals at which these terminal rhymes occur so irregular after all? They come always in the third or the sixth lines in each strophe—and if we consider the remaining third and sixth lines in the other strophes, we find further congruities—*together* in the sixth line of the first strophe, rhymes with *gather* in the third line of the last; there is a rhyme series related to the *singers/fingers/strangers/mingle* group in *winks, indistinct,* and *shrink* and further rhymes in *join* and *point* in the second strophe and in *world* and *hurled* in the third and fourth. In fact, then, after a little unraveling, *all* the teleutons but one (which is, appropriately, *floats* in the penultimate line) are bound into the system of sound relationships which articulate, which *are* the poem's meaning: "all one world." But it is, in Snodgrass's early work, a world made one in part by blindness, by abjuring the clear vision and the firm grasp—hence the evanescence, the unreality of the things in the poem, the phenomena of toying: the amusement park, the fireflies, the pavilion with Easter-colored lights, the small frogs that are "warm singers," I believe, because of the mating season, the stars glinting like jacks in a reduction of the cosmos to a child's game, and the final, crucial likeness of girls drifting across the dancefloor "vague as milk-weed floats / bobbing from childish fingers." Before we conflate a certain prepubertal insistence, which is carried through the poem to this clinching figure, with the *action* of the poem, the locus of its verbs, let us loiter about the image of those milkweed floats, for they will recur, a few poems on in this book, again accorded a curious ambiguity of intent, a sexuality both gathered and dispersed, won and lost in the consciousness of the speaker. In the poem "Winter Bouquet" Snodgrass speaks of the "dry vaginal pods of milkweed" and of the war years when "many a wife / wandered the fields after such pods to fill life / preservers so another man might not be lost." And ends the poem, another of his returning soldier, peace-is-war emblems, with the scatter-ing of the bouquet, "white bursts of quilly weedseed for the wide arms / and eyes of the children squealing where they drift /. . . like an airlift / of satyrs or a conservative, warm snow." In this poem, as in "At the Park Dance," the outright sexual, generative function of the milkweed is scanted, flouted actually, for the elusive, fantastic ("like an airlift of satyrs") and even asexual ("a conservative, warm snow") aspect: "vague as milkweed floats / bobbing from childish fingers." If the pods are vaginal, they are also dry; and if they are seeds, suggesting the same regeneration as the Easter lights earlier in the poem, they escape our grasp, as the lights fade out. And that is the other significant organization of the poem—the image of fading, impressed upon us through-out by the verbs which indicate the transient in their very conver-gence: the *melting* park *darkens,* the firefly *winks* (suggesting the dark rather than the luminous intervals of his cycle), the colored lights *fade out* until they *merge* with the *weathered* (blurred? in any case no longer untouched) trees, and *join* the singing frogs to *achieve love's vanishing point* (the expression is a study in itself, being both that location toward which all impulses tend and one where all are canceled out), where all perspectives *mingle; the lost* and the *unseen* contribute to this intensity of the void, and *beyond,* out of eyesight, the stars, *hurled* there, are *glinting;* finally, the girls *turn* like the milkweed *floats,* and elude childish fingers, *bobbing* on the dance floor.

Every effect, then, every device and technique and principle of organization in this little poem supports its cause in the same way: a unison, a sounding-as-one, but fugitive, costly, and not to be trusted. The experience of convergence, more hinted at than held onto, is less significant to Snodgrass than the separations to be overcome, the divisions registered.

Dissociation—the breakup of personality into what Melville called *isolatos,* "not acknowledging the common continent of men," a place that *contains* the human condition, nor even trusting that we are members of ourselves as well as of one another—dissociation has no further range, no finer ruse than the one Snodgrass, a man ruefully assenting to masks:

> Poets of our generation—those of us who have gone so far in criticism and analysis that we cannot ever turn back and be innocent . . . have such extensive resources for disguising ourselves from ourselves . . .

was to employ at about this period, when his poems were being published in those Ghibelline reviews and anthologies which, among the blood feuds of our postwar poetry, stood for the kempt and the cooked against the Guelph party, which did not stand at all but rather coasted downstream. For if we look Snodgrass up in the "biographies and bibliography" section of the anthology *A Controversy of Poets* (which attempted to muster forces from both factions), we find the following laconic entry:

> Born in Wilkinsburg, Pennsylvania, in 1926. . . . Teaches at Wayne State University in Detroit. Deeply influenced by the Texas poet S. S. Gardons.

And if, concerned to get to the bottom of that *deep influence* and undistracted by something odd in the sound of the name, we should look up S. S. Gardons (who does not appear to have published a volume of verse) in, say, the second selection of the *New Poets of England and America* anthology (almost entirely a Ghibelline affair), we find two poems and the following preposterous entry in the biographical notes:

> Born in Red Creek, Texas, 1929. Works as a gas station attendant in Fort Worth . . .

Now when a man spells his name backward and concocts another biography for his reversed self (slicing three years off his age and adding, with that gas-station attendant's job, a touch of Noble Savagery to a *universitaire* career felt to be perhaps too unremittingly tame), it is evident that he is crucially conscious of the divided nature of his aims, of the separatist impulses which lead him to come down so much harder on the divorce than on the marriage of true minds.

Indeed, I think Snodgrass abandoned the supposititious self because it was insufficiently opposing. The poems by S. S. Gardons are not different *enough* from the poems by W. D. Snodgrass to warrant the labor of sustaining a pseudonym; both of those in the *New Poets of England and America* anthology (others appeared in the *Hudson Review*) fit too neatly into the anfractuosities of *Heart's Needle*—indeed, "To a Child" actually belongs among the torments of the title poem, that excruciating cycle of apostrophes to the seed and symbol of division, the poet's daughter ("an only daughter is the needle of the heart"), the child addressed as the identity lost in divorce proceedings, so that when S. S. Gardons, a highly psychoanalytical type for a pump attendant, reports:

> We have seen the dodder
> That parasitic pale love-vine that thrives
> Coiling the zinnias in the ardor
>   Of its close embrace.
>   We have seen men abase
> Themselves to their embittered wives;
>
> And I have let you see my mother,
>   That old sow in her sty
>   Who would devour her farrow;
> We have seen my sister in her narrow

Grave. Without love we die;
With love we kill each other . . .*

we know he is saying no more, and no less, than W. D. Snod-
grass, who says, in the third poem of "Heart's Needle," to "the
child between them":

> Love's wishbone, child, although I've gone
> As men must and let you be drawn
> Off to appease another,
> It may help that a Chinese play
> Or Solomon himself might say
> I am your real mother

—too neatly and too needfully to fit anywhere else. With one
terrible delineation of "The Mother," generating precisely that
opposing self which Gardons invokes in order to ward off
(which is what, after all, *gardons* means): "She hallucinates in
their right places / their after-images, reversed and faint," the
alter ego is offered up, one may say, on the altar of egoism, and
Snodgrass returns to Snodgrass, to that triumphant or at least
intrepid assertion of his own old wretchedness:

> Your name's safe conduct into love or verse;
> Snodgrass is walking through the universe.

> Your name's absurd, miraculous as sperm
> And as decisive. If you can't coerce
> One thing outside yourself, why you're the poet! . . .
> If all this world runs battlefield or worse,
> Come, let us wipe our glasses on our shirts:
> Snodgrass is walking through the universe.

And the universe, since Snodgrass is but the one poet, unable
to pair off his responses, his responsibility, into that second,
separate self—the universe will not be one but rather, in the
body of this man's poetry, divided against itself, disparate in his

*Howard is quoting the version of these stanzas that appears in *New Poets of
England and America*, ed. Donald Hall and Robert Pack (1962). Snodgrass revised
the stanzas when *Remains* appeared in book form in 1970 (Perishable Press). The
revised version of "To a Child" had not been published when this essay was
written.

despair. *Oppositions* will contrive all of Snodgrass's poetry, in both *Heart's Needle* and in the book that followed it in 1968, *After Experience;* will control what I have called its body, since a living body must have two parents, must branch its passions in two directions until, as Snodgrass says, they may be neither humane nor loyal; will contribute that tone of characteristic *aigreur* we hear in his Orpheus' address to the Powers of the Underworld, "who are all bright worlds' negative":

> . . . And I went on
> Rich in the loss of all I sing
> To the threshold of waking light,
> To larksong and the live, gray dawn.
> So night by night, my life has gone.

Not only the confrontation, the combat of self and others, mothers against fathers, fathers against sons, mothers against daughters, brothers against sisters—Snodgrass articulates every member of the family romance, the family rebellion under the terrible rubric:

> Whom equal weakness binds together
> none shall separate . . .

—but the conflict of self against its accommodating yet refractory body engages this poet's art. Among the most striking of Snodgrass's poems are those that deal with sickness, with dying, with the recalcitrant soma doing battle against the raging psyche. "I was drifting," he says in "The Operation," and all the identity which that enormous pronoun wields is set against that other, that unknown nonperson on the hospital card:

> The body with its tributary poisons borne. . . .
> To the arena, humming, vast with lights; blank hero,
> Shackled and spellbound, to enact my deed.

The sense that our body is not ourselves, yet does our deed, is a cruel one, and made crueller still by any afternoon in the woods. The cardinal sings, and his message, to the victimized poet, hankering after reconciliation, "outspeaks a vital claim" unavailable to opposing human selves "that only in circumference embrace / and by divorce." Here is what the cardinal says, and it is not until the end of *After Experience* that Snodgrass, some fifteen years later, can come up with a comparable song, an equivalent assertion of undivided selfhood:

> "The world's not done to me;
> it is what I do;
> whom I speak shall be;
> I music out my name
> and what I tell is who
> in all the world I am."

For the rest of *Heart's Needle,* and for the ten parts of the title poem in particular, there will be a lyric necessity, a formal requirement to stand over and against singleness of experience, unity of identity. The poet who reminds us—in his accomplished verse making, his *turning,* that is, upon himself—of Verlaine, as we see by setting "Autumn Scene" beside "Colloque Sentimental":

> In the public gardens they are walking.
> The skies appear correct and glum.
> Their heels click drily; they are talking.
> Behind their backs, the elms repeat some shocking
> News of what's to come . . .
>
> Dans le vieux parc solitaire et glacé,
> Deux formes ont tout à l'heure passé.
>
> Leurs yeux sont morts et leurs lèvres sont molles,
> Et l'on entend à peine leurs paroles.
>
> Dans le vieux parc solitaire et glacé,
> Deux spectres ont evoqué le passé . . .

And who reminds us—in his bitter mistrust of precisely the accomplishments he is prized (and paid) for—of Heine, as the next double exhibit proves:

> I memorize you, bit by bit,
> And must restore you in my verses
> To sell to magazines.
> We keep what our times allow
> And turn our grief into play . . .

Sie [die Kastraten] sangen von Liebessehnen,
Von Liebe und Liebeserguss;
Die Damen schwammen in Tränen
Bei solchem Kunstgenuss.

And who reminds us, most of all—not only in his bereft land-
scapes, the scenery of a disquieted soul, but in his agonized
inquest of motives—of Tennyson, the parallel indicated if we set
some of "The Examination" beside a little of Tennyson's "The
Dead Prophet":

. . . "We shall continue, please." Now, once again, he bends
  To the skull, and its clamped tissues. Into the cran-
ial cavity, he plunges both of his hands
  Like obstetric forceps and lifts out the great brain,

Holds it aloft, then gives it to the next who stands
  Beside him. Each, in turn, accepts it, although loath,
Turns it this way, that way, feels it between his hands
  Like a wasp's nest or some sickening outsized growth.

They must decide what thoughts each part of it must think;
  They tap at, then listen beside, each suspect lobe;
Next, with a crow's quill dipped into India ink,
  Mark on its surface, as if on a map or globe,

Those dangerous areas which need to be excised . . .

. . . *She tumbled his helpless corpse about.*
  "Small blemish upon the skin!
But I think we know what is fair without
  Is often as foul within."

She crouched, she tore him part from part,
  And out of his body she drew
The red "blood-eagle" of liver and heart;
  She held them up to the view;

She gabbled, as she groped in the dead,
  And all the people were pleased;
"See what a little heart," she said,
  "And the liver is half-diseased!" . . .

The poet who suggests and sustains these associations—and Snodgrass has translated, we recall, from many German and French poets as well as taught widely in the standard English and American repertory—reaches, in *After Experience,* to a new richness of dialectic energy in the declaration of hostilities, in the choosing up of sides. There are, indeed, two poems here which are the masterpieces of Snodgrass's sundered song, the title poem and another, "A Visitation," which initiate—by their very accommodation in formal terms of the division, the opposition, the partition of voices—that ultimate and utter statement which becomes a closing of gaps, a filling of the rift within the lute. "A Visitation" is a dialogue in terza rima (so that the two voices are joined by their braided rhymes, even when the alternating indented stanzas pursue entirely discrepant lines of statement) between the ex-soldier poet and Eichmann's ghost. It is a dialogue, not a quarrel, in which the offended self realizes (when reminded by the obsequious spirit, "there's something beats the same in opposed hearts") that by the very attempt to fend off, to avert the monster *other* (as by Gardons, explicitly), it will creep upon us:

> . . . All the more cause I should keep you there—
> How subtle all that chokes us with disgust
> Moves in implacably to rule us, unaware.

And the ghost, ending the visitation, replies with a final pun ("you can look through me") which indicates how clearly Snodgrass has seen that the despised *other* can be exorcised only by acknowledgment, by acceptance, by assimilation, as in the rhyming central line of the ghost's last tercet (*somewhere* referring back to the poet's *there* and *unaware*), which indicates that the Eichmann in all of us is a recognized participant:

> My own love, you're all I could wish to be.
> Close your eyes—I'll just wander off somewhere
> Or watch the way your world moves—you can look through me.

The other supreme poem in Snodgrass's canon of Great Divorces is the one from which the second book draws its title, "After Experience Taught Me . . .", and it too is devised as a pairing off: it too consists of two voices, in alternating and indented pairs of lines, the rhymes again imbricating the whole thing together, though the voices are not, this time, in dialogue. "It seemed to me," Snodgrass remarks in an essay about the composition of one of the parts of "Heart's Needle," "and I have often found this to be so, that my poem could develop a structure adequate to my experience only if, like the old sonata form, it carried two separate thematic areas at the same time." Precisely, and for one area, in "After Experience Taught Me," he has taken the opening of Spinoza's essay "On the Improvement of the Understanding" in John Wild's translation:

> After experience has taught me that all the usual surroundings of social life are vain and futile; seeing that none of the objects of my fears contained in themselves anything either good or bad, except in so far as the mind is affected by them, I finally resolved to inquire whether there might be some real good having power to communicate itself, which would affect the mind singly, to the exclusion of all else; whether, in fact, there might be anything of which the discovery and attainment would enable me to enjoy continuous, supreme, and unending happiness.

Casting this into rough pentameters, and with a little significant editing (such as the very modern substitution of "something" for "some real good having power to communicate itself"), Snodgrass achieves some eight lines of his poem, its "first area."

And for his second area, Snodgrass has recreated a lecture he says he heard in the navy on the most effective way to kill a man in hand-to-hand combat. Unlike the cool, abstract, and deliberative discourse of Snodgrass-as-lens-grinder, this second voice is brutal, colloquial and without modulation—it is Gardons-the-commando, and by an inspired piece of carpentry, the military lecture on jiffy-killing is bonded by rhyme with the inquiry into supreme and unending happiness to produce the disconcerting and critical music of this poem ("like the old sonata form") by which the poet had sought to enact his suffered oppositions from the start:

> After experience taught me that all the ordinary
> Surroundings of social life are futile and vain;
>
> I'm going to show you something very
> Ugly: someday, it might save your life.
>
> Seeing that none of the things I feared contain
> In themselves anything either good or bad

What if you get caught without a knife;
Nothing—even a loop of piano wire;

Excepting only in the effect they had
Upon my mind, I resolved to inquire

Take the first two fingers of this hand;
Fork them out—kind of a "V for Victory"—

Whether there might be something whose discovery
Would grant me supreme, unending happiness.

And jam them into the eyes of your enemy.
You have to do this hard. Very hard. Then press . . .

and so forth, to the last, unendurable opposition—

You must call up every strength you own
And you can rip off the whole facial mask.

Wishing to be, to act, to live. He must ask
First, in other words, to actually exist.

Snodgrass, however, is more than a mere intellectual terrorist, and he is not content merely to offer these versions of death-in-life, apparently exclusive and only related by their very unlikelihood together. The poem ends with a further-indented quatrain in yet a third voice, the poet's own, in which the other two speakers transcend their subjects, or are transcended—for the first time in all this poet's work—by a subject which includes them both, and the significances become one, united in an unanswerable but enduring question of the poet to himself:

And you, whiner, who wastes your time
Dawdling over the remorseless earth,
What evil, what unspeakable crime
Have you made your life worth?

In this final quatrain, where the Spinoza-poem and the commando-poem unite, death has taken the role of a continually regenerative process. The enemy in the commando-poem is also what stands between the speaker of the Spinoza-poem and his happiness: the external, superficial self. It is exactly the "facial

84

mask" which the *philosopher* must rip off; and it is the *soldier,* executing a murder, who is asking to actually exist. Only such a violent, assertive response to life as the "unspeakable crime" of self-murder can justify living, and thereby lead to happiness. For it is a self-murder the poem presents, two times over. And this terrifying act of killing a self, even a false self, is the definitive act which runs death at last irrevocably into life, thought into action, all elements into their apparent opposites.

After this poem, Snodgrass no longer needs to divide in order to conquer, no longer needs to double himself—once he had said:

> We shout along our bank to hear
> our voices returning from the hills to meet us.
> We need the landscape to repeat us—

in order to create himself. He ends his second book with half a dozen poems of the unified self, the undistracted voice, speech of Shakespeare's "great creating nature" in whose accents death is heard unsevered from life, in whose rhythms the antagonism of the sexes, of self and body, parents and children, is absorbed, dissolved, fused. A clue to the subject of these poems, their necessary cause, is given by the best of the translations Snodgrass has included, fine English versions of Rilke's "Tapestry of the Lady with the Unicorn" and his "Archaic Torso of Apollo." Yes, the poems are about *art,* about works of art, about—with the exception of "Planting a Magnolia," which is the answer in this volume to the cardinal's overheard assertion in the first—five modern paintings, a Matisse, a Vuillard, a Manet, a Monet, and a Van Gogh. All are written with a release, an expressive leisure, though never a looseness, from the old clinching forms which indicate that Snodgrass has come to terms with his own form, and the terms to which he has come *are* that form,

> That will excite us, without hope,
> Returning in the rumors of
> Obscene blunt beauty that surrounds
> And will survive us.
> Before it dies.

Only art can afford occasion for such transcendence, and Snodgrass has seized it with an authority which his embrace of otherness, his resolution of opposites, his death, if you like, alone warrants. "In nature," he says in an essay, "man alone has the choice to withdraw from the reality in which he lives, and so has the power to die, either metaphorically or literally." Snodgrass has, in these magnificent and explicit poems, died into the work, the created reality, of those other men, and of course made out of just that otherness something altogether his own—someone, as he says in "Manet: 'The Execution of the Emperor Maximilian,' " though I have twisted the tenses in his favor—

> . . . someone has come,
> Declared significance, solved how these things relate
> To freedom, to our life's course, to eternity.

ROBERT PHILLIPS

W. D. Snodgrass and the Sad Hospital
of the World

Lowell's confessional poems seem the result of an attempt to
work out a separate peace between himself and his father's mem-
ory. W. D. Snodgrass's most famous work is clearly the result of
forced separation from his daughter. While the jacket of his book
informs us he is "the father of three children," the poems of the
"Heart's Needle" sequence, which gives the volume its title, are
clearly about the poet's relationship with his first child, a daugh-
ter. And in an epigraph taken from an old Irish story, Snodgrass
reminds us that "an only daughter is the needle of the heart." It
was this needle, pricking the poet's vitals, which hurt Snodgrass
into writing the most admired sequence of confessional poems in
our time short of Lowell's "Life Studies" cycle. The ten poems
of the Snodgrass sequence are in their way as frank and as har-
rowing as the fifteen which compose Lowell's. (Both books
were published in 1959.)

Then, years later, under the pseudonym "S. S. Gardons"—
Snodgrass more or less spelled backwards—he published an
even more startling cycle of confessions under the title *Remains.*
It is a lesser known work than *Heart's Needle,* owing to the
disguise of the author, the limited number of copies printed (two
hundred), and the list price of forty dollars. No review copies
were distributed. One can only speculate the reason for such
anonymity. While the "Heart's Needle" sequence is about wife
and daughter, for whom the poet has responsibility and presum-
ably control, the "Remains" poems are about his father, mother,
and the memory of a sister, dead at twenty-five. The sequence is
apparently so frankly based on actual familial love-hate relation-
ships that the poet probably chose not to hurt his parents further
by exposing them directly. As William Heyen observed, "it is

From *The Confessional Poets* by Robert Phillips (Carbondale and Edwardsville:
Southern Illinois University Press, 1973). The essay originally appeared in differ-
ent form in the *University of Windsor Review* 4, no. 2 (Spring 1969). Copyright ©
1969 by *University of Windsor Review.* Reprinted by permission.

difficult to send one's mother a book in which she is depicted as 'consoled by evil,' or in which one's dead sister is depicted as wearing 'eyeshadow like a whore.' "[1] The important thing for American poetry is that Snodgrass did not repress his desire to write such a book or suppress the poems once written. However limited their readership at present, the *Remains* poems remain.[2]

It was in 1959 that Snodgrass published what amounts to his poetic manifesto. He explained why the use of personae and third-person narratives and adopted poses and postures were, for him, a dead end. It was one of the earliest statements in print supporting a postmodern "confessional" school:

> I am left, then, with a very old-fashioned measure of a poem's worth—the depth of its sincerity. And it seems to me that the poets of our generation—those of us who have gone so far in criticism and analysis that we cannot ever turn back and be innocent again, who have such extensive resources for disguising ourselves from ourselves—that our only hope as artists is to continually ask ourselves, "Am I writing what I *really* think? Not what I think is acceptable; nor what my favorite intellectual would think in this situation; nor what I wish I felt. Only what I cannot help thinking." For I believe that the only reality which a man can ever surely know is that self he cannot help being, though he will only know that self through its interactions with the world around it. If he pretties it up, if he changes its meaning, if he gives it the voice of any borrowed authority, if in short he rejects this reality, his mind will be less than alive. So will his words.[3]

It is this dedication to "sincerity," to the "self he cannot help being," which individualizes the best of Snodgrass's work. In another of his infrequent essays he exclaims, "How could one be a first-rate artist without offending, deeply, those he most loves?"[4] Snodgrass has always written what he must. He is our poet of the antipersonae. Indeed, one of his best poems is literally about just that, concluding, "You must call up every strength you own / And you can rip off the whole facial mask."[5]

This sincerity, for want of a better word, when expressed in poems about the poet's own life, is what makes Snodgrass's confessions more sympathetic than Lowell's. Snodgrass is, somehow, his own best metaphor, a "seemingly miraculous embodiment as an individual of the age's stereotype." Living in suburbia, driving a Volkswagen, puttering in the garden, marrying a minor league beauty queen, his life touches the reader's more deeply than does the artistocratic Lowell's, because in fact it more closely resembles the reader's own. Jerome Mazzaro says it neatly: "Lowell has to stand outside himself to become part of the age; Snodgrass does not. There is, as a result, less irrelevant poetry by Snodgrass and less strain in writing, for his own urgency touches the urgency of his readers."[6]

What Mazzaro does not go on to say, and what needs saying, is that for Lowell reality is deeply rooted in *things*. It was Wallace Stevens, that elegant poet who lived an elegant life, who said, "I am what surrounds me." But it could have been Robert Lowell. The very context and texture of *Life Studies* is, say, venerable stone porches, Edwardian clocks, pedigreed puppies, Rogers Peet pants, chauffeured autos, home billiard tables, and wall-to-wall leather-bound books. At times the sheer weight of possessions burdens Lowell's volume. Snodgrass, on the other hand, happily wears his relative poverty on his shirt-sleeve. Experience has taught him "That all the ordinary / Surrounds of social life are futile and vain." Or, put another way, "There is a value underneath / The gold and silver in my teeth." Snodgrass sees the typical American's materialism as spiritually stultifying. In "Flash Flood" he dramatizes the futility of such materialism by narrating how one act of God or man can splinter "the goods they had used their / lives collecting." He implies that such a severance is far from tragic. Indeed, after the stock market crash of the 1930s people, in his opinion, "then began to live." In this sense his second book, *After Experience,* is an American poetic counterpart of E. M. Forster's English novel, *Howards End;* both books relate, in symbolic acts, the poverty of the inner life of the middle and upper classes when possessions take precedent over persons. One poem is concerned with the "company men" who "will spend their lives / In glossy houses kept by glossy wives," a condemnation which echoes that of *Heart's Needle,* in which he assails "the young who sell / their minds to retire at forty." Another poem compares such men to moths who, trapped, are impelled by a "blind fanatical drive." But Snodgrass's consummate statement on materialism is found in "The Platform Man," a poem which sets forth his personal philosophy (platform) of minimal possessions and minimal expectations. Here he employs the figure of a double-amputee on a platform as symbol for man beggared by man. The poet concludes,

> I'd travel light: taking nothing
> Free and give no quarter.

> The curse is far from done
> When they've taken your daughter;
> They can take your son.

The taken daughter, as we shall see, is the event which gave rise to Snodgrass's most poignant poems.

The materialism of the company man leads to blind conformity, the subject of many other poems. "Lobsters in the Window" is a portrait of men as creatures, "heaped in their common trench." Snodgrass, obsessed with the individual's loss of identity in America, gives us poems on the anonymity of lovers checked into motels under assumed names; servicemen setting out for the East in camouflaged uniforms; businessmen who "dress just far enough behind the fashions / And think right thoughts"; black-robed academicians for whom a committee gives the proper "opinions on fine books" and chooses "clothing fit / For the integrated area where he'll live."

Like Lowell, Snodgrass obviously has experienced alienation in the no-man's-land of mid-century America. But if Lowell is the poet of voyages, always traveling somewhere in search of meaning—Rome to Paris, Boston to Dunbarton, home to lovers' lane—Snodgrass is the poet of withdrawals and returns—the soldier home on leave, the soldier revisiting San Francisco, Ulysses brought home alone to no-man's-land, the postoperative patient returned to consciousness, the wandering lover restored to his beloved, the native returning home after fifteen years, the poet to his favorite writing place, the professor to the classroom, the endless return of the seasons, and especially the bittersweet return of a separated father to his daughter.

Heart's Needle is a book composed of nineteen short poems plus the ten poems of the title cycle. The pieces are characterized by the essential egocentricity of the confessional poet. Indeed, in one Snodgrass exclaims,

> While civilizations come down with the curse,
> Snodgrass is walking through the universe.[7]

Like the "Life Studies" sequence, *Heart's Needle* is arranged roughly in chronological order to conform with the progression of the poet's life. But, instead of childhood traumas and father hatred, Snodgrass's emotional life seems to have begun with the war, and his return from it. This leads into a period of rumination, a teaching career, marriage, fatherhood, divorce, remarriage. Unlike the poems of Lowell and Donald Justice, Snodgrass's reveal no compulsion to return to the child's garden with verses.

The first poem, "Ten Days Leave," strikes the chord of alienation which reverberates throughout the book. The serviceman on leave, feeling vastly changed by war and experience, finds that nothing at all has changed: "His folks / Pursue their lives like toy trains on a track." This image of the oval train track could stand for Snodgrass's deterministic worldview: all things are cyclical; even the "seasons bring us back once more / like merry-go-round horses." Though we return to our point of departure, in our end is not our beginning—either we or the departure point itself may have drastically changed during our absence. The returned serviceman, for instance, feels in his own home like "A tourist whispering through the priceless rooms / Who must not touch things."

"Returned to Frisco, 1946" continues the alienation theme. Stripped of identity by uniform and service number, the soldier shoulders along a rail with the others, "like pigs." Earlier they had scrambled up hostile beaches "like rabbits." Reduced to an animalistic state, the poet returns to the saintly city only to find the Golden Gate Bridge, that rainbow of promise, "fading away astern." On the other hand, Alcatraz has been prettified with flowers. The war has canceled free will. Hope is dimmed, and over all looms the shadow of prison house.

"Mehtis . . . ou tis" is centered on the famous pun from book 9 of the *Odyssey* (in which, at a banquet, Odysseus relates his adventures since leaving Troy, in particular his encounters with the Lotus-Eaters and the Cyclops). In this further exploration of alienation and lack of identity Snodgrass adopts a rare persona in the figure of Odysseus, who disguised himself as No Man and was able thus to save himself. Perhaps, the poet is saying, by abandoning all past identity, one can create a new self. Like Odysseus, the returning warrior might begin again.

The poem, however, is not one of Snodgrass's best. Its lofty allusions, its untranslated title from the Greek, its dedication to a psychotherapist who is never identified as such (though knowledge of whose profession is essential to comprehension of the second stanza addressed to him), are all barriers to communication.

"At the Park Dance," with its dancing couples who are even in physical closeness "loving strangers," is a minor development of the alienation theme. "Orpheus" is something else again.

Snodgrass here, more successfully than in the Odysseus poem, dons the mask of the legendary husband and poet who has lost his beloved. It may not be too much to assume that the poem is his expression of grief over the loss through divorce of his first wife. Though Snodgrass is at his best when speaking in his own voice, Orpheus' is singularly appropriate here. Returned from an expedition, married, and then separated from his young bride, Orpheus, like Snodgrass, paid a heavy penalty for "looking back." We can even compare the verse Snodgrass makes with the Orphic poetry of early Greek writers; in true Orphism one finds the sense of guilt and the need for atonement, the suffering and the ultimate belief in immortality, which characterize his own poetry.

Dedicated to the poet's second wife, "Papageno" is about the poet's search for love after the fracture of his first union. Just as Orpheus had his lyre, Papageno has his flute—both symbols for the poetry Snodgrass employs to call the world to love. Snodgrass here seems to confuse Mozart's Papageno with the opera's hero, Tamino, who possesses the "stealthy flute." Papageno, on the other hand, carries a pipe of Pan and—later—a set of chimes (*Silberglöckchen*). In Mozart's opera *The Magic Flute* Papageno's instrument was bestowed by the Powers of Darkness and had the power to inspire love. So Snodgrass, in the dark time after divorce, "went to whistle up a wife," seeking love and purification.

That his search was a long and dark one is evident in the symbolic landscape—or psychescape—of the next poem, "The Marsh." The dead limbs, rotting logs, and snarled sun are emblems for the poet's state of mind. The low level of the swamp is an equation for the spiritual, negative, and destructive state he has entered. At the time the water's surface is a mirror which presents an image for self-contemplation, consciousness, and revelation. In "heavy waters" Snodgrass recognizes the need to deliver himself out of this state: "Stick in the mud, old heart, what are you doing here?" (An interesting comparison can be made between his swamp poem, Lowell's "Dunbarton," Roethke's "The Premonition" and "First Meditation," Plath's "Full Fathom Five" and "Sheep in Fog," and Kunitz's "Father and Son." All five poets seek purification from the darkest waters.)

In Snodgrass's "September in the Park" the poet has emerged from darkness. But the world in which he finds himself is still hazy, a landscape of marginal things—a dim sun, some dying leaves, and squirrels gathering food for winter. The poet has traveled further inland, away from the bog of despair, but he is still wandering, has still attained nothing to replace that which he has lost. All he has is a memory of his hand upon his wife's breast. True tenderness is felt in these several poems. Whereas Lowell has never written a love poem, only poems of marriage, Snodgrass is capable of transmitting much more feeling in matters of the heart. He achieves this partially through great directness and simplicity, partially through a tone which one critic has described as "dreamy precision," giving us human encounters something like "snowdrops in water, that are so full of implications."[8] Compared to his tender apostrophes, Lowell's wifely poems are harsh indeed.

With "The Operation" the book shifts focus and the poet's quest is partially fulfilled. The dark of the swamp, the hanging smoke of the park, lift. The reader discovers the poet undergoing purification in a dazzling world of white. In the hospital the poet is symbolically reborn; the knife which shaves his body hair leaves him "white as a child." The knife also makes of him a sacrifice, the naked poet on display for strangers to flay. (The poem is related to "The Examination" from his second book, *After Experience;* in that poem it is the poet's brain and not his body which is operated upon.) Through totally delivering himself up the poet regains the world. His last vision is of the world beyond, inverted and slow, but nevertheless quite "gay." He has awakened into a world of flowers and women. We can assume that one of the women by his bedside is the new partner he has spent so long seeking. Hers are the flowers which make the world gay.

"The Operation," then, is about human recovery and resilience. Using bodily recovery from an operation as metaphor, he explores the heart's recovery from lost love. Through sacrifice man can attain something greater than that which has been given up. The poem's two allusions are, as always with Snodgrass, highly relevant. It is not only his own long hospital gown which reminds the poet of Pierrot. "Little Peter" has traditionally been the artist-lover of soaring imagination who must grimly hide his real passion behind a comic mask. The second allusion, to "a schoolgirl first offering her sacrament," functions not only as a parallel to the hospital gown, but, as Donald T. Torchiana says, reinforces the theme of guilt purged through sacrifice.

For better or worse, "The Operation" is the poem which has occasioned scores of imitations by less skillful writers—works which constitute the "my-stomach-laced-up-like-a-football" school of poetry. (The quotation is from Anne Sexton, but Snodgrass's operation poem is the original.) With its clinical observations, its unflinching attention to such details as aluminum bowls and cold sponges, rubber gloves and pared pubic hair, the poem makes successful use of subject matter formerly thought unfit for poetry. The difference between this poem and many of its imitations is a vital one. Snodgrass contrasts the clinical with the emotional, the white-on-white hospital landscape with the world of flowers and love, the anesthetized patient with the recovered husband-lover. The poem is about deliverance from a bad time to a better, the salvation of the spirit. His imitators, by way of contrast, too often use the means and forget the end; they are clinical for the sake of being shocking. They shout, "Look, Ma! No cavity's too sacred to write about! The anus, the vagina, the Caesarian section!" This is a vision far different from and more limited than Snodgrass's sad hospital of the world, in which one dies to become resurrected, is cut to become whole.

It would be nice to leave the poet and his love together in that hospital room. Nice, but contrary to Snodgrass's book and life. So the autobiographical chronicle continues with "Riddle," a poem of separation from Jan, the second love, and "Winter Bouquet," a poem of reunion. In the latter Snodgrass perhaps plays with his name when he inventories those "grasses gone to seed." The dry strawflowers are a symbol for the poet without his love, a husk devoid of past vitality. Only a woman's love can revivify the poet's body/spirit, much as the love of women who gathered pods during the war years to fill life preservers saved shipwrecked men. Both acts save men from being lost. In the third and final stanza, when Jan returns, the poet blows the weed-seed to the March wind. This act of delight and fertility celebrates the reunion, as do the following two "Songs," erotic poems of man's dependence on woman, woman's dependence on man.

"Seeing You Have . . ." and "Home Town" reveal the poet, for all his new connubial bliss, to be haunted by other feelings. The first addresses itself to the fact that the poet is not quite happily monogamous. The second is a portrait of the artist as an older man, rewalking the streets of his youth and compulsively hunting what he has outgrown. It is a poem which invites comparison with Peter Taylor's short story "Drug Store."

The poet's quest continues. He leaves the scene of his youth, and the next poem, "A Cardinal," finds him in a gully within a wood. Yet even in this voluntary withdrawal the poet cannot escape the world about him. Still he hears the uniformed college air cadets marching and counting cadence; trucks and trailers grinding on the turnpike; airplanes soaring in the air; factories turning out consumer goods. Even the woods itself is spoiled by the poet's contemporaries: toilet paper, lovers' litter, and beer cans spoil the habitat. One is reminded of the sweet, spoiled Thames of *The Waste Land.*

A writer of words no one wishes to read, a member of a military service but between wars, the poet finds hope in identifying with the bird of the poem's title. Snodgrass's search for meaning in life is encapsulized in the words of the "song" he attributes to that red bird:

> "I fight nobody's battles;
> don't pardon me for living.
>
> The world's not done to me;
> it is what I do;
> whom I speak shall be;
> I music out my name
> and what I tell is who
> in all the world I am."

It is significant that, once more, as in "Winter Bouquet" and "These Trees Stand . . ." and "April Inventory," the quest for identity is linked to the ability to say his name. A name which, in one poem, he calls "absurd, miraculous as sperm, and as decisive" and which, in many other poems, he changes entirely by reversing the letters and attributing authorship to "S. S. Gardons."

It is equally significant that the creature chosen for projection of the self is, first, a bird and, second, a red one. Birds, of course, are very often used in literature to symbolize human souls. (Think, for instance, of the *Mirach,* in which Mohammed found the Tree of Life in the middle of heaven, about which perched those many brilliant birds, the souls of the faithful.) More specifically, Snodgrass's bird seems to be symbol of thought, imagination, or spiritual relationships. Certainly, as a creature of the Element of Air, it denotes loftiness and lightness of spirit, which can descend to the earth then rise again and again in perpetual mediation between "heaven" and earth, as did Shelley's skylark.

The color of Snodgrass's bird determines its secondary symbolism. The color of blood, of the life force, as well as of fire and purification, the cardinal is a near perfect figure for the poet surrounded by philistines. More brilliant than they, and dedicated to truth and beauty and art, he strikes a strong contrast to those who earn their living praising only "what it pays to praise" (for instance, Snodgrass suggests, soap and garbage cans). Like the cardinal in the wood, the poet is a bright spot in the thickets of commerce. Like "Papageno," the poet/cardinal whistles in the dark to drive the devils off. But whistle though he may, the poet is still, at poem's end, somewhere in the weeds. He has not yet emerged a whole self. He does, though, seem to know better than before who and where he is.

Condemnation of the American middle and upper classes continues in "The Campus on the Hill." The poet has at last progressed from the swamp to the weeds and from the weeds to a house on a hill. The serviceman is now college instructor. But the America which surrounds him is the same. Even within the groves of academe the values deemed important are not those of the mind. The poem rails at the children of the *nouveaux riches* for their unthinking conformity.

And was there ever a more poignantly modern couplet than this:

> The pear tree lets its petals drop
> Like dandruff on a tabletop.

From "April Inventory" these lines from the last poem to precede the "Heart's Needle" sequence convey the poet's frame of mind after all that has gone before. The man who chased girls must now nudge himself to look at his female pupils, so great is their age differential; the poet who has lost hair and teeth has gained a wife and an analyst. Yet, through it all, the poet/protagonist has managed to adhere to his youthful ideals. He has not sold out. His "inventory" is not one of capital gains or material possessions. It is one of humble and modest achievements on the spiritual plane. While the "solid scholars" were pushing ahead for better situations and salaries, Snodgrass was teaching a girl a song of Mahler's; showing a child the colors of the luna moth ("and how to love"); and easing in turn a wife and an old man who was dying.[9]

While not learning a "blessed thing they pay you for," it is obvious the poet has learned how to be William DeWitt Snodgrass. In this poem he can finally name his full name. He is resigned to growing older without getting richer, to the loss of youth and physical beauty, because these resignations are firmly rooted within a great commitment to that which is of more value than youth, beauty, or money. A truly individual comprehension of one song of Mahler's, or of one butterfly's wing, is worth all the books on books. Above all Snodgrass preaches the gospel of gentleness in a violent world, a gentleness which "will outspeak and has its reasons." It is this general gentleness which preserves the poet in a world of specialists.

Just as the writing of the poem "The Operation" marked a turning in Snodgrass's life, the entrance of a feminine muse to inspire and perhaps save him, so too is a similar milestone marked by the "Heart's Needle" cycle. Only it is the subtraction of a loved one rather than her addition which prompts the poetry. Inspired by the enforced separation from his young daughter, Cynthia, the sequence of ten poems—one each for each season over a two-and-one-half year period—shows the experienced father-poet groping for meaning and survival when the world he has created and grown into falls about him.

Appropriately the cycle begins in winter (of 1952), the terminal season, with a poem directed to the lost child. The daughter, born in another winter and during the martial Korean War and, by implication, during the marital war the poet waged with his wife, is seen as a victim of strife. Just as the snows of Asia are fouled by the war's fallen soldiers, so Snodgrass's daughter's mind ("A landscape of new snow") shall be disturbed by marital strife. As in "The Operation," white connotes purity. But the hospital white signaled a new beginning; here the same color portends a terminus, the end of family life as the poet has come to know it. Comparing himself to a chilled tenant farmer, the poet surveys his daughter's purity and his own chances for restraining "the torments of demented summer." We later come to realize that this "demented summer" is a figure for the separation from his wife, which he was unable to forestall.

The next poem, of spring 1953, finds the daughter three years old. Father and daughter are portrayed planting seeds. He cautions her to "sprinkle them in the hour / When shadow falls across their bed." In other words, she should look toward the living in the presence of death or separation. He recognizes now that the daughter, his own seed, shall come to sprout in his absence. Someone else shall have to "weed" her. Yet the poet seems to be saying that she shall grow almost *because* of his absence. There is a recognition of the shadow which has fallen across that other garden bed, the nuptial, and when the poet declares, "Child, we've done our best," he speaks not just for himself and her in regard to the damaged garden, but for himself and his wife in regard to the ruined marriage.

Extremely subtle, these lyrics of "Heart's Needle" paradoxically cut deeper than Lowell's more overt outcries. Poem 3 of the sequence is a skillful symbolic portrait of the father/daughter/mother relationship during the summer after the spring planting. Employing the symbolic action of the child's swinging and tugging between them, Snodgrass communicates at once the tug-of-war between a mother with "custody" and a father with "visiting privileges" and the heavy tug of love on the human heartstrings. The Korean War again forms a counterpoint and counterpart to the domestic clash; both parents are compared first to cold war soldiers who never give ground but never gain any—stubborn and stoic parents between whose stations the child swings back and forth—and, second, to prisoners of war. As with the opposing sides of a battle, "nobody seems very pleased." And with the poem's allusion to Solomon's wisdom the poet implies that, in order to save his daughter, he must first give her up. As in the biblical story, the true parent is the one who, rather than have the baby sawn in two, sacrifices all claim to possession.

Fall 1953. Poet and daughter walk in a public garden (in poem 4). Just as no one can hold back the autumn, the separation is inevitable. That which was lovely and gay is now a ghost of itself; in the poem the dandelion heads have turned gray. Snodgrass renders a symbolic landscape of dwindling and termination:

> . . . the asters, too, are gray,
> ghost-gray. Last night's cold
> is sending on their way
> petunias and dwarf marigold,
> hunched sick and old.

The poet next translates this landscape into the language of sickness and analysis: the morning glory vines become "nerves caught in a graph." But this image immediately melts into one of the broken lines of the poems the poet cannot write. Separation, analysis, and writer's block are all part of one interior landscape.

Still, perhaps all is not futile. In the penultimate stanza the pair find a flower among some late bloomers, a bud which may yet blossom in the daughter's room. Her life may yet flower after his departure. This possibility, however, is negated in the ultimate stanza. The poet tells, in a little parable, of a "friend's child" who cried upon the death of a cricket who used to sing outside her window. The cricket, of course, is another figure for the poet. As William Heyen reads these lines, they are a portent of grief for the daughter and death for the father. But, as Heyen says, "unspoken here is also the realization that he must continue his writing."[10] Herein lies a paradox: only the destruction of his marriage provides sufficient impetus for the renewal of his creative abilities.

The fifth poem concludes the first year, beginning with winter again, and introduces a greater depth of feeling. The daughter's loss finally is hideously real, not future possibility but present reality. Through skillful use of halting enjambment ("Although you are still three, / You are already growing / Strange to me"), the poet conveys emotionally not only the girl's physical development but also her increasing mental alienation from her father. This loss and alienation provoke the strongest image in the first half of the cycle: the poet feels himself a fox caught in a trap, a fox whose only salvation is to gnaw off his paw. That paw, remaining behind, is the flesh of his flesh, the daughter surrendered to the machinery of divorce. As the Bible says (Matt. 5:29), "If thy right eye offend thee, pluck it out, and cast *it* from thee." It is better to enter the Kingdom of Heaven blind, lame, or maimed than not at all.

The poem of the second spring is a memory piece occasioned by a walk on the riverbank with his daughter, who has brought an Easter egg. To interpret this egg as a traditional symbol of hope, potentiality, and immortality seems too painfully ironic. The Easter egg is here more precisely a symbol for the mystery of life, the poem's major theme. The second stanza is literally a rendering of the miracle of birth. The third relates an incident of flooded killdeer nests, the eggs lost to water. The fourth depicts a precarious nest, the fifth, dead starlings and a trapped pigeon. All these imitations of mortality are but preparations for the portrait of the father at his daughter's sickbed, when those miraculous lungs (of stanza 2) become caught and will not take air.

These recognitions of the brevity and destructive nature of life are by way of apology to the daughter for the revelation, saved for the eighth stanza, that the poet has remarried. He has another child, another wife. It is Snodgrass's attempt to make the most of this bad situation, our life, in which we have few choices and those we have may prove destructive to those we love.

The image of the net which snares the pigeon is not unlike the trap which snares the fox of the preceding poem. Both, like marriage and divorce, are traps. In letting the pigeon go to its keeper, the poet is reenacting his letting his daughter go to the custody of his wife. In each case he fears he has brought about destruction. Yet, as Heyen has said, destruction is perhaps "the inevitable outcome of any attempt to live the individual life."[11] We can only try to choose what is best.

Blue July and the poet is swinging his daughter again. Once more the back-and-forth movement of a swing conveys the pendulumlike push-pull relationship. He voices his hope that, though she climbs higher and farther from him, she may fall back to him the stronger for it.

Animals, war, and institutions are the three prevailing motifs of "Heart's Needle." In poem 8 the poet lives "next door to the jail"; the zoo's caged monkeys "consume each other's salt." (The image of caged animals recurs later as well.) When the poet's daughter visits, this autumn, he is Halloween, masquerading as a fox. (We remember the fox's foot left behind in poem 5; the fox, indeed, is the daughter, the life-red creature whose existence is so dear to the poet.) It is an irony that, when the daughter strips off her mask, her father's new neighbors still do not know who she is. As the face she wears in public is not her own, so in the poet's new life she has no essential identity. The false face and the grinning jack-o'-lantern are a pair of masks, the appearances the poet tries to maintain. Yet the jack-o'-lantern's face fronts a hollow core. Behind the grin, as behind the daughter's visits, there is an emptiness. The girl has no real participation in his life, only visits which should become less frequent for her own independence. That such independence is imminent is conveyed through her symbolic act of eating snow off his car. Years before she had, unrealistically, asked her father to catch a star, "pull off its skin / and cook it for our dinner." Her dining fare and her vision are already more down-to-earth. The poet knows he should relinquish his hold on the girl. Yet to do so would be to create an awful void, summarized in the line, "Indeed our sweet / foods leave us cavities."

Animals, institutions, and war are again the motifs for the penultimate poem of the cycle, a piece which must count as the strongest. Set within a museum in Iowa City, the poem's stuffed animals are arrested in motion "like Napoleon's troops." This institution is clearly Snodgrass's microcosm of the larger world, where creatures are pitted against creatures in constant rage. The bison shoving at his calf is not unlike the poet fighting with his wife. The lioness standing over her cub is no less envious than the daughter's mother. The poet and his wife are the poem's two Olympian elk who stand bound and fixed in their everlasting enmity.

These animal images are succeeded by a catalog of the museum's horrors: a two-headed foal, a hydrocephalic goat, a limbless calf, Siamese twin dogs, and more. These are clearly outward manifestations of the poet's inner state, like the dwarf marigold of poem 4, those flowers so "hunched sick and old." Yet these visions are not of flowers but of flesh. And the catalog includes unborn and born, "putty-colored children curled / in jars of alcohol" as well. Man himself has fought no less than members of the animal kingdom. Only those here arrested in alcohol can avoid being born into the world and spilling blood. The poet cannot accept man's nature; he does not understand it, has no answers. He only knows that he lives less than one mile from his daughter and has not seen her for more than three months.

It is a dark, almost suicidal poem, culminating in the terrible vision of a world which "moves like a diseased heart / packed with ice and snow." Unlike that other poem of a poet-scavenger moving among the garbage dump of a civilization—Lowell's "Skunk Hour"—there is here no glimmer of hope.

That hope, nevertheless, is to be found in the tenth and final poem. Winter gives way to spring. Separation yields to reunion. Images of life and recreation crowd the short poem. Nothing has really changed, of course; the seasons merely "bring us back once more / like merry-go-round horses"; the train travels its oval track. But the poet is reconciled! He will not accept the advice of friends who state that he would leave his daughter alone if he truly loved her. (Job's advisors?) His life is inexorably bound to hers, however little of it he is handed. He is like the coons and bears of the park, "punished and cared for," those creatures who stretch forth fingers for whatever scraps are given. After ten seasons of separation she is still his daughter. A book of both separations and reunions ends with the latter.

As poet-critic Heyen summarizes deftly, "*Heart's Needle* remains a poetry without answers, but it is a poetry of total awareness. Inherent in its criticism of the way things are is the ability of the intelligence that informs its lyrics to accept this reality and to struggle against it at the same time. *Heart's Needle,* without caterwauling, free from what Ezra Pound calls "emotional slither," takes on dimensions of the tragic."[12]

With the tenth poem the "Heart's Needle" sequence ends. Which is not to say that Snodgrass's poetic exploration of his relationship with his daughter ends. The second book, *After Experience* (1968), opens with four poems which seem to have been written at the time of *Heart's Needle* and which continue the cycle though collected outside it. (A fifth additional poem to his daughter closes the *Remains* volume.) "Partial Eclipse" uses that meteorological phenomenon as metaphor both for the father's refusal to be blacked-out of the girl's life and for the very nature of the strained relationship. Like the full moon during eclipse, at least "one glint was left." Yet it is only a glint. That which was once full and bright is now "dim as a ghost." "September" is a brief chronicle of loss. The heron they saw together is gone, the newts in the creek are gone, and, of course, the daughter herself is gone. The dry landscape reinforces the impressions.

The ephemeral nature of human relationships is the subject of "Reconstructions." In each of three opening stanzas Snodgrass slowly builds his evidence: a plant left behind, the Indian gift of a doll, a pathetic owner/pet drama. Yet it is not relationships in general which agonize the poet, but that between himself and his daughter. And he realizes that in saying she did not mind leaving the plant behind, in snatching the doll away, and in leaving the sitting dog trembling for her command to relax, the daughter is reenacting roles she herself has been forced to observe or play during her parents' separation. She has turned grief into play. And nothing can be done to change this state of affairs. At the poem's conclusion the daughter is left at her mother's; the dog is given away. Always outward, away from the poet himself, the loved ones go.

"The First Leaf" seems to bid farewell to the subject which has sustained Snodgrass for fourteen poems. The daughter is now more than six years old and going away for a full year. The season is autumn and the first leaf which falls from its branch and spins across the windshield is like the daughter herself, torn free from her origins to spin out into the world. (Snodgrass together with Roethke seems intuitively to know, moreover, that the leaf is one of the eight "common emblems" of Chinese symbolism, being the allegory of happiness. With the fall of the leaf, happiness drops to dust.) The reader is told the daughter will travel by train, and when the poet posits the image of cattle transported in a trailer before his car, like men shipped to battle, we know he is associating by image the impersonal and mechanical process by which such a separation is decreed. The poet admits to a sense of guilt at having a life of his own at the expense of hers. He has been able to remarry only by shedding her mother; able to write poems again only through finding the subject of his daughter's loss. The result of all this suffering, then, is that "Now I can earn a living / By turning out elegant strophes." Another Snod-grassian irony. From out of the wreckage of his family life the poet has found a new life and new creativity. As someone once observed, some eggs must be broken to make an omelet. But what a terrible price to pay for a handful of poems! We feel the weight of his loss in the last four lines, carefully controlled and understated, yet unmistakably bereft:

> You move off where I send you;
> The train pulls down its track.
> We go about our business;
> I have turned my back.

That he did not, could not, turn his back is evident in the later poem, "To a Child," with its themes of fertility and futility. Published in *Remains* in 1970, it gives evidence that Snodgrass has not yet abandoned the relationship as his primary subject. Yet for all its obsessive quality the subject has been handled in all fifteen poems with great emotional control. So obviously hurt into writing, the poet is, nevertheless, never mawkish or self-pitying. These are dry, brittle poems. Even in extremely personal revelation, Snodgrass somehow preserves a proper aesthetic distance between his psyche and his Smith-Corona. The "Heart's Needle" cycle and the five subsequent poems which might have belonged to it is an artistic victory over the defeats and pains of quotidian existence.

One of Snodgrass's most successful techniques for achieving this distance is a borrowed one, T. S. Eliot's "objective correlative." In the poem in which the poet-father first acknowledges that his daughter has become a stranger to him, for instance, he shifts from the personal to the ostensibly impersonal. Snodgrass leaps from the situation at hand to the image of the fox who "backtracks and sees the paw, / Gnawed off, he cannot feel; / Conceded to the jaw / Of toothed, blue steel." The paw, as we have said, must be equated with the lost daughter, the trap with the divorce. But by translating the details of his life into meta-phoric terms, Snodgrass avoids sentimentality without losing sentiment and forcefully communicates the full measure of his personal loss. Indeed, "Snodgrass is walking through the uni-verse" in his poems: Snodgrass the man is seen by Snodgrass the poet as a character in a drama viewed from afar.

Another check on direct emotional overflow is the use of his symbolic landscapes, really poetic psychescapes, as in the fourth poem of the cycle. Those dwarf marigolds, old and sick, are an objective projection of the father's subjective state when he realizes he must part with his little girl. The device is most effective in the ninth poem in which the poet contemplates the unnatural condition of their separation as well as the nature of man; the poet wanders through that museumscape of cysts, fistulas, and cancers. The poet is no Shelley, falling and bleeding upon the thorns of life. Rather, he records in apparently cool fashion the outer signs of his inner state. This technique is developed to near perfection in Snodgrass's second book, in the poem "What We Said," whose twenty-eight lines detail scenery which mirrors every human grief. But the poems in *After Experience* also reveal the danger of this device when overworked. The symbols and symbolic acts show signs of strain. The moon obligingly disappears on cue, a kind of *deus ex machina,* in sympathetic synchronization with the daughter's departure; furtive lovers drop aspirin in a vase of motel flowers, unconsciously performing an act of sympathetic magic as they express their desire for a life with continuity, if not permanence.

Sometimes, of course, these symbolic landscapes and acts coalesce for Snodgrass to form a magnificently reverberant poem, as in "Powwow," a trenchant comment on the destruction of the culture of the American Indian by the American "Americans." In performing their ceremonials now, the Indians "all dance with their eyes turned / Inward—like a woman nursing / A sick child she already knows / Will die." At the poem's conclusion the tourist drives away from the performance "squinting, / Through red and yellow splatterings on the windshield." The bright guts of insects that go with him resemble the bright war paint of the Indians, who also flung themselves against the oncoming force and shall not live again. Here image and intention are one. (Many confessional poets have written of the shadow images that slide across their bedroom walls, notably Delmore Schwartz in "In the Naked Bed in Plato's Cave" and John Berryman in "Beethoven Triumphant"; Snodgrass alone seems to find inspiration in the objects which cross his windshield.)

Such achievement is unfortunately rare in *After Experience.* Too often the landscape, the carefully planted symbol, the internal pun, seem too deliberate, too academic. The Snodgrass of *Heart's Needle* was a taker of risks; too many of the purely personal poems in *After Experience* smack of the ingrown nail—everything growing inward, with too much consciousness of Self and Craft. The four new poet-daughter poems seem blurry, heavy carbons of the sharp originals. They were, perhaps, written at the time of the cycle and deliberately withheld from the book for that reason. And, as if aware his situation is no longer so unique, his revelations no longer so revealing, in the second book Snodgrass coarsens his language as if that alone might still shock. Elegance has fled from the poetry, the fine elegance of, say, "Winter Bouquet." When the poet passes a drive-in now, it must be described as one of the "hot pits where our teens / Fingerfuck."

Not that Snodgrass need resort to gutter language to shock. The title poem, "After Experience," describing an act of self-defense so acutely painful no one can read it without a wince of the eye, a flop of the stomach, is ample evidence of his rhetorical powers. Aside from the purely personal and confessional poems with the manner, if not the power, of *Heart's Needle,* the poems in the second volume must be categorized in three other distinct groups. First come the more objective poems, including the supremely successful "A Flat One," which amplifies the hospital imagery of "The Operation" but makes the act of saving a life seem a selfish gesture and comments on modern life in a more devastating way than any other poem in recent American literature; "Lobsters in the Window," which imagistically recreates the primordial life as it comments on mass conformity; and "The Platform Man," a poem in which guilt and mutilation fuse in a most beautifully placed and seemingly inevitable pun; as well as an uneven group of five poems attempting to reexperience particular paintings by Matisse, Vuillard, Manet, Monet, and Van Gogh. The last, a very fluid poem utilizing many quotations from the artist's letters, is the most successful of the group.

A third category is a generous selection of translations, fourteen in number, from Rilke, Bonnefoy, Rimbaud, and others. Though unqualified to comment on the linguistic veracity of these translations, we can say they are among the book's most moving poems. Snodgrass has managed to find in other languages poems which reflect his own plight—such as von Eichendorff's "On My Child's Death," that poet's loss by death paralleling Snodgrass's through divorce. In rendering these poems into the American idiom, Snodgrass has found a voice which at times seems more authentic than his own. As statements on grief, the translations are crucial to an understanding of Snodgrass and where the poet presently has arrived. (In the same year he published *After Experience* Snodgrass also published a quite different series of translations, the *Gallows Songs* of Christian Morgenstern, on which he collaborated with Lore Segal. This poet of fancy and lyricism, for whom "time and space are not realities," seems less suited to Snodgrass's personal vision than, say, Rilke and Rimbaud. To compare his translation of Morgenstern's "The Moonsheep" with that of E. M. Valk proves the point.)[13]

The fourth category is not a group at all, but a single poem, "The Examination," the only satire in the Snodgrassian canon. It is a dark allegory on the examining of Ph.D. candidates by university faculty members, perhaps the result of his own examination in literary history for the Ph.D. in English at Iowa. During the course of the poem's examination the victim is physically and spiritually dismembered. The penultimate stanza concludes, "Well; that's a beginning. The next time, they can split / His tongue and teach him to talk correctly, can give / Him opinions on fine books and choose clothing fit / For the integrated area where he'll live." The poem is an elaboration of the theme of Berryman's "Dream Song #8," in which officials of an institution tell the patient, "if you watch Us instead, / yet you may saved be. Yes," this after "They blew out his loves, his interests." Snodgrass's poem also stands comparison with Swinburne's "In Sepulcretis," in which a man is dismembered by those who "Spy, smirk, sniff, snap, snort, snivel, snarl and sneer." Swinburne's conclusion is, "This is fame." Snodgrass would probably disagree, and say, "This is life." Snodgrass's poem seems to have started a spate of such poetic allegories in our time, of which a late example is Erica Jong's "The Book," from her *Fruits & Vegetables* (1971), in which another examining committee decides "to repossess my typewriter, my legs / my Phi Beta Kappa key, one breast, / any children I may have, / & my expresso machine."

After Experience, like Anthony Hecht's second collection, *The Hard Hours,* bears testimony to the effort of a truly excellent poet to push a unique vision and practice beyond viability. Snodgrass's major achievements remain *Heart's Needle* and sections of the tougher *Remains.* But when in the second volume he does connect, as he does at least nine times in the hefty book, it is with poems which probably shall endure. "What We Said," "The Platform Man," "Leaving the Motel," "A Flat One," "Powwow"— and, for sheer singularity, "The Examination"—are all poetic events for which we should be grateful.

If *After Experience* seemed too varied a collection, the "Remains" poems of "S. S. Gardons" is a highly unified sequence.

Just as a daughter lost through divorce was Snodgrass's subject for the ten poems of the "Heart's Needle" sequence, the loss of a sister by death provides the occasion for this new eight-poem cycle. The sequence begins with a poem on the poet's mother and ends with one addressed to his daughter. In between the quality of his experience is rendered with infinite detail. In all eight the pivotal experience is the sister's death, which occurs ironically enough on Independence Day. Only through death does the mousy sister achieve a kind of independence from sickness, a dull life, and a domineering mother.

The title, *Remains,* reverberates with meaning. On one level it refers to the bodily remains from which the spirit of the girl has departed, and on which the undertaker has undertaken an elaborate cosmetic job (in "Viewing the Body"). But "to remain" is also to be left behind, which is the case with the survivors of the dead girl. To remain is also not to be included or comprised, which is the situation of the poet himself, an alien in a small town which thrives on conformity and misfortune. Finally, the title may be intended for the manuscript of the poems itself, which is blurbed by the publisher as the literary remains of "S. S. Gardons":

> This sequence of poems was collected by his friends after his disappearance on a hunting trip in the mountains. From the condition of his abandoned motorcycle, it was impossible to determine whether he suffered foul play, was attacked by animals, merely became confused and lost, or perhaps fell victim to amnesia. At present, the case is listed as unsolved.[14]

For the time being, at least, Snodgrass has chosen to phase out his nom de plume.

Remains opens with portraits of Snodgrass's mother and father. The first is portrayed as one who "moves by habit, hungering and blind"; the second, one who exacts "no faith, no affection" and whose entire life has been a "programmed air of soft suspension" which he survives in, "cradled and sustained." To such a couple were born the poet and his sister, "The Mouse" of the poem by that title. Like the small mouse they once found outdoors, the sister—small and dull, yet ever so much more precious than the found creature—dies. Yet, unlike the mouse, she is unmourned by the brother. As children, they were taught to "be well-bred," not to cry over dead animals, so that when the genuine, human tragedy presents itself, the poet "wouldn't spare one tear." His upbringing bars the display of true emotion, an observation which holds true in relation to the writing of these poems themselves. William Heyen observes, "the potential for bathos is certainly here, but the metrical control and hard rhymes, because the employment of conscious technique always implies the poet is attempting to control highly emotional matter by mind, stop the voice from breaking, stave off the purely melodramatic."[15] The brother/sister relationship here is reminiscent of that of Tom and Laura in Tennessee William's moving *The Glass Menagerie,* with the mousy sister especially resembling Laura.

The mouse analogy is carried into the next poem, "Viewing the Body," in which the girl's gray life is contrasted with the gaudiness of her death,

> Flowers like a gangster's funeral;
> Eyeshadow like a whore.
> They all say isn't she beautiful.
> She, who never wore
>
> Lipstick or such a dress.

Rather, "gray as a mouse," she had crept about the dark halls of her mother's house. The shadow sister of the youthful hero of Housman's "To an Athlete Dying Young," this girl paradoxically achieves her only glory through dying. Yet it is a false victory, as all deaths must be, and the worldly trappings are grotesquely unsuitable as props for this girl's earthly departure. The red satin folds of the coffin are "obscene." The deadly circumstance and pomp seem a hideous parody of her life-style.

Exactly one year after her death the poet and his wife are back in the parents' house, sensitive to the family's awareness of the anniversary. The girl's unworn party dress is still closeted, her stuffed animals still shelved. The poet senses that his young wife is unforgiven by the family for being alive—why her, and not the sister instead, the sister, whose deathday is ironically the wife's birthday? More metaphysical than most others of Snodgrass, this poem shifts into speculation on the kingdom of the dead, a wondering at where, "Into what ingrown nation has she gone / Among a people silent and withdrawn." Entering the still mournful house after some Independence Day fireworks display, the poet realizes the full extent of his personal alienation: "No one would hear me, even if I spoke."

"Disposal," the next piece, is in many ways redundant. Though it carries forward the action of the cycle—the dead girl's personal effects are finally disposed of—it contributes little new to the appraisal of the girl. Her one party dress unworn, she lived in dresses sewn of canceled patterns and markdowns. The poet's preoccupation with the gaudy casket is again manifest; he compares her daily dress with the way she was laid out in death:

> . . . Spared of all need, all passion,
> Saved from loss, she lies boxed in satins
>
> Like a pair of party shoes
> That seemed to never find a taker . . .

The last two poems shift focus from the dead to the surviving. Out of morbid curiosity the poet makes his journey (another Snodgrassian journey!) home on the first "anniversary" of the girl's death, as we have seen, to find nothing changed. He has survived, the parents have survived, but his mother and father seem more like the living dead. That they do not even acknowledge the world about them is communicated symbolically by the two stone lions which guard their house entrance: ". . . someone has patched / Cement across their eyes." The poem carries other symbolic freight as well, including some cherries from a tree the parents still try to protect from neighborhood boys. Is it too much to suggest that these cherries are symbolic of the virginity they also tried, too successfully, to protect from neighboring males? The cherries which now rot in their lawn are one with the now rotting virgin in her grave.

The final poem, "To a Child"—already mentioned in conjunction with the "Heart's Needle" cycle—is an inventory of past events, the cyclical nature of life, and its ironies. The child addressed is obviously the daughter of the earlier book, to which this poem might rightly be appended in some future edition. This is a bittersweet catalog, like the earlier "April Inventory"; the poet concludes there is much for the living to learn from another's death, be it that of a sister or merely that of "the glow of rotten / Wood, the glimmering being that consumes / The flesh of a dead trout." The verse moves forward into a region of parasitic existences which suggest the lives of his parents. He urges his daughter, who has observed both his sister's death and her mother's pregnancy, to attain the possibility and the meaning of love. Without love we die. Yet—the final irony—"With love we kill each other." Love is for the poet the mistress without whom he cannot live yet with whom he cannot live.

This last is a horrifying group of poems, less sentimental and more sensational than "Heart's Needle," which it echoes in part; compare the conclusion of the latter, "We have to try," with the line from the earlier, "We try to choose our life"; compare, "And you have been dead one year" with "And you are still my daughter." The tone, the rhythm, and the effect are the same. Which is why Snodgrass can never truly disguise these poems, no matter what name he appends to them. In each book he speaks in a voice of suffering and guilt of marginal characters and separations.

NOTES

1. "A Note on S. S. Gardons," *Western Humanities Review* 25, no. 3 (Summer 1971): 253.

2. *Remains* was finally reprinted by BOA Editions in a trade paperback edition in 1985, making it available to the general public for the first time. For the new edition Snodgrass dropped the name Gardons and substantially revised the poem "Diplomacy: The Father."

3. "Finding a Poem," *Partisan Review,* Spring 1959.

4. "Master's in the Verse Patch Again," *The Contemporary Poet as Artist and Critic,* ed. Anthony Ostroff (Boston: Little, Brown, 1964), 114.

5. "After Experience Taught Me . . . ," in *After Experience* (New York: Harper and Row, 1968), 39. All references to poems in this book are to the original hardbound edition.

6. "Public Intimacy," *Nation,* 16 September 1968, 252.

7. All quotes from *Heart's Needle* are from the original edition (New York: Alfred A. Knopf, 1959). No paperback has been published.

8. Donald T. Torchiana, "Heart's Needle: Snodgrass Strides through the Universe," in *Poets in Progress: Critical Prefaces to Thirteen Contemporary Americans,* ed. Edward B. Hungerford (Evanston: Northwestern University Press, 1967), 114.

9. Torchiana, who seems to know Snodgrass personally, identifies the Mahler song as the *Lob des Hohen Verstands* and the girl as Rachel Chester, a promising young painter; the girl of the moth lore lessons, as one of Jan Snodgrass's daughters by a previous marriage; and the dying man as Fritz Jarck, whom Snodgrass had attended in a hospital. This must surely be the same Old Fritz of the later poem, "A Flat One" (in *After Experience*).

10. "Fishing the Swamp: The Poetry of W. D. Snodgrass," *Modern American Poetry: Essays in Criticism,* ed. Jerome Mazzaro (New York: David McKay, 1970), 358.

11. Ibid., 359.

12. Ibid., 361.

13. The Valk translation is readily available in *Modern European Poetry,* ed. Willis Barnstone (New York: Bantam Books, 1966).

14. "A Prefatory Note on the Author," unsigned preface to *Remains: Poems by S. S. Gardons.* Limited edition. (Mt. Horeb, Wis.: Perishable Press, 1970). All references are to this edition.

15. *Western Humanities Review* 25, no. 3 (Summer 1971): 253.

J. D. McCLATCHY

W. D. Snodgrass

The Mild, Reflective Art

It is not difficult to believe W. D. Snodgrass's boast that he is descended, on one side of his family, from Robert Herrick and, on the other, from Robert Burns. His lyricism is not only the most consistent among the confessional poets, it is the most insistent: "without some sort of external modification, like conventional stylistics," he has written, "it is extremely difficult to create a structure and tone complex enough to keep the language alive at all points." His syllabics and stresses and rhyme schemes are not meant to chasten his subject, but to balance its emotional demands and accommodate contradictory experiences and feelings: a language "alive" to the life it records. That life, in its meter-making argument, does not touch the extremes of madness or longing that aggravate the work of Sexton, Lowell, Plath, and Berryman. His family is not burdened with fame or wealth; his history is not haunted with attempts at suicide or perfection. Just as his verse is the successor to the severe, homely lyrics of Hardy and Frost, so too his losses and betrayals are the familiar ones, circumscribed by the small-town society to which our playwrights and novelists have accustomed us. In his poem "These Trees Stand . . ." Snodgrass describes his own poetry when he tells of a night nurse on ward rounds and "the mild, reflective art / Of focusing her flashlight on her blouse." The light he shines back on his own life reflects a sincerity, both technical and moral, that never excludes subtlety: complex but not complicated. The same strictness with which he measures his song is apparent in the lines he draws to trace his self, his story. In an early essay on D. H. Lawrence Snodgrass predicts the direction of all his own later work: "To know one's needs is really to know one's own limits, hence one's definition."[1] The

From J. D. McClatchy, *White Paper: On Contemporary American Poetry* (New York: Columbia University Press, 1989). Copyright © Columbia University Press. Reprinted by permission. Originally published in the *Massachusetts Review*, Spring 1975, the essay was revised for *White Paper*.

need for love which limits trust, the need for growth which limits security—the dilemmas that gather definition, itself continually revalued in his effort to say, with Parolles, "Simply the thing I am / Shall make me live."

Quoted on the dust jacket of *Heart's Needle* (1959), Robert Lowell wondered at Snodgrass's poetic origins: "He flowered in the most sterile of sterile places, a post war, cold war midwestern university's poetry workshop for graduate poets." Snodgrass's first models were consistent with such an atmosphere and curriculum; the congealed symbolism and obliquities of Empson and early Lowell. But his stylistic shift was more of an adjustment than a rejection:

> [The teachers at Iowa] were marvelous teachers, though at a certain point, I felt that they were teaching me to write learned, symbol-laden poems that any good modern poetry committee could write. They all thought I was wrong, and were really concerned for me. And they said, "You mustn't do this, you got a brain, you can't write this kind of tear-jerking stuff." But above all they had really taught me how to pack a poem with meaning, and from that it's a fairly easy jump to how to pack a poem with feeling, which to me tells a lot more. They were worth opposing. . . . You know, I had people like Robert Lowell, Berryman, all those people came there to teach, and they were worth fighting, too.[2]

This kind of respectful impatience began with his reading, the jaded quality of which drove him back to the poet's private intentions and personality which, in turn, revalued the poem:

> I remember when I was in school, we were all taught to write obscure, brilliant, highly symbolized poems about the loss of myth in our time, and, you know, it suddenly began to occur to me that I didn't care about the loss of myth in our time; frankly, I was glad to be rid of the stuff. . . . But we were all writing poems about what we thought "The Waste Land" was about. None of us had bothered to find out that "The Waste Land" isn't about that at all. We thought it was about that because you could make doctoral dissertations by talking about all the learned allusions in "The Waste Land" and how it was about, you know, the need for a "meaningful myth" in our lives; nobody had noticed it was about Eliot's insane wife and his frozen sex life. He had helped disguise this, with

Pound's assistance, by his editing of the poem. We believed people's doctoral statements about the poem. We believed Frost and Eliot when they said their poems were about other things than their own sex lives, and we can now look at the poems and see that that just isn't so at all.

The way he listened developed into the way he spoke, though as with other confessional poets it was the force of example which allowed his discovery. Some of these examples were local and personal; a young poet at Iowa named Robert Shelley was one:

> Just as I was writing imitation Lowell, he was writing imitation Hart Crane. Then all of a sudden he struck on a very simple, direct, lyrical style that really floored me—it was exactly the sort of poem all the critics were saying you couldn't write because our age was too fragmented or complicated or something. He only finished half a dozen of those poems, however, before he committed suicide. So all of a sudden, his style came onto the market—we were all very fond of him and now it seemed not only permissible but even a good thing to take that style he'd only begun and go on to develop it.[3]

A more recognizable influence was that of Randall Jarrell, whose own last books, *The Woman at the Washington Zoo* (1960) and *The Lost World* (1965), were decidedly more relaxed and autobiographical than his earlier work, and whose muted, civilized voice—along with those of Ransom and Roethke—Snodgrass came to recall:

> Lowell was my teacher at Iowa, but I'd been writing like him even before he came there (I think). I worked with Jarrell at a writer's conference in Boulder, Colorado, and he helped jar me out of that style. I showed him the same poems that practically all the best critics (Warren, Ransom, etc.) had liked and he didn't like any of them. He liked, instead, a piece I'd paraphrased from Ovid and two of Rilke's *Sonnets to Orpheus* (which later appear with a larger group of them in *After Experience*). So I began to suspect that it might really be better to simply say it, straight out, simply and directly. I could see that even with my modern heroes, Rilke and Rimbaud, there was always either a sense of direct surface narrative or else a musical and lyric thrust to carry you through the poem—meantime, I

was beginning to suspect that when most of us there at Iowa put the subrational up on the surface of the poem (as Rimbaud, for instance, had done) we were not making any discoveries that he hadn't already made.[4]

Rimbaud's poem *"Mémoire,"* for example—Snodgrass's translation of which appears in *After Experience*—sinks its pretext beneath fragmented symbolic equivalents. Snodgrass doesn't refuse to use symbols; in fact, he depends on them frequently, just as he employs satire or parable or personae, if that is what a particular poem requires. But, unlike Rimbaud, he foregrounds the actual experience drawn from life, always allowing subject to dominate symbol and trusting his musical substructure to carry the expressive, unconscious force of both his pretext and his poem. In a rather formal statement about his work he puts it this way:

. . . the poet's voice must embody not the expedient certainties of his daily life and belief, but rather in its style, in its way of treating details and images (how discrete are they, how firm, how extensive?), above all in its sounds, its subrational structure of aural textures and rhythms. It is here he must hope to find those meanings which may remain beyond the consciousness of his own period, but which may be deep enough to endure into the consciousness of another.[5]

Snodgrass's reliance on a kind of notational expressiveness was likewise determined by examples "beyond the consciousness of his own period":

But I think my chief influences were musical. The last-century Germans you speak of came to me chiefly through musical settings—especially Mahler's *Kindertotenlieder*. I tried translating some of these and while my teachers like Lowell and Engle could help me very much on those poems which they truly loved and understood, they wouldn't let *me* write such poems. A second big influence there was a set of Spanish and Italian songs of the 16th and 17th centuries by Hugues Cuenod which appeared just then—I still remember the first day I heard them—my hair simply stood on end. And I wanted to do something as directly and stridently passionate. At least I thought that would be a real and significant blunder—to go on writing as we had been wasn't important enough even when it worked.[6]

The qualities he cites in the song literature—simplicity and passionate directness, sustained by the unobtrusive subtlety of their settings—are among the most distinctive characteristics of Snodgrass's own verse and version of the confessional impulse. One might even assert the direct influence of the *Kindertotenlieder* on the "Heart's Needle" sequence. The poems by Friedrich Rückert were written after the deaths of two of his young children, and their settings by Mahler have become associated with the death of his own youngest daughter shortly after he completed the song cycle. Rückert's texts stress not so much the death of his children as the emptiness their loss has left, and Mahler's music points up the poignance of the poems by its restraint. The sequence closely links variations of grief, each with its own distinct tone and rhythmical structure, heightened by the music's unembarrassed and delicate pathos.

The convergence of these influences can only be considered as part of the transformation of Snodgrass's style, because style—in his phrase, "that quality of voice which suggests qualities of mind"—is finally, for this poet, a moral and psychological concern. The "sincerity" he sought for the texture of his verse made similar demands on his subject, and, having discovered *how* he could speak, he had further to discover what he needed to say. The value of the poem as product was inextricably bound up with the process of its composition: to compose is finally to expose. "Am I writing what I *really* think?" was the question— the criterion—that insisted itself. Abandoning rhetorical disguises meant forgoing psychological defenses as well:

> For I believe that the only reality which a man can ever surely know is that self he cannot help being, though he will only know that self through its interactions with the world around it. If he pretties it up, if he changes its meaning, if he gives it the voice of any borrowed authority, if in short he rejects this reality, his mind will be less than alive. So will his words.[7]

The effect of this demand for self-knowledge on the compositional process may be a reason for Snodgrass's relatively small body of work and is reflected in the rigor with which he pursues the nuances of both an experience and its voice. His generalized account of his procedure with any given poem implies the sincerity he calls for, even as it provides a miniature of his career itself:

> In working on an actual poem I almost always find myself starting it much the way we were taught at Iowa. I make a very compacted, intellectualized, and obviously symbolical poem with a lot of fancy language in it. But then, as I go on working at it, the poem happily becomes plainer and longer, and seems much more "tossed off." The first version often seems very labored and literary and intellectual. The final version, if I'm lucky, will seem very conversational, and sort of "thrown away." It will also be much longer.[8]

The process, in other words, is one of "realizing" an experience back toward the casual immediacy with which it first occurred.

This commitment to a relentless probing and revelation is not easily achieved, and in Snodgrass's case derives from psychotherapy, which provided both its stimulus and model. The simultaneous discovery of self and voice, and of the sincerity necessary to both, is evident in this account by the poet of his therapy at the University Hospital in Iowa City:

> In many ways that therapy really consisted of just stating and restating the problem until you finally got it in your own language—until then, you really hadn't said anything. So long as you were talking about "castration anxiety," etc., you were acting so superior to the problem, that you belied the very existence of the problem in the way you set out to describe it. Until you said that in your own language, you hadn't really accepted its existence, much less dealt with *your* experience of it (as opposed to someone else's abstractions about it).
>
> Or to say the same thing another way, I began to notice that one of the two of us in that room sounded like a psychiatry textbook and it wasn't *him*. (Perhaps I should note that he—the doctor—wasn't *really* in the room at all because the whole thing was part of an experimental technique.) Anyway, all this led me to question the tone and the subject matter of my poems. I was surprised to notice that my doctor wasn't much interested when I talked about those abstractions; he sat up and took notice when I talked about my daughter. He wasn't inclined to question me about those things where I

could sound impressive; more often he asked me how I was planning to pay my rent.

I'd gone into that therapy because (partly) I'd not been able to write for two years. I recall that my doctor specifically asked me if that wasn't because I wasn't writing about things I cared enough about to get me past the resistance.

I might also comment that some years later I went into deep analysis in Detroit. That, of course, affected my work but in ways that were less obvious (if, perhaps, more far-reaching). It had a very large hand in the poems I did based on paintings.[9]

Week after week, alone in a strangely familiar room, speaking out loud to himself, over and over, the guilts and fears and inadequacies, until his language caught their reality, and problems became self. The formality of his verse underscores the authority of his struggle, and if the effect of song is finally—with whatever self-consciousness—celebratory, then Snodgrass reminds himself and his readers of Rilke's words: "for the poet whose aim is praise, the great test is how much of the world's misery and sorrow can be digested into that praise."[10]

There was considerable misery to be digested by Snodgrass before the praise and prizes which greeted the eventual publication of *Heart's Needle*. The isolation of his decision and the discouragement by his teachers were prolonged over the five years he worked on the "Heart's Needle" sequence, begun in 1953:

> When I started writing these poems, my teachers were concerned for me and didn't like the poems at all. Lowell, I recall, was particularly distressed. But several years later I sent the whole cycle of poems to Donald Hall and Louis Simpson who were editing their first anthology—they got very excited about them and Hall showed the whole group to Lowell, who entirely changed his mind about them. He got me a publisher later when no one else would publish my book and, in general, he opened all the doors for me. He later wrote me to say that he took those poems as one of his models in the *Life Studies* pieces.[11]

By this time Snodgrass had absorbed his training sufficiently to use it rather than be used by it, and had eliminated from his final collection its aspects of "insincerity." While a few poems in the book—"Mehtis . . . ou tis," "Orpheus," "Riddle"—are stiffer than the rest, and so seem throwbacks, none is merely an exercise.

The three poems which open *Heart's Needle* comprise an initiatory account of the poet's return home, both chronological and spiritual, from World War II on. "Ten Days Leave" is a study in disorientation and alienation, the artificiality of the past and detachment of the present, much like Hemingway's story "Soldier's Home." His specific model, though, was probably William Meredith's 1944 poem "Ten-Day Leave," whose stanza scheme and central dream-metaphor Snodgrass adopted for ironically different purposes. The war-jarred poet returns in person to his service dream of home:

> Supposing it were just his old mistake?
>
> But no; it seems just like it seemed. His folks
> Pursue their lives like toy trains on a track.
> He can foresee each of his father's jokes
> Like words in some old movie that's come back.

But his new awareness stumbles over the inadequacy of metaphor to restore the familiar; the poem proceeds by analogy, each stanza testing—*like, as if, supposing, seems, recalls*—a dreamscape at which he wonders: "How real it seems!" It is the principle of unreality that dominates until resolved in the third poem, just as the perspective shifts from the "he" of this poem, to "we" in the next, and finally to "I" in the third. "Returned to Frisco, 1946" resumes the stance and structure of "Ten Days Leave" to describe his last landing. As soldiers, they had "scrambled like rabbits / Up hostile beaches," and now, under the twisted banner of Owen's "old lie," they assault "our first life," "our old lives." But the new enemy seems like his own family; the new fear, like his old habits. The liberty he had fought to give others and been granted himself leaves him

> Free to choose just what they meant we should;
> To turn back finally to our old affections,
> The ties that lasted and which must be good.
>
> Off the port side, through haze, we could discern
> Alcatraz, lavender with flowers. Barred,
> The Golden Gate, fading away astern,
> Stood like the closed gate of your own backyard.

The illusion of choice is left bewildering in this poem, since Snodgrass came to find, through psychotherapy, that it depends on a sense of self-identity that can at once accept and transcend the past. "Mehtis . . . ou tis," dedicated to the psychiatrist he never saw, R. M. Powell, works the returning soldier motif into the story of Odysseus. Like the Greek hero, the poet's "defiant mind" allowed him escape from the dark cave and return to a self centered with a guilt that proves reality:

> Unseen where all seem stone blind, pure disguise
> Has brought me home alone to No Man's land
> To look at nothing I dare recognize.
> My dead blind guide, you lead me here to claim
> Still waters that will never wash my hand,
> To kneel by my old face and know my name.

The quest for his "name," a definition discovered through needs and limits, continues throughout the book—in "Home Town," "A Cardinal," "These Trees Stand . . . ," and "April Inventory"—and serves as the light by which he reflects on his personal and social relationships.

The next twelve poems explore the ruins of his first marriage and the reconstruction of his life with new love. This section opens and closes with similar poems—"At the Park Dance" and "Home Town"—which dramatize the poet's isolation, after the shocks of war and divorce, from his accustomed community. The virtue he makes of this necessity is his resolve to learn from the experience. The last stanza of "Home Town" abandons the poem's narrative of habitual fears and desires pursued on small-town curbs, and the poet turns inward to ask himself the anxious question:

> Pale soul, consumed by fear
> of the living world you haunt,
> have you learned what habits lead you
> to hunt what you don't want;
> learned who does not need you;
> learned you are no one here?

This is the lesson also learned in "Orpheus" and in "The Marsh," where Snodgrass explores the emotional underworld and swamp of his first marriage. As Orpheus, the poet descends to ask Time and Experience for the woman he can only remember but not now love. Though he accuses himself of "mistrust," by figuring the experience into a self-justifying myth, complete with a bleak, modernist cityscape, Snodgrass evades the pain by means of the pattern, so that the actual experience is diminished in its detail, though its self-pity is coddled by the high style:

> It was the nature of the thing:
> No moon outlives its leaving night,
> No sun its day. And I went on
> Rich in the loss of all I sing
> To the threshold of waking light.
> To larksong and the live, gray dawn.
> So night by night, my life has gone.

This theme is more convincing in later poems to his daughter, where the loss that allows song is combined with a more realistic guilt.

The companion poem to "Orpheus" is "Papageno," which employs the same rhyme scheme to present the complementary poet: folkloristic rather than mythological, a birdcage replacing the lyre. And this poem sets the tone and style for those that follow: gentle, witty, lyrical, wondering, celebratory. It is not "my stealthy flute" that can "whistle up a wife"; love, in the person of his second wife Janice, to whom the poem is dedicated, finds him:

> I beat about dead bushes where
> No song starts and my cages stand
> Bare in the crafty breath of you
> Night's lady, spreading your dark hair,
> Come take this rare bird into hand;
> In that deft cage, he might sing true.

The "Night's lady" is no longer the Eurydice he could not lead back, but the Papagena who saves him from death—even though Snodgrass's description seems confused with that of Pamina, daughter of the Queen of the Night in Mozart's *Die Zauberflöte*. This entire group of poems rises from "the burned out bed / of ashes" ("September in the Park") to tell about recovery and renewal. Guilt is not only purified through sacrifice but through more vitalistic and seasoned cycles which turn memories into hopes and which naturalize the necessity of suffering. Despite the self-addressed caution in "Seeing You Have . . . ," Snodgrass grounds these poems in joy and in "Riddle" even turns his pride into a series of conceits—self-consciously echoing the metaphysical poets—and puns on the "divorce" that has united the lovers. And, while poems like "Winter Bouquet" and the two titled "Song" are domestic and erotic, "The Operation"—another of the hospital poems favored by the confessionalists—works toward its simple recognition through ritual (robes to arena to angel to bowl) and allusion (Pierrot and Christ). It is a remarkable poem, blending the realistic and the visionary into an account of his struggle toward the still point of a confident marriage: his wife's gift crystallizing the dark, rushing world he watches through it:

> I lie in night, now,
> A small mound under linen like the drifted snow,
> Only by nurses visited, in radiance, saying, Rest.
> Opposite, ranked office windows, glare; headlamps, below,
> Trace out our highways; their cargoes under dark tarpaulins,
> Trucks climb, thundering, and sirens may
> Wail for the fugitive. It is very still. In my brandy bowl
> Of sweet peas at the window, the crystal world
> Is inverted, slow and gay.

If the first two groupings of the book's poems deal with Snodgrass's sense of "new life," with himself after his return from war, and with his second wife after his divorce, then a third group—"A Cardinal," "The Campus on the Hill," "These Trees Stand . . . ," and "April Inventory"—move still further out to sift the continuing life of his social and professional relationships. "A Cardinal" is the book's pivotal "crisis poem," Snodgrass's version of "Resolution and Independence," which both sums up the poems that precede it and summons up those that follow and exemplify it. The first part of the poem—the opening twelve stanzas—presents the heartache and drowsy numbness of the poet, not half in love with easeful death but stunned by the mediocre, postwar technocracy and stunted by his inability to signify his presence as a poet in it. The question forced on him— what is *mine?*—is worked through a series of contrasts: poet/ nature, poet/city, nature/city. The "marketable praise," "this heavy prose / of factories and motors," deadens his own "scared silence," "blank pages," and unmarketable rhymes. Realization cannot lessen alienation; though he hears "the ancient pulse of violence" throbbing beneath suburban advertising jingles, his own sense of helplessness in a society whose enterprise freely excludes him—even as the insects and birds withdraw from the woods in which he seeks a meaningful solitude—leaves him voiceless: "Meantime, I fuss with phrases / or clamp my jaws in silence." The second part of the poem abruptly introduces its symbolic cardinal—the bird figure familiar to poetry from Shelley's skylark to Stevens's sparrow—though it is less a symbol in the sense of embodying an absolute correspondence than a focus for the poet's modulating awareness of himself. Snodgrass's own predicament screens his first, Jacobean understanding of the "old sleek satanic cardinal," no different from industrialized vultures and whose song, like theirs, is a "Hosannah to Appetite." But the poet goes on to realize his "Darwinian self-pity" and to listen again to the cardinal as "he outspeaks a vital / claim to know his needs" and "sings out for survival." What the cardinal says is, of course, what Snodgrass is learning of himself:

> "The world's not done to me;
> it is what I do;
> whom I speak shall be;
> I music out my name
> and what I tell is who
> in all the world I am."

Mere appetite is changed to assertion, itself a style in which the self is to be discovered. The uselessness of poetry is converted into the importance of self. Here is the end of the poem:

> All bugs, now, and the birds
> witness once more their voices
> though I'm still in their weeds
> tracking my specimen words,
> replenishing the verses
> of nobody else's world.

Just as he has listened to learn, so too he speaks to his daughter in the paired poem of assertion "These Trees Stand . . . ," in which he urges his separation from her as an example, in a touching lesson of pride in the absurdity of isolation:

> Your name's absurd, miraculous as sperm
> And as decisive. If you can't coerce
> One thing outside yourself, why you're the poet!
> What irrefrangible atoms whirl, affirm

Their destiny and form Lucinda's skirts!
She can't make up your mind. Soon as you know it,
Your firmament grows touchable and firm.
If all this world runs battlefield or worse,
Come, let us wipe our glasses on our shirts:
Snodgrass is walking through the universe.

The other two poems in this group also take up the question of survival, set in the stale academic atmosphere of 1950s America. "The Campus on the Hill" details Snodgrass's frustration at Cornell, where he had moved to teach after Iowa, and at the version of survival among his students. While the world breaks around them, they hope to survive by staying inert:

They look out from their hill and say,
To themselves, "We have nowhere to go but down;
The great destination is to stay."
Surely the nations will be reasonable;
They look at the world—don't they?—the world's way?
The clock just now has nothing more to say.

That last line, and the poem's title, are meant to recall Edwin Arlington Robinson's villanelle, "The House on the Hill":

And our poor fancy-play
    For them is wasted skill:
There is nothing more to say.

There is ruin and decay
    In the House on the Hill:
They are all gone away,
There is nothing more to say.

That same empty disgust is Snodgrass's attitude here, and his condemnation is severe, even as it seems to depend in part on his own helplessness. A much richer account of the same situation is Snodgrass's best known poem, "April Inventory"—richer because more personal. The satire is muted and includes himself, so that his survival sounds more authentic. This elegy for d'antan opens with the cruelest month reminding of nature's renewal which taunts his steady decline: "In thirty years I may not get / Younger, shrewder, or out of debt." But, unlike those isolated manipulators, the "solid scholars" who have gotten "the de-

grees, the jobs, the dollars," he has sought values which recover
self, has pursued his arguments in human incidents:

> I taught my classes Whitehead's notions;
> One lovely girl, a song of Mahler's.
> Lacking a source-book or promotions,
> I showed one child the colors of
> A luna moth and how to love.
>
> I taught myself to name my name,
> To bark back, loosen love and crying;
> To ease my woman so she came,
> To ease an old man who was dying.
> I have not learned how often I
> Can win, can love, but choose to die.

This humility before the primacy of the self's needs allows
Snodgrass a pride in his losses, which the Roethkean last stanza
moralizes:

> Though trees turn bare and girls turn wives,
> We shall afford our costly seasons;
> There is a gentleness survives
> That will outspeak and has its reasons.
> There is a loveliness exists,
> Preserves us, not for specialists.

Everything he has learned through these poems is relearned in
the second half of the book, the "Heart's Needle" sequence, ten
poems to Cynthia, his daughter by his first marriage, one for
each of the seasons during the two and a half years, from the
winter of 1952 until the spring of 1955, of his divorce and re-
marriage.[12] As both a completely other person and still a part of
himself, his daughter provides Snodgrass a unique occasion to
confront his selfhood at a point where all its relationships con-
verge. That point is also an extremely painful one—a point
where, like the trapped fox, he has had to gnaw off his own paw
to escape, where legal estrangement becomes existential estrange-
ment, where he cannot explain his maturity to her innocence and
so has to revalue both, where the limits of self-pity and bitterness
cannot be distinguished from the needs for growth and regret.
To maintain such a developing complexity within the scheme of
a single poem is a difficulty Snodgrass overcomes, first of all, by

the voice he has achieved. William Heyen once described it as "urgent but controlled, muted but passionate, unassuming but instructive." And in addition to his voice, there is the verse; each poem is given an independent rhythmical structure—sometimes elaborate, sometimes simple—which varies the angle of feeling and perception, and can accommodate rather than avoid his revelations of loss and resolve. At the same time, the poems are closely linked, not only by the central relationship which they trace, but by a series of motifs—bed, snow, fox, trap, bird, color—which recur, gathering new meanings into old. And these techniques combine finally to portray a world of self-willed, separate individuals whose shared—and disillusioned—experience makes possible a tentative but necessary union. What Snodgrass says in the first poem could be used to summarize his technique throughout:

> And I have planned
>
> My chances to restrain
> The torments of demented summer or
> Increase the deepening harvest here before
> It snows again.

The introductory poem offers the bleak background of his daughter's childhood. Born during the Korean War, she did not warm the frigidity of his marriage, a cold war in its own terms:

> Child of my winter, born
> When the new fallen soldiers froze
> In Asia's steep ravines and fouled the snows,
> When I was torn
>
> By love I could not still,
> By fear that silenced my cramped mind
> To that cold war where, lost, I could not find
> My peace in my will. . . .

That inverted reference to Dante introduces to the sequence the important theme of will, which necessitates his own actions and his attempt to teach his daughter that their consequences are important in ways she may come to understand for her own life. The second poem translates an actual occurrence into a parable, giving it a form in which the child can understand her own experience. The garden which father and daughter have planted, and which she has unwittingly walked on and overwatered, recapitulates her own childhood: "Child, we've done our best." And the advice he offers, which predicts their separation, catches up his own failure as well:

> Someone will have to weed and spread
> The young sprouts. Sprinkle them in the hour
> When shadow falls across their bed.
> You should try to look at them every day
> Because when they come to full flower
> I will be away.

The third, fifth, and ninth poems of the sequence are the most bitter, and the third is perhaps the most painful since it describes the first shock of separation from his daughter. The middle of the poem distances the event by recalling newspaper accounts of the Korean War as metaphors of the failed marriage and its victim:

> We read of cold war soldiers that
> Never gained ground, gave none, but sat
> Tight in their chill trenches.
> Pain seeps up from some cavity
> Through the ranked teeth in sympathy; . . .
>
> It's better the poor soldiers live
> In someone else's hands
> Than drop where helpless powers fall
> On crops and barns, on towns where all
> Will burn. And no man stands.

The eerie stillness of this violence then draws back a time "I tugged your hand, once, when I hated / Things less; a mere game dislocated / The radius of your wrist." The necessity now to "appease another"—a mother—extends the game-image, as the poet tries to hold back the reality of loss, to hope he is saving what he surrenders: "It may help that a Chinese play / Or Solomon himself might say / I am your real mother." With the fourth poem the separation has settled into its awkward round of visits, and the tension between the poet and the father is strained as Snodgrass mocks the golden-lads-and-girls-all-must myths by which we try to make sense of dislocation:

We huff like windy giants
scattering with our breath
gray-headed dandelions;
Spring is the cold wind's aftermath.

The grief he feels and has caused is linked to a guilt at his inability
to perform either role, which the last stanza gently displaces:

Night comes and the stiff dew.
I'm told a friend's child cried
because a cricket, who
had minstreled every night outside
her window, died.

The fifth poem completes the first half of the cycle, bringing it
around again to winter and the dark, closed landscape of his
separation, and to the same images of the first poem:

Winter again and it is snowing;
Although you are still three,
You are already growing
Strange to me.

What is strange to him is her growth apart from him:

You chatter about new playmates, sing
Strange songs; you do not know
Hey ding-a-ding-a-ding
Or where I go

Or when I sang for bedtime, *Fox*
Went out on a chilly night,
Before I went for walks
And did not write.

And it forces him to concede, as does the fox, "the paw, /
Gnawed off, he cannot feel; / Conceded to the jaw / Of toothed,
blue steel."

But this realization, which informs the second half of the cycle,
is one in which Snodgrass will discover his own motives. This
begins with the lengthy sixth poem, the background and composi-
tion of which Snodgrass himself has described in his essay "Find-
ing a Poem" and need not be repeated here. But it is important to

note the patterns which his recognition assumes. The poet is meditating on the time passed since his daughter's first acceptance of life at birth: "You took your hour, / caught breath, and cried with your full lung power." A series of metaphors follows to describe the marriage breakup—birds whose nests were flooded, trees ruined in storms—and the survival by sacrifice:

> . . . Crews
> of roughneck boys swarmed to cut loose
> branches wrenched in the shattering wind, to hack free
> all the torn limbs that could sap the tree.

The "July Fourth" storm he mentions—an Iowa City tornado of 1953—recalls subliminally his own sister's death on that date of the asthma his daughter suffers from: "Your lungs caught and would not take the air." His sister's refusal of breath had been a denial of life, and Snodgrass now fears Cynthia will not choose her own life:

> Of all things, only we
> have power to choose that we should die;
>   nothing else is free
> in this world to refuse it. Yet I,
>   who say this, could not raise
> myself from bed how many days
> to the thieving world. Child, I have another wife,
>   another child. We try to choose our life.

By casting the present dilemma into the shadow of the past, Snodgrass has discovered as well the dimensions of his own decision and has come to understand the necessity, for himself and his daughter, to choose the unavoidable. If he cannot grant her his presence to learn by, he can offer his daughter his example: to turn betrayal of others into trust of self, denial into decision. The balance thus achieved, for himself and in his relationship, is apparent in the seventh poem:

> Here in the scuffled dust
>   is our ground of play.
> I lift you on your swing and must
>   shove you away,
> see you return again,
>   drive you off again, then

> stand quiet till you come.
>   You, though you climb
> higher, farther from me, longer,
>   will fall back to me stronger. . . .
>
>   Once more now, this second,
>   I hold you in my hands.

The eighth is an account of the new "household" set up by the two. No longer the romantic one of constancy, where a small girl plots with her father to catch a star, "pull off its skin / and cook it for our dinner," their relationship has all the realism of packed lunches and "local restaurants." Though the ending reiterates only regret and resentment, his acceptance is one by which loss gives strength:

> As I built back from helplessness,
>   when I grew able,
> the only possible answer was
>   you had to come here less.

Though the "sweets" they eat on her visits leave "cavities," their anxious motto has become "We manage."
    The ninth poem relapses to the blank bitterness of early poems:

> A friend asks how you've been
>   and I don't know
>
> or see much right to ask.
>   Or what use it could be to know. . . .
>
> Nothing but injury will grow,
>   I write you only the bitter poems
>   that you can't read.

But the scene of remembrance—before cases of posed stuffed animals in a Natural History Museum—reveals the self-hatred at the roles and feelings he finds himself locked into at his worst. The "little bobcats" arched in their "constant rage" remind the poet that it was here, the year before, that his daughter and stepdaughter "pulled my hands / and had your first, worst quarrel, / so toys were put up on your shelves . . . I forced you to obedience; / I don't know why." The reason lies in the epigraph from Simone Weil with which Snodgrass prefaced his essay on Dostoyevski: "A harmful act is the transference to others of the degradation which we bear in ourselves. That is why we are inclined to commit such acts as a way of deliverance." If acceptance is its own deliverance, then the poet is, for the moment, caught in a refusal to yield to himself:

> The window's turning white.
> The world moves like a diseased heart
> packed with ice and snow.
> Three months now we have been apart
> less than a mile. I cannot fight
> or let you go.

The last poem resolves the relationship; it is the final changed return, rich with natural and seasonal imagery and steadied by the most constant rhythm in the cycle: "The vicious winter finally yields" and "our seasons bring us back once more." Her return, like that of the spring and its rites, has occurred often enough for him finally to believe it is desired rather than allowed, and the sequence ends with their escape into themselves and each other:

> If I loved you, they said, I'd leave
> and find my own affairs.
> Well, once again this April, we've
> come around to the bears;
>
> punished and cared for, behind bars,
> the coons on bread and water
> stretch thin black fingers after ours.
> And you are still my daughter.

At the same time Snodgrass was writing *Heart's Needle,* he published a few poems about his parents and their responsibility for his sister's death. They appeared under various pseudonyms because Snodgrass did not want them to come to his mother's attention, and they were only gathered finally in a small, expensive, limited private edition called *Remains,* published in 1970 under the anagram S. S. Gardons, for whom Snodgrass had devised a cryptic life and disappearance. His reluctance is understandable, considering the terrible honesty with which these portraits are drawn, but as he asks in an essay on Ransom, "How could one be a first-rate artist without offending, deeply, those he most loves?" These are raw poems, but not heartless: their forgiveness persists in their understanding. The rage of his memories and the intensity of his analysis are controlled in a verse which turns a revenging wit into a search for origins. His own survival—prior to that of war and divorce—has depended on escape, just as his alternative self, his sister, retreated beyond will into a suicidal surrender. This book is Snodgrass's unflinching view of the remains.

The opening pair of poems—"The Mother" and "Diplomacy: The Father"—assumes the personalities of each parent to reveal their unconscious motives. A perverse inversion of her nature and role is the key to "The Mother," and Snodgrass uses careful conceits and turns of phrase to spot this, as in her view of her own children:

> Born of her own flesh; still, she feels them drawn
> Into the outer cold by dark forces;
> They are in love with suffering and perversion,
> With the community of pain. Thinking them gone,
>
> Out of her reach, she is consoled by evil
> In neighbors, children, the world she cannot change,
> That lightless universe where they range
> Out of the comforts of her disapproval.

The type of the devouring mother is apparent in the dark, poisonous images of cave—"labyrinth of waste, wreckage // And hocus-pocus"—and spider:

> And the drawn strands of love, spun in her mind,
> Turn dark and cluttered, precariously hung
> With the black shapes of her mates, her sapless young,
> Where she moves by habit, hungering and blind.

Though she feeds on her own family to nurture imaginary hurts, Snodgrass sketches her as a driven creature in that last line. In the companion poem his father is one of the sapless, black shapes, and Snodgrass uses his Polonius-like voice and advice to reveal and dismiss him simultaneously, though with more regret than he can manage for his mother, if only because his father seems trapped in more awareness of his situation. The comparative self-justification—"as in yourself" is the second line of every stanza in this speech to his son—urges power, which stresses his own impotence, and force, which uncovers his lack of passion. The compromises he has made to live with his wife and world are still tinged with possibilities despaired of:

> Friend, this is lonely work. Hankerings will persist
>   for true allies, those you love; you will long
> some days to speak your mind out or just assist
>   someone who, given that help, might grow strong
> and admirable. This is your black hour,
>   the pitiless test.
>
> But think back: what did they ever do for you?
>   As in yourself,
> so in those who take your help, your thought, your name,
>   seek out their old strengths, their hidden talents
> to aid and abet, to buy out. Your fixed aim,
>   whatever it costs you, must still remain a balance
> of power in the family, the firm, this whole world through.*

What his father has missed is himself and the qualities of self Snodgrass had learned in *Heart's Needle:* love, trust, growth, passion, dedication. Against these he measures his father; against his father, himself. Yet in his own way this father has provided an example in reverse for Snodgrass's sense of his own fatherhood, and this draws the two men into a complex similarity. In his father's last words to him, Snodgrass points up that connection to himself, and to those who recall his relationship to his own daughter:

> Your life's the loving tension
> you leave to those who'll still take your instruction.
> You've built their world; and air of soft suspension
>   which you survive in, as cradled and sustained
>   as in yourself.

The following four poems center on the events and causes surrounding his asthmatic sister's death. "The Mouse" is a memory poem, recalling the course of their childhood together, how

---

*McClatchy is quoting from the 1970 Perishable Press edition of *Remains.* As Robert Phillips noted earlier, "Diplomacy: The Father" was revised when *Remains* was reissued by BOA Editions in 1985.

they would weep over a dead mouse, as in Hopkins's "Spring and Fall: To a Young Child." And later he cannot weep and knows why: by expanding the memory into metaphor, he describes their avenging fury of a mother as a cat

> That pats at you, wants to see you crawl
> Some, then picks you back alive;
> That needs you just a little hurt.
> The mind goes blank, then the eyes. Weak with dread,
> In shock, the breath comes short;
> We go about our lives.
>
> And then the little animal
> Plays out; the dulled heart year by year
> Turns from its own needs, forgets its grief.
> Asthmatic, timid, twenty-five, unwed—
> The day we left you by your grave,
> I wouldn't spare one tear.

The poet's prose version of these events, if less vivid, is more direct:

> It seemed to me that she, disapproving the life around her and unwilling to find any other, had withdrawn into a very destructive and self-deceiving relationship with her mother. This, of course, had satisfied none of her real needs, but she was unable to change her course; she developed a severe case of asthma. . . . When her problem became progressively worse and she reached the age at which it must have been clear that she would never marry or have any independent career, she took the logical last step. On the morning of the Fourth of July . . . , her heart simply quit beating. To die on Independence Day seemed an act of terrible and destructive blamefulness, yet this may have been, in its way, the easiest solution of her dilemma—she had died spiritually (that is, as an animal moved by aims and opinions) years before.[13]

This too is the subject of the book's most powerful poem, "Fourth of July," with its stark narrative and weary, end-stopped lines, choked on the smoke that seeps through the city, his home and family, which compose a land of the dead. The public celebration counterpoints the private numbness:

She stopped a year ago today.
Firecrackers mark the occasion down the street;
I thumb through magazines and keep my seat.
What can anybody say? . . .

It is a hideous mistake.
My young wife, unforgivably alive,
Takes a deep breath and blows out twenty-five
Candles on her birthday cake.

The ironic contrast between the two women—the sister he could not rescue and the wife who rescued him—barely allows him to tolerate his own angry resignation:

It is an evil, stupid joke:
My wife is pregnant; my sister's in her grave.
We live in the home of the free and of the brave.
No one would hear me, even if I spoke.

This is the same voicelessness as in "A Cardinal" and again is caused by the obscuring of the self: his sister's life and the poet's identity among an oppressive family. When he does speak he does so away from his parents—at the public isolation of a funeral, or the privacy of a bedroom, or in a poem. "Viewing the Body" and "Disposal" are macabre descriptions of his dead sister and her empty room, and the poet's violence—in her casket she lies with "eyeshadow like a whore"—emphasizes his outraged sense of waste.

The final two poems are the remains of the family tragedy: its survivors, his parents and himself. "The Survivors" is his last glance back, searching for what he has already found: "We wondered what might change / Once you were not here; / Tried to guess how they would rearrange / Their life, now you were dead." Everything is overgrown or disrepaired, and the two stone lions on the front steps have their eyes patched with cement. Blind too are the ghostly parents, who attend at a dead ritual of separation:

Only at night they meet.
By voiceless summoning
They come to the living room; each repeats
Some words he has memorized; each takes his seat
In the hushed, expectant ring

By the television set.
No one can draw his eyes
From that unnatural, cold light. They wait.
The screen goes dim and they hunch closer yet,
As the image dies.

If "nothing is different here," then the last poem, "To a Child,"
stakes out the life he has made for himself by means of a warning
prayer to his daughter. The poem is familiar because it is close to
those in "Heart's Needle"—though muted by the mood which
the other poems in *Remains* cast over it—and is, in fact, a spin-
off of the sixth poem in the earlier sequence. In "Finding a
Poem" Snodgrass recalls revising first drafts of that poem, and
the deletions he felt necessary: "Finally, I had to give up my lines
about stone-skipping and the Sunday lovers on the riverbank.
This nearly broke my heart, but I promised myself to work them
into a later poem." They settle finally into "To a Child":

Still, I guess we often choose
Odd spots: we used to go stone-dapping
On the riverbanks where lovers lay
Abandoned in each others' arms all day
By their beached, green canoes;
You asked why they were napping.

The odd spot he and his daughter have come to is a field for "our
talk / About the birds and the bees." That talk is preceded by
stanzas describing episodes and lessons in the forms of natural
love. In their own way they rehearse the facts of life, the facts of
his own and of their life together:

And I mailed you long letters
Though you were still too young to read; . . .

They threw my letters out.
Said I had probably forgotten. . . .

We have watched grown men debase
Themselves for their embittered wives

And we have seen an old sow that could smother
The sucklings in her stye,
That could devour her own farrow.

> We have seen my sister in her narrow
> Casket. Without love we die;
>   With love we kill each other.

As in the ending of "Heart's Needle," Snodgrass attempts to affirm life in the face of his child's imagining herself dead. The earlier poem closed with the example of self-affirmation; this poem is more tentative, more desperate:

> I sit here by you in the summer's lull
> Near the lost handkerchiefs of lovers
>   To tell you when your brother
> Will be born; how, and why.
> I tell you love is possible.
>   We have to try.

Nine years elapsed between *Heart's Needle* and the publication of *After Experience* (1968). Perhaps that length of time itself accounts for the variety of work in the later volume, but Snodgrass was probably also intent on displaying his interests and achievements apart from those confessional. The diversity of *After Experience* is reminiscent of the example of Snodgrass's old master Lowell. Nearly half of the book is occupied with twenty-four translations and a series of long poems which are interpretative recreations of the subjects and energies of five impressionist paintings. And of the remaining poems several are set pieces, which their titles alone indicate: "A Character," "Flash Flood," "Exorcism," "Edmund to Gloucester," "The Men's Room in the College Chapel," "Powwow," and his academic satirical allegory "The Examination." The influence of Vietnam is felt in an increased political note to the work, in such poems as "Inquest" and "A Visitation."

Snodgrass seems, then, intentionally to have restricted his confessional impulse, but it does shape a significant portion of the book even though the poet's use of it has changed along with his intervening experience. The book's title hints at Snodgrass's personality in these poems: it is wary, hard-edged, guarded, perhaps more pessimistic, certainly more *experienced*. The shift between first and second books has been from awareness to understanding.

The title poem is an extreme example of the essentially dramatic nature of this process. In his effort to demonstrate the final similarity between two seemingly opposed views of life, Snodgrass alternates the phrases of two speakers: the first is Spinoza, the opening of his essay "On the Improvement of the Understanding"; the second is a lecture Snodgrass says he heard in the navy on the most effective way to kill a man in hand-to-hand combat. The brutal details of ripping off "the whole facial mask" undercut, but do not destroy, the philosopher's exalted argument; the purposes of Snodgrass's juxtaposition are closer to a comment he once made in an interview: "Your ideas are normally just the way you disguise your feelings so that you can do what you want without admitting you're doing it. All right, so our disguises are a part of us. . . . Most people, by taking off their clothes, don't demonstrate much except that they aren't very interesting. . . . I'm much more interested in the kinds of disguises we put on all the time. Our disguises can reveal a lot more about the way we feel."[14] What Snodgrass says here was put more succinctly by Valéry: "There is no theory that is not a fragment, carefully prepared, of some autobiography." This is why the poem's last stanza points its accusation at the poet himself as well as at the reader:

> And you, whiner, who wastes your time
> Dawdling over the remorseless earth,
> What evil, what unspeakable crime
> Have you made your life worth?

This is finally the function of the book's "ideas," and the effect of its probing hesitancy: Snodgrass sets (his critics would say, reduces) his actual experience to a moral scrutiny, in order to discover and evaluate the real feelings and motives beneath the disguises and rationalizations, the autobiography beneath the theory. His concern is not for belief, but for character, and, if this deprives the book of the immediacy of *Heart's Needle,* it does lend a larger, more penetrating perspective, which is apparent when the poems in *After Experience* about his daughter and his first wife are compared with earlier ones.

The cumulative narrative arrangement of poems in *Heart's Needle* was concentrated and consistent. In this book it is more oblique, but a reader can still easily follow the chronology of events in Snodgrass's experience: his uneasy relationship with his daughter, the troubles in his second marriage, the love affairs, the professional disappointments. What Snodgrass has done, though, is to intersperse his narrative poems with lyrical, depersonalized ones, which serve as choric interludes by framing his experiences with more distance. In fact, the opening poem of the collection, "Partial Eclipse," seems addressed, at first, to the generalized "you" of the traditional lyric, until later we see it, along with the three, more direct poems that follow it, as a continuation of the "Heart's Needle" address to his daughter. They would be harsh poems, if they were not hardened. In the "eclipse" of their relationship that time has clouded over, "something, one glint was left," and in the next poem ("September") even that dims:

> I hoped to spot that small Green Heron
> We saw together down the marsh
> This August. He'd gone off on an errand.
>
> Then too, of course, this *is* September.
> The newts in the creek had gone, already.
> I don't know where. I can't remember
> Your face or anything you said.

The next two poems seek the reasons in the girl's own emerging maturity. What disturbs the poet, in "Reconstructions," is the way in which her parents' characters are reconstructed in the child:

> You offered me, one day, your doll
> To sing songs to, bubble and nurse,
> And said that was her birthday;
> You reappeared then, grabbed her away,
> Said just don't mess with her at all;
> It was your child, yours.
>
> And earlier this summer, how
> You would tell the dog he had to "Stay!"
> Then always let him sit
> There, ears up, tense, all
> Shivering to hear you call;
> You turned and walked away.

There is a measure of self-disgust in this realization since, in reflecting her father's behavior, she reminds him of what he has made her "real" existence for himself, of his own "reconstructions": "I memorize you, bit by bit, / And must restore you in my verses / To sell to magazines." The final poem in this group, "The First Leaf," merely elaborates this guilt:

> Next year we'll hardly know you;
> Still, all the blame endures.
> This year you will live at our expense;
> We have a life at yours, . . .
>
> You move off where I send you;
> The train pulls down its track.
> We go about our business;
> I have turned my back.

The "enduring blame," what time can and cannot erode, is also the occasion for the poems about his first wife, "Mementos, 1" and "Mementos, 2." Both involve the accidental discovery of a memory—a photograph and a dress, the first in a desk drawer, the second in "the third-floor closet," both suggesting the dark, hidden nature of the unconscious. The photograph in "Mementos, 1" is at once his idealized memory and the evidence of his immaturity:

> you stand
> Just as you stood—shy, delicate, slender,
> In that long gown of green lace netting and daisies
> That you wore to our first dance. The sight of you stunned
> Us all. Well, our needs were different, then,
> And our ideals came easy.

His later "needs" were determined by growth and the imperative escape from marriage's "lies, self-denial, unspoken regret," which forced his sense of reality and the genuine "first meeting." The blame that endures is a helpless one and is here transferred to a poignant longing: "I put back your picture. Someday, in due course, / I will find that it's still there." In "Mementos, 2" his discovery of "that long white satin gown / and the heavy lead-foil crown" his wife once wore as the local "Queen of the May" stirs erotic memories—roots, hair—that embitter other memories of her neurotic fears that his love "might stain" her. "Yet the desire remains," and in that contradiction he finds forgiveness of a sort:

> I thought of our years; thought you
> had had enough of pain;
> thought how much grief I'd brought you;
> I wished you well again.

A series of poems go on to detail the difficulties in his second marriage, and the poet's strong sense of will—his ability to make a life for himself—is shaken by undercurrents of fatalism: "The curse is far from done; / When they've taken your daughter / They can take your son" ("The Platform Man"). Even his affairs are hedged in by circumstance or doubt; there seems a self-sought claustrophobia in "A Friend" and "Leaving the Motel," where moral conclusions are either forced or suspended.

Two other poems in *After Experience* deserve mention in a discussion of Snodgrass's confessional work. "Leaving Ithaca" looks back to a poem like "April Inventory" and is in many ways more winning. It is a more modest and relaxed poem yet more carefully worked. Dedicated "to my plaster replica of the Aphrodite of Melos," the poem turns this battered and mended piece of kitsch into his enduring symbol of Love, around which other loves have lived and died: "Well, we must both look second-hand. / Lady, we've cost each other":

> Now, of course, we have to move again
> And leave the old house roughhewn as we found it,
> The wild meadows and unworked fields around it—
> No doubt it would have spoiled us to remain.

The poet's survival depends on the persistence of love, as in a line addressed to both the statue and his wife: "Lady, we are going to have another child." The echo of his earlier affirmations is fainter and more defeated but continues Snodgrass's most urgent and appealing uses of his experience as exemplary:

> We'll try to live with evils that we choose,
> Try not to envy someone else's vices,
> But make the most of ours. We picked our crisis;
> We'll lose the things we can afford to lose
>
> And lug away what's left in orange crates. . . .

This same tenacity structures the narrative of "A Flat One" (hospital slang for a corpse), an extensive revision of a poem written for John Berryman at Iowa, about the death of Fritz Jarck, an old World War I veteran in a V.A. hospital where Snodgrass was working at the time. It is a cunningly detailed poem, complete with a Foster Frame bed and autoclave, that builds to a crucial self-examination on a man's moral and human response to pain and the suffering of others. The poet's initial resentment is self-ishly uncomprehending:

> Old man, these seven months you've lain
> Determined—not that you would live—
> Just to not die. . . .

> They'd say this was a worthwhile job
> Unless they tried it. It is mad
> To throw our good lives after bad;
> Waste time, drugs, and our minds, while strong
> Men starve. How many young men did we rob
> To keep you hanging on?

But he hesitates into his discovery: "You stayed for me— / Nailed to your own rapacious, stiff self-will." Stretched out on a Foster Frame bed would have given the old man a crucified look, but that reference is less important than the fumbled conclusion, where the poet lurches to learn what he has since taught himself to exemplify:

> I can't think we did *you* much good.
> Well, when you died, none of us wept.
> You killed for us, and so we kept
> You, because we need to earn our pay.
> No. We'd still have to help you try. We would
> Have killed for you today.

We would have killed for you today.
Something vicious lurks under the sentiment, and it recurs in several poems throughout *After Experience*. "Edmund to Glouces-ter" gives voice to the villain of a "bitched world." Like the book's title poem, which undermines its own consolations, "The Men's Room in the College Chapel" explores the place of sex and excrement that lies subversively beneath high-minded be-liefs. In "Inquest," with its villanelle-like pattern insisting on its obsessive repetitions, the speaker cross-examines his mirrored reflection. The figure—in the mirror, in the speaker's con-science, and in his subconscious, both in this poem and in the one following, "A Visitation"—is clearly Adolf Eichmann. Snod-grass is fascinated, here as elsewhere, with choked-back guilts and justification's twisted reasoning. Feelings he first discovered in himself and in his marriages he begins to notice in—or project

onto—history itself: in either a person or a people, forces move in "implacably to rule us, unaware."

Such poems could be said to have led to *The Führer Bunker,* a project that has preoccupied Snodgrass for two decades since *After Experience.* But, in fact, the roots of the project go back much further. When he first enrolled in the writing workshop at Iowa he intended to study play writing, not poetry. Even earlier he had begun to make a play out of Hugh Trevor-Roper's *The Last Days of Hitler.* The dramatization got nowhere, but the idea was rekindled in the early 1970s when Snodgrass began fashioning monologues for the leading actors in the drama of the last month of the Third Reich. Twenty of them were published as a book-length poem-in-progress in 1977. Others followed, and in his *Selected Poems 1957–1987* Snodgrass chose a new grouping of fifteen, along with a note to say that the cycle now consists of over seventy poems, which have been variously drawn on for staged performances.

Perhaps the final shape and purpose of the poem will eventually come clear. (I hesitate to call it a play; though possibly conceived as a sort of anti-*Faust,* its dramaturgy is too weak, and its details too impacted, for it to hold the stage. A closet drama, then—or bunker drama.) In a note to the 1977 edition Snodgrass wrote that his intention went beyond a mere account of the horrifying details: "The Nazis—like some others one may have encountered—often did or said things to disguise from the world, and sometimes from themselves, their real actions and intentions. My aim is to investigate the thoughts and feelings behind the public facade which made those actions necessary or even possible. My poems, then, must include voices they would hide from others, even from themselves." But even that explanation is vague, and the question remains: Is the poem a stuffed owl? (A question made more pointed still by the project that subsequently engrossed the poet—a long sequence called *The Death of Cock Robin.* Most of these poems are written in doggerel; all are related to paintings by DeLoss McGraw and spoken by a character called "W. D." With a few exceptions, like the bravura "A Darkling Alphabet," these latest poems are not only a disappointment but a puzzle: Why would a poet with such gifts, even in his search for diversity and new "voices," deliberately parody those gifts and wreck a career?)

The Führer Bunker is best read, I think, as a peculiar extension of Snodgrass's earlier work. There are two couples in the poem, Hitler and Eva Braun, and Joseph and Magda Goebbels. They stand as perverse extremes of traits the poet had earlier documented in his own experience. Adolf Speer (whom Snodgrass interviewed as part of his research) functions as a kind of bad seed / wise child of these marriages and as close to a stand-in for the author himself as we're given. We are encouraged to make these connections by the epigraph that now prefaces the sequence: "Mother Theresa, asked when she first began her work of relief and care for abandoned children, replied, 'On the day I discovered I had a Hitler inside me.' " But aren't such comparisons too slick? They risk trivializing the tragic life of history, and distorting the true dimensions of the domestic life as well.

The grotesque delusions of his cast (Bormann's mushy letters home, Eva Braun singing "Tea for Two," Magda Goebbels's villanelle to explain murdering her own children) are his theatrical focus, but his subject finally is, in Arendt's now over-used phrase, the banality of evil. That banality now outweighs the more intriguing parallels to themes in Snodgrass's previous books, but they are crucial. Snodgrass himself has pointed out that the Nazi leaders were each failed artists, and as a distorted analysis of the artistic temperament the poem can take its place as a kind of *Inferno,* written after but to be read before the purgatorial confessions of *Heart's Needle.* During their conversations Speer told Snodgrass: "We were like the Greeks when they got to Asia Minor and had all that limitless space before them." *The Führer Bunker* is a poem about *limits,* from the point of view of those who won't or can't recognize them.

Turning to *The Führer Bunker* is not unlike the experience, after having read Hardy's exquisite lyrics to his dead wife, of then turning to read *The Dynasts.* Myself, I search the second half of the *Selected Poems 1957–1987* for poems like the 1986 sequence called "A Locked House," which involves the breakup of a marriage. "Mutability," "The Last Time," and "A Locked House" itself would be reckoned among Snodgrass's strongest work. In the last named poem he remembers driving home with his wife as they worried, needlessly, about their locked house and secure marriage. But with the years things happened "none of us ever guessed," and the house stands again locked but because abandoned rather than waiting:

> The house still stands, locked, as it stood
> Untouched a good
> Two years after you went.
> Some things passed in the settlement;

Some things slipped away. Enough's left
That I come back sometimes. The theft
And vandalism were our own.
Maybe we should have known.

The painful memories these poems sift for moral bearings have consistently resulted in Snodgrass's best work. Though, as they demonstrate, he has not entirely forsaken the confessional mode, he has sharply modified it for his own purposes. For a poet so concerned with survival, perhaps this was a necessary tactic after the enormous success and influence of *Heart's Needle*. But it is his confessional poetry that remains as the heart of his achievement. In "April Inventory" he mentions teaching his classes "Whitehead's notions." One of those notions is that "the canons of art are merely the expression in specialized form of the requirements for depth of experience." At its best Snodgrass's mild, reflective art has specialized in precisely that depth of experience.

NOTES

1. W. D. Snodgrass, "A Rocking-Horse: The Symbol, the Pattern, the Way to Live" (1958), *In Radical Pursuit* (New York: Harper and Row, 1975), 133.

2. "W. D. Snodgrass: An Interview," *Salmagundi* 22–23 (Spring–Summer 1973): 165.

3. W. D. Snodgrass to J. D. McClatchy (WDS to JDMcC), from a letter dated 28 May 1973.

4. *Ibid.* The "paraphrase from Ovid" referred to is "Europa," which was never collected but appears in *Botteghe Oscure* (1953), 12:325–27.

5. Quoted in William Martz, ed., *The Distinctive Voice* (Glenview, Ill., 1966), 256.

6. WDS to JDMcC, from a letter dated 28 May 1973.

7. W. D. Snodgrass, "Finding a Poem" (1959), *In Radical Pursuit*, 32.

8. Philip L. Gerber and Robert J. Gemmett, eds., " 'No Voices Talk to Me': A Conversation with W. D. Snodgrass," *Western Humanities Review* 24, no. 1 (Winter 1970): 71.

9. WDS to JDMcC, from a letter dated 6 February 1974. See "Poems about Paintings," *In Radical Pursuit*, 63–97. Snodgrass's critical essays are all strongly psychoanalytical in their method as well and often distinctly autobiographical in their account of his approach to an understanding of the texts involved. *In Radical Pursuit* includes readings of *A Midsummer Night's Dream, Don Quixote,* the *Inferno,* and the *Iliad,* and with each he is concerned to reveal and explore "the unconscious areas of thought and emotion" in these expressions of their artists' personali-

ties. By equating exegetical criticism with consciousness and even ideology, Snodgrass's purposely "radical" stance demonstrates the continuity and integrity of his relationships to texts—whether lived, written, or read. The true work of art is finally an "important act in our lives" and, like every other such act, is "both propelled and guided by the darker, less visible areas of emotion and personality." See also "Poetry Since Yeats: An Exchange of Views," *Tri-Quarterly* 4 (1965): 100–11.

10. W. D. Snodgrass, "Four Gentlemen; Two Ladies," *Hudson Review* 13, no. 1 (Spring 1960): 130.

11. WDS to JDMcC, from a letter dated 28 May 1973.

12. It is interesting to note that Snodgrass had originally titled each poem in the sequence. On a typescript of "Heart's Needle" sent to Theodore Roethke on 25 August 1957 (and now in The Theodore Roethke Collection, Suzzallo Library, University of Washington), Snodgrass wrote the following titles over each of the poems, and under each added the season it recounts:

1. The Cold War (Winter 1952)
2. Planting (Spring 1953)
3. The Separation (Summer 1953)
4. Evening Visitation (Autumn 1953)
5. Loss of Feeling (Winter 1953)
6. Reviving (Spring 1954)
7. Fledgling (Summer 1954)
8. Ferment (Autumn 1954)
9. Deadlock (Winter 1954)
10. Returning (Spring 1955)

These titles have the simplicity of lieder titles, and are another indication of the influence of such songs on Snodgrass's sequence. I am indebted for this information to William Heyen and Richard Blessing.

13. This is drawn from the version of "Finding a Poem" as it originally appeared in the *Partisan Review* 26, no. 2 (Spring 1959): 280. In reprinting the essay in *In Radical Pursuit* Snodgrass repressed this section, withdrawing the painful family privacy from public view, and says only that his sister was "closely involved with her family" and that "it would be hard to say *why* she died."

14. "W. D. Snodgrass: An Interview," 161.

PART FOUR

Reviews 1975–89: In Radical Pursuit, The Führer Bunker, Selected Poems, *and Fine Press Editions*

RICHARD HORWICH

Critical Feast

Most collections of essays have about them the odor of left-
overs—dishes already served to earlier guests or not-quite-
successful concoctions rescued from the bottom shelf of the
refrigerator. It's a pleasure, then, to report that, when W. D.
Snodgrass turns from poetry (*Heart's Needle, After Experience*) to
criticism, he serves up a veritable banquet, full of nourishment
and taste.

For the twelve essays which make up *In Radical Pursuit,* unlike
the off-duty musings of some poets, are neither superficial chat
nor supertechnical obfuscation. Instead, we have here the prod-
ucts of real intelligence, harmoniously ordered and rigorously
applied to subjects worthy of it. In an age when kitsch and pop
culture still mesmerize, it is refreshing to find a critic who, as
eight of these pieces demonstrate, is as much at ease with Shake-
speare, Cervantes, Dante, and Homer as he is with such modern
masters as Roethke, Ransom, Lawrence, and Dostoyevski; in
addition, he introduces them to us with four quite personal, and
quite fascinating, studies of the creative process itself, as he appre-
hends it through his own work and that of his contemporaries.

What primarily distinguishes Snodgrass is the sheer originality
of his thought; his essays are as full of surprises as his poems. He
tells us in the preface that he doesn't write unless he has something
new to say, and what might be another man's boast turns out here
to be only the literal truth. As a teacher of Shakespeare, I can
particularly relish the novelty of Snodgrass's approach to *A Mid-
summer Night's Dream* in "Moonshine and Sunny Beams," which
seems to me as fruitful as anything since Northrop Frye's book on
the comedies appeared almost ten years ago. And "Poems about
Paintings" gives us not only new insights into Van Gogh,
Vuillard, Matisse, Manet, and Monet and a valuable description of
the way Snodgrass turns his thoughts and feelings about their
works into poems—but also, as a sort of bonus, those poems

New Republic, 15 February 1975. Copyright © 1975 by *The New Republic.* Re-
printed by permission.

themselves, which rank with Auden's "Musée de Beaux Arts" as examples of their genre. If, at any rate, the measure of good criticism is whether it sends us back to the primary work with a different perspective or a new set of questions, *In Radical Pursuit* certainly catches up with what it's pursuing. I defy anyone to read the essay on Lawrence's story "The Rocking-Horse Winner" without leaping up midway through, as I did, to ransack the bookshelves for a look at the story itself.

Snodgrass's bloodlines lead back to Freud and the "new critics," but not in any slavish way; his prose, always entertaining, is free of the jargon of many psychoanalytic studies and the fussiness of much close textual analysis. At its worst academic criticism mires us in the work under scrutiny, cutting us off both from the author's inspiration and our own responses to it. At the other extreme psychoanalysts and their disciples sometimes exalt the author's importance above that of his creation, as though a literary work were just a set of clues to the psychology of its creator, a strategy for disguising his truths instead of his means of revealing them. But *In Radical Pursuit* successfully crosses and recrosses the gulf between art and life—the life which the artist depicts, the life out of which he creates his art, and his own life as well.

For Snodgrass is an artist, and his literary knowledge, taste, and intuition are always in evidence, tempering and enriching the analytic disciplines he practices. Thus, he grounds his view of the *Inferno* as Dante's self-psychoanalysis in a concrete understanding of medieval history and poetic convention; similarly when he traces the relationship between Roethke's poetry and his troubled life, we know that Snodgrass is working as much from the empathy of a fellow poet as from any Freudian postulates about the artist's psyche.

Snodgrass goes to the heart of the matter, even when the matter is his own life. He never spares himself; we learn a great deal about the sort of man he is from these essays, and not all of what he tells us is becoming to him. But the measure of his success is that his own recollections never seem an intrusion upon the works he is illuminating for us. What finally emerges is a man both brilliant and humble, whose personal honesty is no less impressive than his literary gifts.

MICHAEL WOOD

From "In the Literary Jungle"

Criticism is full of failed leaps toward generality, and it is good to see W. D. Snodgrass, undaunted, line up to try his hand at things like the Industrial Revolution ("Work became a burden, an imprisonment; the modern itch for fun was born"); political theory ("Raskolnikov and his story may indeed stand as exemplifying the history of revolutionaries and their actions in the Western World ever since the French Revolution"); and cultural diagnosis ("In the name of self-expression, the average man will create a world of total sameness and conformity"). These attempts are not encouraging, though, and the appearance of "the average man" is downright depressing.

I admire the impulse behind Snodgrass's essays a great deal—he wishes to connect literature with the most familiar and unknown (unknown because familiar) experiences of daily life—but the essays themselves issue too often in helpless, narrow simplicities: "If Dante had ever become closely acquainted with the human, physical Bice Portinari, wouldn't he probably have found her ill-tempered, neurotic, as hard to live with as most humans?" Homer's Achilles is "driven by the self-centered passions of a spoiled three-year-old. Could it have been different with Hitler? Stalin? General MacArthur? With the Wall Street tycoons? With men?" Can we imagine Dante's Francesca living happily with Paolo, if her husband were magically put out of the way? "Do we *seriously* believe she would be more faithful to him? Too plainly most of us are equally unhappy with whomever we marry. . . ."

Most humans; most of us; Snodgrass's all too frequent use of the demotic *we* is meant to suggest we are all in the same boat. What it actually suggests is that Snodgrass doesn't know how time-bound and tiny his boat is. We are all neurotic, spoiled,

From *New York Review of Books,* 17 April 1975. Reprinted with permission from *The New York Review of Books.* Copyright © 1975 Nyrev, Inc. Mr. Wood reviews two other books of criticism, *A Homemade World: The American Modernist Writers,* by Hugh Kenner, and *A Map of Misreading,* by Harold Bloom.

aggressive, unfaithful, and unhappy: such a projection of middle-class American worries on to the whole of literature is amazing and can probably be performed by honest and decent men only with the assistance of Freud and his tempting myths of the darkness of the psyche. Snodgrass looks into his heart, or for that matter into his remarkable poems, finds there such apparent universals as repression and guilt and resentment and angst, and by an imperceptible slip in his logic, mistakes his heart for the world. No doubt it is true that neurosis, aggression, unhappiness, and the rest lurk everywhere, in some form or another, but that is not the same thing as saying that everyone is neurotic, aggressive, and unhappily married.

Snodgrass says in his preface that he never writes prose until he feels "fairly sure" that he has "something new to say about a subject." There is a clue here to what is wrong with *In Radical Pursuit,* to the reason why it is interesting when it speaks to particulars, like Snodgrass's own poems or his teaching experiences and dull when it tackles the work of others, whether it is that of Roethke or Ransom, Lawrence or Dostoyevski, Shakespeare, Dante, Cervantes, or Homer. Snodgrass is precise about personal details and oddly clumsy about most of the texts he chooses to discuss. That is the mark, perhaps, of the man who has something to *say* about literature. Criticism, like literature itself, doesn't *say* anything—at least not about literature. It may say plenty about other things, but its relation to literature is mimetic, parasitic. I don't think, as Harold Bloom does, that criticism *is* poetry (although I do think a lot of irritating criticism tries to be), but it should be clear that criticism is not a statement or a set of statements, but an *act,* a quest, as Bloom says, borrowing the idea from Paul de Man, for images for the experience of reading.

From "Harold Bloom on Poetry"

W. D. Snodgrass began in the shadow of Lowell's *Life Studies*, but with an individual lyricism that presaged a turn away from confessional verse. The turn is very evident in *The Führer Bunker*, a cycle-in-progress of twenty dramatic monologues, spoken by Hitler, Goebbels, Eva Braun et al. I started reading this with anticipated dread and distaste, though with admiration for Snodgrass's audacity. His audacity is more than matched by his astonishing skill in ordering his intractable material and in combining his own inventions with the verifiable details of the last days of Hitler. Granted the immense difficulties he has taken on, Snodgrass demonstrates something of the power of a contemporary equivalent of Jacobean drama at its darkest.

New Republic, 26 November 1977. Copyright © 1977 by *The New Republic*. Reprinted by permission. "Harold Bloom on Poetry" appears in "The Year's Books" (pt. 1). Mr. Bloom also includes one sentence on W. D. Snodgrass's *Six Troubadour Songs* (Providence: Burning Deck), which I have omitted here, and brief reviews of the following books: *Day by Day*, by Robert Lowell, *Henry's Fate*, by John Berryman, *Collected Poems*, by Howard Nemerov, *Houseboat Days*, by John Ashbery, *Selected Poems, 1951–1977* and *The Snow Poems*, both by A. R. Ammons, *The Compass Flower*, by W. S. Merwin, *Millions of Strange Shadows*, by Anthony Hecht, *The Duplications*, by Kenneth Koch, *The Book of the Body*, by Frank Bidart, *China Trace*, by Charles Wright, *Lateness*, by David Shapiro, *Soothsayers and Omens*, by Jay Wright, *Keeping Time*, by Judith Moffett, *Comforting the Wilderness*, by Robert B. Shaw, and *The Reading of an Ever-Changing Tale*, by John Yau.

PETER L. SIMPSON

Review of *The Führer Bunker*

W. D. Snodgrass makes an auspicious reappearance on the scene in the other book that launches the BOA series, showing that its founder, poet-editor-scholar-ranconteur A. Poulin, is as incisive as ever. *The Führer Bunker: A Cycle of Poems in Progress* is the work of a major historical imagination. Through a series of monologues from all the figures who were party to the final holocaust Hitler brought upon himself, Snodgrass conveys the eerie horror and banal concerns that could be promoted so spectacularly into the Nazi regime. The condensed form and chilling detail of Snodgrass's art reduces these last cruel days to their human essence. This is a truly important work, letting us in on what Hitler and his motley gang did know—making the unspeakable speakable. This is an ambitious effort, full of insights into the extremest of dangers still present if not clear.

St. Louis Post-Dispatch, 20 December 1977. Reprinted by permission. Mr. Simpson also reviews *Cedarhome*, by Barton Sutter.

ROBERT PETERS

The Führer Bunker
W. D. Snodgrass

W. D. Snodgrass's *The Führer Bunker* is a rare example of ambitious, ongoing verse sculpture. The monologue is the medium, the event unifying the projected work (now over half-completed) is the suicide of Hitler and a clustering of followers: Goebbels, his wife, his five children, Eva Braun. Voices of survivors include Speer, Heinrici, Weidling, Bormann, and Fegelein. The focus is on the bunker in Berlin chosen by Hitler as his final refuge. The duration of time is one month, the final month culminating in the suicides. There are twenty monologues. They constitute, as Snodgrass calls them, "a cycle of poems in progress." I gather that he is not exactly certain of the final count—there are already nearly a dozen completed monologues not appearing in this collection. I admire Snodgrass's courage in presenting an incomplete work for public scrutiny. Since he is a poet of stature (*Heart's Needle* remains one of the handful of fine books of its decade), he will be widely reviewed, and there is a danger, I should think, that the reviews may discourage or dissuade him from further writing in this mode. *The Führer Bunker* is gargantuan: few poets have the energy or the daring to attempt work on this scale. The scope reminds one of Robert Browning's *The Ring and the Book,* that multi-faceted slant on domestic murder, examined through the various voices of the principals involved—and of Tennyson's *Idylls of the King*. In a real sense Snodgrass seems to be working at what seems possible for him as an almost epic form. And, despite the flaws in *The Führer Bunker,* it will be around for a long time to inspire writers who've come to realize the sad limitations of the locked-in, private, first-person, obsessional poem.

The problems raised by the poems are these: There is a general sameness of voice. The monologues are usually long (the best—

From *The Great American Poetry Bake-Off* by Robert Peters (Metuchen, N.J., and London: Scarecrow Press, 1979). Originally published in *The American Book Review* (December 1977). Reprinted by permission.

the Hermann Fegelein, for example—are short). The cadences of succeeding lines border on the monotonous, a monotony the frequent end-rhymes, well-turned rondeau (spoken by Magda Goebbels) don't quite modify. After reading the poems to myself and then hearing them read by De this past summer at Yaddo, I've concluded that the fault is primarily one of voice: Snodgrass's technical skills are as much in evidence as ever, but I rarely feel in these Bunker poems that the master's voice has a real chance to be heard. He seems to strive for the manner and presence of a stagable work; as a result, the voice is too often in language and timing Shakespearean. There's considerable fustian; namely, in this passage from Hitler's first monologue:

> Who else sold out? Bremen? Magdeburg?
> They would go on in this pisswallow, in
> Disgrace, shame. Who could we send to make
> Their lives worth less to them? In our camps,
> You gas them, shoot, club, strangle them,
> Tramp them down into trenches, thick as leaves.
> Out of the ground, at night, they squirm up
> Through the tangled bodies, crawl off in the woods.
> Every side now, traitors, our deserters, native
> Populations, they rise up like vomit, flies
> Out of bad meat, sewers backing up. Up
> There, now, in the bombed-out gardens,
> That sickly, faint film coming over
> The trees again. . . .

Or this moment from the last of Hitler's monologues depends, I feel, for its effect on a peculiar staginess of tone, cadence, and diction:

> Tell me I have to die, then. Tell me.
> What have I counted on? Tell me
> The odds against me. You can't be
> Sure enough. My name. My name on
> Every calendar. Relentless, each year,
> Your birth comes around. My death:
> My lackey; my lickass general. My Will
> Scrubs it all out, all of you, all gone. . . .

Yet, despite my quibbles over a sameness of tone and a stagey language, the sequence is complex in brilliant forms. I've already mentioned Snodgrass's achievement in sustaining the rondeau form, one of the most demanding, playful forms in poetry. Magda Goebbels is enamored of the rondeau; confronted with her tragedy (she's about to poison herself and her five children), she sings on in this form. Her monologue (19 April 1945) turns on twenty-eight three-line stanzas, all arranged in four parts, each embroidered around two (and only two) end-rhymes per section; and, as a further bravura stroke, the word *true* (and rhymings thereon) dominates three of the sections. Here is how section 1 begins:

> How can you do the things you know you'll do?—
> One last act to bring back integrity.
> I've got just one desire left: to be true.
>
> You can't pick how you'll live. Our times will screw
> Your poor last virtues from you, ruthlessly.
> How can you do the things you know you'll do?
>
> My mother drove me on: get married to
> Quandt. Rich. Kind enough. If elderly.
> I've got just one desire left: to be true.

Speer's stanzas, in the initial poem by him, are arranged to reflect the incredible sense of order in Speer's architect mind: his pattern is of a pyramid dissected from top to bottom; later, as Hitler's fate moves to its consummation, Speer's order is greatly jostled—the pyramidal form is now vestigial, is of fewer lines, and is broken with more conventional lines carrying disaster news. Speer's second monologue concludes with this moment of self-realization:

> Why let
> Me live? Time
> For one cigarette.
> He has forbidden us all
> To smoke, then sends us all
> Up the chimney. Up the chimney?
> Idiot. Use your eyes: if he gets his way,
> We won't have a chimney standing. No doubt
> He knows that I will not obey. Perhaps he knows
> That I am going to betray him. And no doubt he knows
> That I am faithful. That I evade my better self. That I
> Neglect my knowing.

Goebbels, Hitler's propaganda chief, usually favors the tacky tetrameter couplet:

> The rest is silence. Left like sperm
> In a stranger's gut, waiting its term,
> Each thought, each step lies; the roots spread.
> They'll believe in us when we're dead.

And less seriously perhaps:

> Our little Doctor, Joe the Gimp
> Comes back to limpness and his limp;
> Hephaistos, Vulcan the lame smith
> Whose net of lies caught one true myth:
> His wife, the famous beauty, whored
> By numbskull Mars, the dull warlord.

Goebbels achieves a zingy, at times almost Gilbert-and-Sullivanesque lilt, fraught with a marvelous irony. During his first appearance, though, Goebbels, occupied burning his personal papers before moving into the bunker to die, employs a collage form made up of newspaper headlines in bold-face print (**BERLIN'S DEFENDER / STRIPS FOR ACTION. NAZIS DUMP STRASSER / ESCAPES TO ITALY**); mottos rendered in a form of Gothic script (*Give all thy worldly goods / Unto the poor and follow me.*); and his ubiquitous rhymed couplets, here primarily reviewing his numerous love affairs as he tosses photographs into the flames. The couplets eerily emphasize his cynicism:

> You can't help start
> Hankering to keep some small part
> Of this world. You wear satins, ermine,
> Rouge and rings, gross as Fat Hermann.
>
> . . . . Now we can get down to what
> Counts—cleaning out the whole vile lot.
> Ernst Roehm was right: only a man
> Who has no possessions can
> Afford ideals. We learn once more
> To do without. Where but in war—
> The leveler—do all things meet?
> Rich and poor, now, dig in the street
> Together; walls bombed out, in flame,
> Bury weak men and strong the same.

Goebbels moves from the fireplace to his piano. Headline: **EDU-CATION MINISTER / PLAYS GERMAN SONGS**. The tune he renders first is a sentimental war song: The glowing sky behind him (Berlin is burning) is "the blood of soldiers flowing. / Lord have mercy on our souls." Clubfoot Joe, as he calls himself, waxes Hesse-esque, with one of those sentimental little home, bucolic-nature ditties so engaging to the German soul:

> Within my father's garden,
>> Two little saplings grow;
> The one of them bears nutmegs,
>> The other one bears cloves.
>
> The nutmeg's fresh and lovely;
>> The cloves are sharp and sweet.
> Now comes the time of parting
>> Never again to meet.
>
> The winter's snows are melting;
>> Far off these streams will flow.
> Now out of my sight you vanish;
>> Out of my thoughts you go.

Eva Braun's brother-in-law, Hermann Fegelein, a lecher, was caught trying to flee Berlin, was jailed, questioned, and finally shot. His is the most scatalogical conscience of the lot; there's little subtlety in his mind as he juxtaposes his sexual exploits with his own impending assassination:

> *spreadeagled in*
> *the hall with her pants off radio girl*
> *I could have had her anytime I wanted*
> *shit*
>> [three days ago when I said shit
> they squat   say this was a test
> at the last minute the reprieve
> no]

Bormann apparently betrayed him to Himmler, or so he believes:

>> [martin came in
> to finger me   said I was with himmler
> in some sellout to the west   I wish
> to sweet shit Id of known]

                         but I screwed them
    every one   shit not that blackhaired slut
    on the sofa   margaret cocktease
    turned me down

His bitter consolation is that he foresees the Russian avengers:

                   oh you'll just pray for vaseline
    [sweet jesus no   they cant just
    can they
              shit   shit   shit

Having devoted the past four years myself to reworking his-
torical material into possibly new poetic forms (Ann Lee, founder
of the Shakers; King Ludwig II of Bavaria; Elisha Kent Kane, the
American Arctic explorer), I do see some of the enormous prob-
lems Snodgrass confronts, and I empathize with him and greatly
admire his achievement, despite my reservations. I am sure these
poems (and the completed version when it appears) will be
widely read, discussed, and imitated. They deserve much atten-
tion. In converting these slabs of marble into sculpture Snodgrass
may not be Rodin or Giacometti, but he is a St. Gaudens, and that
is no mean achievement.

HUGH KENNER

From "Three Poets"

Six Troubadour Songs

In the hundred years since the reclamation of Provençal songs commenced, we've acquired words to some two thousand five hundred of them, though eight out of nine have lost their tunes in transit. All that time our sense of what the songs are like has been altering, and a Tennysonized taste for the troubadour as moonlit crooner has now been supplanted by a hearty sense that, as Mr. Snodgrass phrases it, "Troubadour songs have only two subjects: one, let's go Crusading and kill lots of Moors; two, let's go get . . . the boss's wife."

His versions, fortunately, are less reductive, and we're given not only the well-known ballad of the man who got his way for a week with *two* boss's wives by pretending to be a deaf-mute and then had to pleasure them 188 times ("My breech-strap near broke at that rate, / Also my reins"), but

> Such sweetness swells through these new days,
> The woods take leaf; each bird must raise
> In pure bird-latin of his kind
> The melody of a new song. . . .

This is Guillaume IX's "Ab la dolchor del temps novel," in a version that, like the original, goes bravely to a tune Mr. Snodgrass has detached from another poem entirely; Guillaume's tune is lost.

All six poems are accorded tunes, to which the English sounds have been carefully fitted. Sometimes the Provençal sounds have been matched as well:

> Near a hedgerow, sometime recent,
> There I met a shepherd lassy
> Full of mother wit and sassy

New York Times Book Review, 1 January 1978. Copyright © 1978 by The New York Times Company. Reprinted by permission. Mr. Kenner also reviews *The Body Is Made of Camphor and Gopherwood*, by Robert Bly, and *China Trace*, by Charles Wright.

gives an impression of Marcabrun's rhyme sounds, *mestissa, massissa,* and, if for "*Farai un vers de dreyt nien*" English has nothing better to offer than "Sheer nothing's all I'm singing of," cankered with consonantal collisions, that's a lesson about English; not about the translator's craft. The translator's ear is unstopped.

The Führer Bunker

Twenty poems: twenty Nazi monologues (Hitler, Speer, Goebbels, Eva Braun, Martin Bormann, et al.) presumed to have been spoken "1 April–1 May 1945." It doesn't work, for the reason Mr. Snodgrass himself pinpoints: "A reader unfamiliar with history of World War II may find many details in these poems outrageous, chilly, monstrous, downright incredible." And "Eva Braun's favorite song *was* 'Tea for Two.' "

The facts are everywhere so bizarre there is little for a poet to invent:

> *Tea for two*
> *And two for tea*
>   I ought to feel ashamed
> Feeling such joy. Behaving like a spoiled child!
> So fulfilled. This is a very serious matter.
> All of them have come here to die. And they grieve.
> I have come here to die. If this is dying,
> Why else did I ever live?
>   *Me for you*
>   *And you for me*

No way to surpass "Eva Braun's favorite song was 'Tea for Two.' " This is "A Cycle of Poems in Progress," meaning there will be more; and why Snodgrass should be wasting his gift on attempts to outdo "the banality of evil" I can't begin to guess, any more than he can guess what really went or ought to have gone through those minds, that month, not even though, he says, "Former Minister Albert Speer granted me a most provocative interview and Herr Herbert Graf of the U.S.I.S. clarified many problems for me." Those deaths, in that bunker, were self-conscious bad art—perhaps the one thing poetry can't transcend.

DANA GIOIA

From "Poetry and the Fine Presses"

Critics moralized endlessly about W. D. Snodgrass's last book, *The Führer Bunker,* asking whether a poet should write with such obvious fascination about Hitler and his *ungemütlich* gang. They seemed surprised as schoolgirls that poets could be fascinated with evil. (Does no one read Milton or Marlowe seriously anymore?) This critical breast beating was touching to behold, but it mainly served to deflect attention from the underlying literary issue of how a writer as good as Snodgrass could have written poems generally so lax and ineptly sentimental. After this macabre romp with Adolph and Eva I hesitated in picking up *If Birds Build with Your Hair* from Nadja, but I am happy to say that this new collection shows Snodgrass at his best again—witty, wise, and endlessly inventive.

The poems in *If Birds Build with Your Hair* are contemporary pastorals. Owls, barns, cherry trees, and dying elms may not be the subjects one would expect from a poet who has become famous writing on Matisse, Goebbels, and professorial lust, but then Snodgrass has never been predictable. Writing about country life, he manages to avoid the stereotypes of nature poetry and addresses his subjects with fresh intelligence and humor. A discursive poet at heart, Snodgrass occasionally has given two or even three images where one might do, but this indecisiveness is often part of his charm—as in "Old Apple Trees," which, despite its fancifulness contains the most realistic apple orchard I know:

> Like battered old millhands, they stand in the orchard—
> Like drunk legionnaires, heaving themselves up,

Reprinted by permission from *The Hudson Review,* Vol. 35, No. 3 (Autumn 1982). Copyright © 1982 by The Hudson Review, Inc. The other books reviewed are as follows: *The Wolf Last Seen,* by John Quinn, *Games of Chance,* by Thom Gunn, *There Are Things I Tell to No One,* by Galway Kinnell, *The Quiet of the Land,* by William Stafford, *Witnesses,* by Edgar Bowers, *The Defense of the Sugar Islands,* by Turner Cassidy, and *Many Houses,* by Charles Gullans.

Lurching to attention. Not one of them wobbles
The same way as another. Uniforms won't fit them—
All those cramps, humps, bulges. Here, a limb's gone;
There, rain and corruption have eaten the whole core.
They've all grown too tall, too thick, or too something.
Like men bent too long over desks, engines, benches.
Or bent under mailsacks, under loss.
They've seen too much history and bad weather, grown
Around rocks, into high winds, diseases, grown
Too long to be willful, too long to be changed.

This passage shows why one returns to Snodgrass's best work with such pleasure. It is not simply because he is so clever and entertaining, but because he is so true to experience.

Nadja has done an excellent job in printing Snodgrass's book with Univers monotype on rich beige paper, but unfortunately they have bound it with an odd zigzag cross-stitching, which makes the book difficult to open easily and read unless one uses both hands. A moment's inattention and blam! the book slams shut. This hardly creates a genial atmosphere in which to contemplate country life.

GAVIN EWART

One Poet, Many Voices

On the evidence of his *Selected Poems 1957–1987* W. D. Snodgrass is one of the six best poets now writing in English—though who the other five are would be arguable. He writes mainly in rhymed stanzas, a technique that has never entirely gone out of fashion in Britain but which has been ridiculed in certain quarters in the United States. British and American literary cultures are not exactly in synch, but they do overlap. In Britain Anthony Hecht and Richard Wilbur are as easily appreciated as W. H. Auden. Mr. Snodgrass, whose Pulitzer Prize–winning first book, *Heart's Needle,* was published in England in 1960, only one year after its American appearance, is certainly one of the poets who can make the Atlantic crossing easily.

It is a measure of Mr. Snodgrass's traditionalism and accessibility that his quality can often be defined by comparing him with poets of the past. *Heart's Needle* contributes seventeen of its thirty poems to this volume, and these are still among the best by Mr. Snodgrass. The resemblances to other poets are striking (conscious or not). In "Ten Days Leave" we have Wilfred Owen.

> He steps down from the dark train, blinking; stares
> At trees like miracles. He will play games
> With boys or sit up all night touching chairs.
> Talking with friends, he can recall their names.

There's a hint of Donne in "Riddle":

> If they act as a microscope
> Of mounted powers it shall be magnified
> Like an airy globe or beach ball that expands
> Between them so vast they could never hope
> To grasp it without all four of their hands
> Opened wide.

New York Times Book Review, 13 September 1987. Copyright © 1987 by The New York Times Company. Reprinted by permission.

Lines like "You have the damnedest friends and seem to think /
You have some right to think" are everyday speech like that of
Donne. Even A. E. Housman seems a ghostly presence:

> I go out like a ghost,
> nights, to walk the streets
> I walked fifteen years younger—
> seeking my old defeats,
> devoured by the old hunger . . .

And, just as Housman, in unguarded moments, could seem trite,
so can Mr. Snodgrass: "The blossoms snow down in my hair; /
The trees and I will soon be bare."

These similarities do no harm to the poems. This is still an
American scene, rural Frost rather than Housman, though,
when Orpheus is singing of "That flowered bride cut down in
Spring, / Struck by the snake, your underling," the formal rhym-
ing and exactitude bring Marvell to mind. In a much later satiri-
cal poem there are conscious echoes of Marlowe and Tennyson.
Well, Auden and Louis MacNeice literally quoted Shakespeare in
"serious" verse.

Although not all of the *Heart's Needle* poems are rhyming
lyrics, the approximate rhyming of some of them (meter/
motors, hills/still, sergeants/bargain) reminds one of Auden's
practice in the 1930s—except for the rhyming of singulars with
plurals—and so does their fluidity, the sense flowing on easily
from stanza to stanza. A phrase like "Heaven's vault" reminds us
that this is, in some respects, a very old-fashioned kind of
verse—but outstandingly successful in such poems as "Riddle,"
"Home Town," "A Cardinal," and "The Campus on the Hill."
And the eighty Thomas Hardy-like stanzas of "Heart's Needle"
itself contain memorable lines:

> Like nerves caught in a graph,
> the morning-glory vines
> frost has erased by half
> still scrawl across their rigid twines.
> Like broken lines
>
> of verses I can't make.

Mr. Snodgrass's next book, *Remains,* had its share of moving
poems. Of those included here "The Mouse" and "Viewing the

Body" work as a pair. "The Survivors" gives a true, unsentimental description of bereavement. "The Boy Made of Meat" is a poem for children, about the revolt of a vegetarian child too often stuffed with steak; the poem is very nicely done, relaxed, humorous, pleasant.

Of the forty poems in *After Experience,* a record of disillusion, twenty-four are here, including eight that are first-class. The most remarkable are "The Examination," a surrealist dissection of the American eagle, and "A Flat One," which is about keeping a patient alive to no purpose. Others, in freer forms, concern paintings; a poem about Van Gogh, "The Starry Night," is the most interesting. But Van Gogh's last words ("*Zoo heen kan gaan*") need a note, as they have in the Oxford edition of *After Experience,* in which we are told that the phrase can mean "This is the way to go," "I'd like to die like this," or "I want to go home."

"The Führer Bunker" is a long sequence in which the Nazi leaders and Eva Braun take turns at dramatic monologues. It is extraordinarily effective and inventive. Himmler speaks like a machine with the voice of one of the Daleks in the "Dr. Who" television series. Eva Braun sings "Tea for Two" (she used to annoy Hitler by singing such songs). Magda Goebbels gives cyanide to her six children, in a "This-is-the-house-that-Jack-built" nursery rhyme:

> This is the needle that we give
> Soldiers and children when they live
> Near the front in primitive
>   Conditions or real dangers;
> This is the spoon we use to feed
> Men trapped in trouble or in need,
> When weakness or bad luck might lead
>   Them to the hands of strangers. . . .
>
> Open wide, now, little bird;
> I who sang you your first word
> Soothe away every sound you've heard
>   Except your Leader's voice.

A sinister quotation from Goebbels stands as an epigraph: "Even if we lose this war, we still win, for our spirit will have penetrated the hearts of our enemies."

All the poems from *If Birds Build with Your Hair* are here, giving us contemporary life in a traditional setting ("Some say better not get involved; / Send Hallmark if you care"), with the bonus of imagination, mostly verbal, as in "Bees hum / Through these branches like lascivious intentions" and:

> Polish ciocias, toothless flirts
>   Whose breasts dangle down to there,
> Triple sea-hags say: headaches if
>   Birds build with your hair.

Selected from *A Locked House* are several poems about people breaking up—"Mutability," a rather hesitant villanelle; "The Last Time," which is about the absent-minded caress of a loved one before the breakup of a marriage, and the best poem in this section; "A Locked House"; and "A Seashell." "Old Jewelry" has an obsession with the emotional significance of things that is very reminiscent of Hardy and Philip Larkin. The most inventive work is "The Death of Cock Robin" from "Kinder Capers." Fantasy tribes—the Brutish, the Merkans, the Ruffians, the Youmans—appear, and one character, "W. D.," is almost equivalent to "Henry" in John Berryman's *Dream Songs*.

The last section, "Darkling," has one supreme poem—"The Poet Ridiculed by Hysterical Academics," including the lines:

> Where are the beard, the bongo drums,
>   Tattered T-shirt and grubby sandals,
> As who, released from Iowa, comes
>   To tell of wondrous scandals?

Mr. Snodgrass has a pleasant kind of mind, great originality, and a terrific talent for verse that is not-quite-for-children, but in general the poems here that are unhappy, rather than playful, are the best.

WAYNE KOESTENBAUM

Form and Discontent

When Emily Dickinson wrote, "After great pain, a formal feel-ing comes," she might have been describing meter's power to anesthetize poets who ache. W. D. Snodgrass's *Selected Poems* pits form against feeling and tries to reconcile them. Because of his preponderance of sorrow and his habit of disclosing secrets, he has been labeled—with Sylvia Plath, Anne Sexton, Robert Lowell, and John Berryman—a confessional poet. Snodgrass made his debut in 1959, with *Heart's Needle,* a book of high craftsmanship, marked by a yoking of mandarin style with sensa-tional content. He retained his allegiance to form; in his late, comic poems the formal feeling seems even to have left behind the pain. But without an undertow of grief, mere meter soon grows pleasureless.

Snodgrass's control succeeds because it keeps his discontents only uneasily at bay. In a fine early poem, "April Inventory," he uses rhyme and meter to deny the "violence" he often perversely rhymes with "silence," as if the only antidote to suffering were to shut up about it:

> Though trees turn bare and girls turn wives,
> We shall afford our costly seasons;
> There is a gentleness survives
> That will outspeak and has its reasons.
> There is a loveliness exists,
> Preserves us, not for specialists.

Snodgrass's assumption that girls, like leaves, are fated to fall, marks "April Inventory" as a relic of 1959. But his tetrameter lines, in their taut perfection, bear witness to loveliness, despite the shadow cast by his anxiously iterated "There is."

Darker specialists inhabit *The Führer Bunker,* a series of dra-matic monologues spoken by Hitler and his companions in the

From *Village Voice,* 17 November 1987, p. 63. Copyright © 1987 *The Village Voice.* Reprinted by permission of the author and *The Village Voice.*

last days of the Third Reich. In "Magda Goebbels" Dr. Joseph Goebbels's wife lulls her six children to sleep with Nazi pieties as she slips them cyanide:

> This is the serum that can cure
> Weak hearts; these pure, clear drops insure
> You'll face what comes and can endure
>   The test; you'll never falter.
> This is the potion that preserves
> You in a faith that never swerves;
> This sets the pattern of your nerves
>   Too firm for you to alter.

The poet distrusts anything that refuses to swerve, including poetry: Goebbels's children will be "preserved" in death as, in the earlier poem, loveliness "preserves us." Snodgrass intends the connection between despotism and poetry. He prints Heinrich Himmler's monologues on a graph-paper grid, so we can see that each poetic line has the identical number of letters. Such self-consciously excessive artistic control stands for Himmler's policy of social control: only a fanatic cares so much about form.

Magda Goebbels, teaspoon of poison in hand, tells her children, "We shape you into pure form." She is a malign muse-mother; all of Snodgrass's work implicitly takes place in her dark nursery. He seeks art's roots in the crib, calling the Parthenon's white marble "ordinate and clean as / Nursery furniture." In other nurseries, not so clean, he finds the origin of evil. In "The Boy Made of Meat," a poem for children, a boy becomes the meat he eats. Here Snodgrass draws from Christina Rossetti's violently oral "Goblin Market" and the story of Hansel and Gretel, demonstrating that there is a fine line between eating and being eaten. Loathing meat, the boy is promised "ice cream with toppings sweet and sour," treats that will "make those boys just bulge with power!" No song Snodgrass sings is ever innocent.

Graciously, he elides the horror; his perfect pitch, rhythm, and rhyme bring pleasure. He can sound like Keats: "and game colts trail the herded mares." He can sound wrenchingly himself: "what must not be seized / Clenches the empty fist." His most emotional poems end with flat understatement. Affectingly simple declarations—"It is an evil, stupid joke: / My wife is pregnant; my sister's in her grave"—risk the bathos they try to avoid. But this master inspires reverence. Surrounded by riches, a reader becomes "a tourist whispering through the priceless rooms."

ROBERT McDOWELL

From "Collisions in Poetry"

As everyone ought to know, W. D. Snodgrass won the Pulitzer Prize in 1960 for *Heart's Needle*, his first collection. Since then he has published seven volumes of poetry, many in hard-to-find limited editions. Now, with Soho Press's release of his *Selected Poems 1957–1987*, we have our first opportunity to see Snodgrass in perspective, and the vision is impressive. Though I do not much care for the label and will make little of it in these comments, it must be said that Snodgrass founded the confessional school in poetry. Later Lowell, Plath, and Sexton would be grouped with Snodgrass and eclipse him in celebrity. This is odd and so American, for it is clear that he has more depth and style than any of them.

In an era that prizes varieties of counterfeit style rather than substance and the style it generates Snodgrass provides a valuable example of dissent. When he writes unerringly of the cruelty of children, the guilt of parents, and the trials of lovers, he is never self-serving or sentimental. This alone sets him apart from his late confessional peers. His grasp of history distinguishes him as well. Whereas in Lowell historical awareness is manipulated only to bolster a defective personality, in Snodgrass it contributes to the creation of a community worldview. "We must live with intent," the poet tells us. In these poems the "I" is not *I*, but all of us. Snodgrass insists that we accept responsibility not only for our lives but for our social inventions too. In short, Snodgrass's poetry embodies belief in a social contract much larger than the popular contract that confines itself to the petty kingdom of the Self.

> Your credit has finally run out.
> On our steel table, trussed and carved,

Reprinted by permission from *The Hudson Review*, Vol. 40, No. 4 (Winter 1988). Copyright © 1988 by The Hudson Review, Inc. The other books reviewed are as follows: *New and Selected Poems*, by Marvin Bell, *Lovesick*, by Gerald Stern, *Flesh and Blood*, by C. K. Williams, *The Minute Hand*, by Jane Shore, *No Sign*, by Sydney Lea, *The End of Beauty*, by Jorie Graham, and *Archer in the Marrow*, by Peter Viereck.

You'll find this world's hardworking, starved
Teeth working in your precious skin.
The earth turns, in the end, by turn about
And opens to take you in.

("A Flat One")

If this book confirms the poet's long human reach, it also showcases his polished versatility. The casual reader familiar only with Snodgrass's purposeful bitterness in an early poem like "Fourth of July" may be surprised to discover here the lovely observations of nature from *If Birds Build with Your Hair* (1979), the slashing humor of "Kinder Capers"(1986), and the witty, disturbing poem for children of all ages, "The Boy Made of Meat" (1982).

Readers of this book, which also outdistances the others discussed here in design, will discover poem after poem with integrity's weight in them. We do not much associate integrity with poetry anymore. But I must use the word here. Like Yeats, Snodgrass writes a formal poetry of aggression that challenges our smug conventions and asks us to be wiser, more humane. "The burning witness of his senses" seems true.

LARRY LEVIS

From "Not Life So Proud to Be Life: Snodgrass, Rothenberg, Bell, and the Counter-Revolution"

I

Postmodern; Postmodernist; such terms sound as if someone died. Someone did, and the form of that death put an end to the Modernist Imagination. For modernism, constellating itself after symbolism—and despite its disjunctiveness and even its embrace of disintegration as a mode—was nevertheless an attempt at permanence and restorations of all kinds. As Yeats phrases it in the closing stanza of "Sailing to Byzantium": "Once out of nature I shall never take / My bodily form from any natural thing / But such a form as Grecian goldsmiths make / Of hammered gold and golden enameling." If Freud is right in *Civilization and Its Discontents,* and if "Man has become a kind of prosthetic god," then much in the labyrinth of modernism can be looked upon not merely as swerves and detours but also as the representations which such a "prosthetic" god might make—both to pass the time and to carve something that would outlast the rancor of his incarceration.

For all its formally revolutionary aspects, this desire for aesthetic permanence in Yeats and others was endlessly recuperative of a *past*—Byzantium for Yeats, Renaissance Italy for Pound, an orthodox Christian piety for Eliot, a revisionary dialogue with romanticism for Stevens—all are attempts at a cessation of time, and, with it, a consequent repression of the anxiety of chrono-

From *American Poetry Review,* January–February 1989. Copyright ©1989 by Larry Levis. Reprinted by permission. Larry Levis wrote this review when he was working on the essay "Waiting for the End of the World: Snodgrass and *The Führer Bunker.*" I have deleted the passages on *The Führer Bunker,* as Levis develops these more fully in his essay. Levis's introductory passages (secs. 1 and 2) provide a context for his treatment of Snodgrass's *Selected Poems,* so I have included them. Levis also reviews *New and Selected Poems,* by Jerome Rothenberg, and *New and Selected Poems,* by Marvin Bell.

logical change in which one is "fastened to a dying animal / It knows not what it is." Yet this immuring of the Self in a past is willed: "Once out of nature I shall never take" suggests some of the vestigial anxiety still present in such a project, for the use of *shall* is an invocation of Will. And to Will is, quite simply, not to Know. And *shall*, that article of faith, would hardly be necessary in the orthodoxy of belief: "Thy Will Be Done" is the abandonment of Self and its surrender, not a petition for its transmutation into hammered gold.

If the verb troubles me in Yeats's line, it is the modifier *prosthetic* that is troubling in Freud's statement, and I suspect that he meant it to be troubling in just this way. For the connotations of *prosthetic,* medical in common usage, remind me that an artificial limb is just that, artificial; that shocking, miserably hard, dark rubber that both amputates and begins at someone's wrist signifies the loss, however partial, of an original body, just as it does in Freud's figure. If we replaced the original and originating Body, our "prosthetic" nature *is* Nature itself, which will join us to matter, to the physical world; we are organisms that will die, anyway, into matter, deities that will become "sods" to every high requiem. Therefore, the post-Freudian figure of man as "the angel who shits" is inescapable, and when Robert Bly at a reading slips on a gorilla mask to recite Shelley's "Ode to a Skylark," or when the Beatles call an album *Rubber Soul* (prosthetic gods, prosthetic souls), they are dramatizing both the loss of a certain imaginative fertility in myth and a knowledge, what "one cannot possibly not know," by which our time has violated and liberated us at once, and their mode of doing so is a Postmodernist self-mockery that now accompanies the imagination as faithfully as a left hand made of glass.

II

After Hiroshima Oppenheimer paid a visit to President Truman, and when Truman had admitted him to his office, the author of the first atomic bomb said: "I feel as if I have blood on my hands." In a gesture uncharacteristic of most presidents before or since, Truman leaned forward and stretched out his arms: "Here," he said, "wipe them on my sleeves." Someone *had* died. And if Truman's reply is uncharacteristic of most politicians, it is characteristic of postwar poetry, which would "rip off the whole facial mask" in order to *know.*

And if the Postmodernist sensibility retains a desire for permanence, the mode of accomplishing it has changed. That is why most artists would tacitly agree, as a *working credo,* that art is more important than life, for without such a belief one is enormously compromised and vulnerable to conscription by the purposes of others. When Faulkner peevishly responded to an interview: "*Au contraire,* Keats's 'Ode on a Grecian Urn' is worth any number of little old ladies," most poets I know would only smile in assent. Yet there is a devilish pleasure in interrogating his assertion, as there is in the interrogation of any piety or truth that is at least three weeks old. Just how many "little old ladies"? *Any* number? Twelve? Thirty-two? Four hundred eighty-nine? Six million? Uh, oh. There is the magic number of the century that causes all smiles to cease together, and there is the problem.

Though Marx foresaw the possibility of quantitative accumulation producing qualitative change, he could not have foreseen its shape in the death camps and Hiroshima. But genocide and nuclear warfare ended modernism as an *imaginative possibility.* Six million is too many. It is, in fact, unthinkable, and it "doth tease us out of thought / As doth eternity." But it is fact, not metaphor, and therefore it has become the problem and violation that we know, and it is why Theodor Adorno wrote: "Poetry after Dachau is a barbaric act." But if that is so, then so is everything else a barbaric act, including the existence of Adorno or of myself writing of him. And although Eliot never intended such a circumstance when he said that "poetry is perpetually in need of re-barbarization," that is what has happened, and happened *in fact.* And though the political leaders of this century, whether totalitarian or democratic, can still mostly be absorbed in the lacerating, abstract metaphor that Stevens provides for them— "A tyrant in a varnished car," one "whom none believe" yet one "whom all believe that all believe"—it is the abstract mode itself that came to be suspect in much Postmodernist work; stunned as it is by the fact of what has happened, only the unadorned frailty of the voice sounds convincing: "But the Germans killed them all. / I know it's in bad taste to say it quite this way. / But it's true. / The Germans killed them all" (Louis Simpson, "A Story of Chicken Soup"). It is precisely this impoverished lack of authority in the voice that *is,* ironically enough, convincing in Louis Simpson's "A Story of Chicken Soup." It is convincing because of its willingness to say something as terrible and as unqualified as what has happened in fact.

III

Long after Modernism perished, it lived on as a worshipped deity in the institutionalized altars of academia. And the work of Snodgrass begins with his apostasy at one of its cathedrals, the University of Iowa in the 1950s. In retrospect even his heresy has within it a kind of indwelling American iconoclasm and revisionary puritanism:

> I remember when I was in school, we were all taught to write obscure, brilliant, highly symbolized poems about the loss of myth in our time, and, you know, it suddenly began to occur to me that I didn't care about the loss of myth in our time; frankly, I was glad to be rid of the stuff. . . . But we were all writing poems about what we thought "The Waste Land" was about. None of us had bothered to find out that "The Waste Land" isn't about that at all. We thought it was about that because you could make doctoral dissertations by talking about all the learned allusions in "The Waste Land" and how it was about, you know, the need for a "meaningful myth" in our lives; nobody had noticed it was about Eliot's insane wife and his frozen sex life. He had helped disguise this, with Pound's assistance, by his editing of the poem. We believed people's doctoral statements about the poem. We believed Frost and Eliot when they said their poems were about other things than their own sex lives, and we can now look at the poems and see that that just isn't so at all.[1]

The intimation, of course, is that Snodgrass understands the Modernists' real concerns, however they may be masked by mythical method, and so, in a curious appropriation of them via his own obsessions, he has created a new allegiance with that sexuality which the priesthood of Modernism had either ignored or censored. He is not rebelling against the Modernists (whom he elsewhere has called "definitive") so much as he is adopting them, in all their repressed, censored splendor, as grandparents. His struggle will be against those priests who have gelded them and locked them in the sacristy of new criticism.

And yet part of his unbridled attack depends upon a reversal, for, as Paul Gaston has noted, in Snodgrass's art an older form is used, a durational and spoken lyrical form, in which the content is new. In modernism, new forms were created to house the "treasure-trove" of the past. At least some of Snodgrass's work is involved in demythologizing, dismantling, a clearing away of what, after the war, must have felt suddenly archaic and false, a mode which in itself had become "a tyrant in a varnished car" and which had spread into the outlying culture like some contagious sleep, one in which all sleepers are alike. It is appropriate that "Fourth of July" is placed in *Remains,* Snodgrass's second collection published under the pseudonym S. S. Gardons and in a limited edition. For the speaker is both anonymous and representative of what most inhabitants feel about the "monolithic piety," or living falsehood, of their culture. What is more intriguing is the phenomenon of a confessional poet traveling under an assumed name, for it suggests that the future of confessional work lies in another direction, as if the exhibitionist had become an agoraphobic, a transformation not uncommon, in life or in art:

> Hearing some politician fume;
> Someone leads out a blonde schoolgirl to crown
> Queen of this war-contract factory town;
> Skyrockets and the last guns boom.

> I keep my seat and wonder where,
> Into what ingrown nation has she gone
> Among a people silent and withdrawn;
> I wonder in the stifling air

> Of what deprived and smoked-filled town
> They brush together and do not feel lust,
> Hope, rage, love; within what senseless dust
> Is she at home to settle down;

> Where do they know her, and the dead
> Meet in a vacancy of shared disgrace,
> Keep an old holiday of blame and place
> Their tinsel wreath on her dark head?

> We tramp home through the sulfurous smoke
> That is my father's world. Now we must
> Enter my mother's house of lint and dust
> She could not breathe; I wheeze and choke.

> It is an evil, stupid joke:
> My wife is pregnant; my sister's in her grave.

We live in the home of the free and of the brave.
No one would hear me, even if I spoke.

It is, and it has always been, Snodgrass's willingness to make
what Camus in *The Plague* would call a complete "condemnation
of things as they are" that distinguishes this poet; it is also part of
what his power comes from, for no one transgresses a taboo,
which in this case was a rebellion against the kind of poem his
mentors prescribed, without releasing a certain amount of psy-
chic energy. Yet Snodgrass's "condemnation" is not quite or not
yet nihilism; nihilism knows it needn't wait to see if things im-
prove, and nihilism, as George P. Eliot maintained years ago,
doesn't care so much about getting the rhymes right. Snodgrass
cares, and waits. And the value that rushes into the poetry of
confessionalism, this most identifiably American of all Postmod-
ernist modes, is simply life itself, the detailing and almost Flau-
bertian observation of it whether it occurs in a threadbare zoo in
Iowa City where a father and daughter go to see the raccoons or
in the smell of a linen chest at 91 Revere Street. After wholesale
genocide and nuclear death it can almost be said that what one
experiences with his senses and mind is a value per se, and that
the record each "poor, passing fact" makes of such an impover-
ished world and culture is the only wealth that anyone might
expect. But it is not the only value that can be posited, or striven
for: "I tell you love is possible. We have to try," Snodgrass adds.
   It is this very domesticity and representativeness that makes
Heart's Needle, and, I would argue, *Remains,* American classics of
our time, just as these qualities are what will make Lowell en-
dure any present chorus of critical jackals who seem themselves
victims of that "monolithic piety" of American culture. Yet the
usual ethical charge against any poet of the confessional mode
had to do with what appeared as an indecent display of private
disclosures of their own lives, of unalleviated obsessions, of an
almost pathological introversion or public manicness. The sub-
jects it took up, after all, were madness, divorce, cruelty, vio-
lence, suicide, even homicidal impulses, and the general reading
public, who, as Leslie Fiedler pointed out, is not interested in
enjoying poetry so much as it feels obligated to judge it, or to
judge the poet or the life of the poet, probably wondered why
they couldn't all be kindly old soothsayers like the Frost they had
so mistaken for a kindly odd soothsayer. Certainly they had
trouble with a druggie like Poe or a Fascist like Pound. And yet
in all fairness it seems now that it was the imitators of Lowell,

Sexton, Plath, Berryman, and Snodgrass, followers and medio-
cre talents who displayed each psychic scar they could find, and
who held up their traumas like medals, and who chanted a rosary
of petty complaints until their very stridency passed for hysteria,
and who then made a shrine of hysteria or of an irresponsible
cruelty they mistook for masculinity, who made the mode repug-
nant by sensationalizing and sentimentalizing it. The eventual
result of their vanity, of their whole effort, is this: I cannot
remember even one of their names.

And yet it appears true, as Yeats observed, that "all that is
merely personal soon rots, unless it is packed in salt or ice." And
What Lowell called the "perfect little stanzas" of the *Heart's Nee-
dle* sequence is exactly that salt, that ice. The new content, the
intimacy of its disclosure, is distilled into variations upon some
very old forms of English prosody. What might have become
"merely personal" is never idiosyncratic; it is representative not
only of the pain of an absentee father but also of the entire
impoverishment of a culture. It is the tenacity of the father with
his obsessive love that matters and that mirrors his larger com-
munity; it is his love's embarrassing persistence that makes him
representative, that throws the values of America into relief by
displaying their dispossession. Furthermore, this fellow walking
hand in hand with his daughter on her weekend visit will not be
nice about it, will not shut up and go away, will not adjust, will
not even adopt, for appearances, the correct, liberal attitudes. All
this is emphasized in the poem's close, which is its recapitulative
coda, complete with its diminished Lear and innocent Cordelia
in their confinement:

> In full regalia, the pheasant cocks
>   march past their dubious hens;
> the porcupine and the lean, red fox
>   trot around their bachelor pens
>
> and the miniature painted train
>   wails on its oval track;
> you said, I'm going to Pennsylvania!
>   and waved. And you've come back.
>
> If I loved you, they said, I'd leave
>   and find my own affairs.
> Well, once again this April, we've
>   come around to the bears;

> punished and cared for, behind bars,
> the coons on bread and water
> stretch thin black fingers after ours.
> And you are still my daughter.

Still; my; to pack in salt or ice means what I hear as that slight variation of the trimeter in the last line: not three iambs but two iambs followed by a spondee, the possessive *my* rising up a little against the recumbency of the iambic pattern, its accommodation. For everything else has been wrested away from the speaker here but this knowledge, this "still" and "my" by which his feeling continues. These too, he might have been tricked out of, or might have given up in the foolish acceptance of neighborly good advice. But to "concede" *that* is to concede (an important word in the sequence) all that this father is, all that he feels. And as J. D. McClatchy argues in his brilliant essay on Snodgrass, "The Mild, Reflective Art," Snodgrass's "controlling concerns—identity and choice—are existential in nature, and confessional in revelation."[2] But in Snodgrass, that which is "confessional in revelation" often confesses to a hard-won self-knowledge. In "April Inventory" his aggression is a kind of self-preservation, and therefore it is a value, perhaps the oldest value, one always accompanied by its faithful antagonist, the *thanatos* of every *eros:*

> I taught myself to name my name,
> To bark back, to loosen love and crying;
> To ease my woman so she came,
> To ease an old man who was dying.
> I have not learned how often I
> Can win, can love, but choose to die.

And yet the joyous knowledge of the poem's final stanza depends upon a change of pronoun and point of view; the *we* and its discovery of *loveliness* is necessary as counterpoint to the isolated *I* and its self-destructive nature; a *we* that is possible only through the wizening of age that occurs in the penultimate stanza and that affords the seer-like, almost gleefully posthumous tonal change:

> Though trees turn bare and girls turn wives,
> We shall afford our costly seasons;
> There is a gentleness survives
> That will outspeak and has its reasons.

> There is a loveliness exists,
> Preserves us, not for specialists.

If the whole poem had not cautioned us with its ironies, this stanza would be one that could only be spoken by an imposter, a Polonius, a spokesperson for "monolithic piety." But because they exist against a panorama of confessional revelations of lust, professional irresponsibility, and all sorts of dalliance and pleasures in life, they plead their case from seasoned experience, experience in which a decent amount of fun and the offensive laziness necessary for every poet has been emphasized, and vindicated.

But this *we* is a change that is indicative of larger changes to come in Snodgrass's work. Although the confessional mode remains prominent in the first half of *After Experience,* and although these poems do not disappoint me, they lack the vital, and sometimes aggressive, energy of the earlier work. Curiously, the most powerful poem in their order centers not upon the poet's life, but upon the man, Old Fritz, dying in a hospital as the poet, who at that time was a young orderly, contemplates the subject in "A Flat One." After the inevitable slow death it is his meditation that seems, characteristically again, representative in the kind of choice he makes in the final reversal of the closure:

> They'd say this was a worthwhile job
> Unless they tried it. It is mad
> To throw our good lives after bad;
> Waste time, drugs, and our minds, while strong
> Men starve. How many young men did we rob
> To keep you hanging on?
>
> I can't think we did *you* much good.
> Well, when you died, none of us wept.
> You killed for us, and so we kept
> You, because we have to earn our pay.
> No. We'd still have to help you try. We would
> Have killed for you today.

Old Fritz is a veteran, has "killed for us," and, although Snodgrass is willing to rebel against any suspect piety of the past, he cannot wholly rebel against that culture which has, after all, so inevitably become a part of him. Here he chooses what he can only believe is the last decency available.

The sequence of poems on paintings and painters that concludes *After Experience* is abruptly abstract in mode rather than confessional; it attempts to confront, in one of its most haunting manifestations, the principles aswirl beneath all action, that eros that is unjudgeably constant as occasioned by Monet's "Les Nymphéas":

> And I am shared out. I become these things:
>   These lillies, if these things are lillies
> Which are dancers growing dim across no floor;
>   These mayflies; whirled dust orbiting in the sun;
> This blossoming diffused as rushlights; galactic vapors;
>   Fluorescence into which we pass and penetrate;
> O soft as the thighs of women;
>   O radiance, into which I go on dying . . .

The attempt by Snodgrass to enlarge the focus of his lens in *Heart's Needle,* to suggest that the personal *agon* of the poem is in some way reciprocally reflected by the contemporaneous Korean War, that there is some causal connection or even synchronous connection between the private and public war, is what M. L. Rosenthal considers a major flaw in the poem; but, if it is, Snodgrass's tenacity in a later historical cycle might come to be seen as a gesture in which such a flaw is recuperated, relieved, and even explained by the later revisionary work, *The Führer Bunker,* for his tenacity is a reflex of his desire for overall coherence and unity over a life's work in a variety of modes, and certainly in a range of different voices. . . .

The best of the poems in this collection are so central to our lives and to our thought that I think the book should be read by anyone interested in poetry at all.

For the Garamond type, the thick, laid paper, the sewn bindings, the care taken to provide even graph paper for the acrostic, telegraphic poems of the idiot Himmler; for the design and cover art, for the kind of painstaking, scrupulous attention to detail that is only appropriate for this poet, I have nothing but praise. The book, like the poems within it, is meant to last, and its publisher, Soho, should be commended.

NOTES

1. As quoted in J. D. McClatchy, "W. D. Snodgrass: The Mild, Reflective Art," *Massachusetts Review* 16 (Spring 1975), 282–83.

2. McClatchy, "W. D. Snodgrass," 282.

PART FIVE   *Retrospective Essays: The Later Work and the Early in Light of the Later*

GERTRUDE M. WHITE

To Tell the Truth

The Poems of W. D. Snodgrass

W. D. Snodgrass, in his early fifties, is well known in the comparatively small world of academia. He has taught for many years: at Wayne State, Cornell, Syracuse, Old Dominion of Virginia, and Delaware, among others; has taken part in writers' conferences; and has written many essays and critical articles for scholarly journals, on literature generally and poetry particularly. He is known more hazily to a somewhat wider audience as the author of *Heart's Needle,* a collection of lyrics which won the Pulitzer Prize nearly twenty years ago, in 1960. He is included in most anthologies of contemporary poetry, usually grouped with the "confessional" poets of our period: such figures as Robert Lowell, John Berryman, Sylvia Plath, and Anne Sexton, to name only a few.

But Snodgrass is not, to the run–of–the–mill reader of poetry— if any such reader there be—as well and favorably known as he ought to be. The reason, I think, lies in his most striking characteristic: his resolute, uncompromising, almost frightening honesty. Far from the lies for which Plato banished poets from his ideal republic, Snodgrass's verse tells the truth, however painful to himself or to others. It neither fakes, evades, exhibits ego for the sake of exhibitionism, nor grinds the axe of fad or ideology. It demonstrates what he himself has declared to be requisite for "the terribly hard work that writing is . . . a complete removal from any ulterior motive, an absolute dedication to the object and the experience."[1] The depth of its sincerity, technical and moral, is, he declares, "a very old-fashioned measure of a poem's worth,"[2] and the painstaking effort to discover and to get into words "not what I wish I felt. Only what I cannot help thinking"[3] is evident in everything he has written.

As a confessional poet, Snodgrass presents an odd spectacle. It

From *Odyssey* (Oakland University, Rochester, Michigan) 3, no. 2 (1979). Reprinted by permission of the author.

is true that he began conventionally, with a recording of painful personal experience: a failed marriage, the difficult readjustment of his relationship with a cherished only daughter, the death of his younger sister, alienation from parents. But when we ponder the path he then took, the term *confessional* seems a misnomer. Following *Heart's Needle* and *After Experience,* his next volume of lyrics, came a series of translations: Christian Morgenstern's *Gallows Songs,* Provençal troubadour songs, traditional Hungarian songs. Then *In Radical Pursuit,* a collection of critical essays and lectures distinguished for their unflinching probing of the poet's most personal experience and, still more, for the objectivity and integrity with which they use that experience to illuminate the creative process. Then—and this is really startling—*The Führer Bunker,* a collection of dramatic monologues by Hitler, Albert Speer, Joseph Goebbels, Goebbel's wife Magda, Eva Braun, and others: damned souls who destroyed so many others before their own Götterdämmerung.

And it is not subject matter only that separates Snodgrass from the confessional tribe. From the beginning his verse exhibits a mastery of technique and form, a control of metrics, an ability to use conventional poetic structures for unconventional purposes that sharply distinguishes it from much if not most contemporary poetry. "Free" verse too often means poetry as shapeless and runny as soup. Snodgrass can write stanzas that actually scan and rhyme in the most unexpectedly traditional way. He likes melody and can handle a long, swinging line and a refrain, as in many of the folk songs he translates. He uses such seemingly outmoded forms as octosyllabic couplets and terza rima. And—yes—when he abandons rhyme and meter for a less structured pattern, he does not abandon form itself but shapes lines and stanzas as controlled as, though different from, those of traditional verse.

According to James Joyce, the artist moves from lyrical to dramatic method; from egocentric to impersonal point of view. Certainly this is true of Snodgrass. And he is himself very aware of it. In an interview with Paul L. Gaston on the publication of *The Führer Bunker* Snodgrass is quoted as saying, "When I got through with the pseudonymous book" (a book of poems called *Remains,* probing the death of his sister and, in order to spare the feelings of his mother, attributed to an invented author, S. S. Gardons) "I felt, OK, that's enough of that. I really don't want to do that anymore."[4] And in reply to Gaston's suggestion that his career has been consistently directed from poems of the personal life, highly private poems, to poems which are "entirely in the world and entirely critical," Snodgrass replied, "Certainly. I hope that's correct. Of course, one doesn't think consciously about things like that."[5]

From the beginning, however, Snodgrass seems to me to have been different in attitude and purpose from the typical confessional poet. Even his most private poems are poems not of statement but of discovery. That is, although they are *personal* they are not truly *subjective,* for they move from the self into the world, using the self not to exhibit a private world—like, for example, the poems of Sylvia Plath and Anne Sexton—but to illuminate the public world we all share. So, too, in his criticism Snodgrass uses the insights and experiences gained from his own psychoanalysis not to exhibit his psyche but to explore and more fully explain the world of Dante, of Shakespeare, of Cervantes. Self-knowledge gained from analysis and experience becomes a tool for understanding others and the world in which we live.

In his interview with Paul Gaston Snodgrass himself seems puzzled by his choice of the subject matter of *The Führer Bunker.* "I don't think I can tell you much about the things that come from my personality, about what drove me personally. All I know is that I was very much interested in this period. As soon as the war was over, I began reading the Nazi books and memoirs. I really wanted to know what the hell could somebody think, or feel, that would make them feel those acts were necessary. How could they even think they were possible?"[6] But surveying the poet's career as a whole it is, I think, possible to hazard a guess as to why the subject attracted him.

The interviewer himself puts his finger on it. He identifies, as one of the most prominent themes of *Heart's Needle,* that of personal autonomy, the assertion of the will: "We try to choose our life."[7] And *The Führer Bunker,* as Gaston says, dramatizes two perversions of this principle. Hitler, who thinks himself free and autonomous, is at the mercy of inner compulsions of which he has no understanding. Speer, on the other hand, has voluntarily sacrificed his own will in his capitulation to Hitler. In their abdication of self-knowledge and will they have brought about the destruction of millions. Against this "spirit that denies" stands the knowledge and rational will of the poet who explores and asserts in order to create, to bring order out of chaos. His effort to enter into, to understand, and to dramatize spirits seemingly wholly alien to his is his most dramatic assertion of his own autonomy and the choice he freely makes: to reject nothing human, nothing done, however horrible, by men who, as Snodgrass says, were "not so different from you."[8] The poet is most fully himself, most completely individual, when he transmutes private knowledge and experience, through an act of creative imagination, into knowledge and acceptance of all that is human.

"The healthy organism grows not in accordance with what has been done to it, but what it wants to become."[9] Snodgrass's paraphrase of the words of an unnamed American biologist, as he himself must know, is a description of and commentary on his own poetic progress and achievement. It is his eye-on-the-experience, on the object of knowledge, on the self not as end but as means, his constant effort to understand and accept the realities of experience and to find the strength to live inside human limitations, that has kept him balanced, sane, humble, humorous, and—within reason—hopeful, where so many others have spun off into exhibitionism, neurosis, madness, despair, suicide.

The process of exploration, understanding, acceptance is not wholly—not even primarily—intellectual. Passion, commitment, volition, action are more central to the process of making poetry than is the detached intellect. Snodgrass rejects those intellectuals who "live only to demonstrate their detachment from all positions, their utter superiority to any belief or any feeling. To them, the greatest sin is passion or energy. *Our* problem, I think, is to discriminate, yet not lose the ability to believe and act."[10] This conviction led him to depart from the advice of his early teachers at the University of Iowa who tried to teach him "how to pack a poem with meaning," for "from that it's a fairly easy jump to how to pack a poem with feeling, which to me tells a lot more."[11] But neither ideas nor feelings can be simply stated without losing poetic power and meaning.

A very great deal must be left to the tone of voice, the choice of language, the suggestiveness of words. . . . Why, finally, is all this tact required? Why must ideas and emotions be repressed from conscious statement into details and facts; repressed again from facts into the texture of language, the choice of words, connotations; repressed finally into technical factors like rhyme and echoes of other words. . . . We are concerned here with problems of inmost belief and of strong emotion. . . . We simply do not credit people's conscious statements in these areas. And for very good reasons—most people simply do not use their conscious minds for the discernment or the revelation of the truth. They use their conscious minds to disguise themselves from others and from themselves.[12]

Such statements tell us a great deal about Snodgrass's verse and the direction it has taken. Concerned above all else with truth-telling and convinced that it is neither possible to tell the truth nor to be believed through rational statement and surface meaning, he has sought ways of telling it through the qualities of language itself, through the connotations and sounds of words, through rhyme, rhythm, and cadence, the musical substructure of verse, through tone and voice and persona. "There is always a kind of invented persona,"[13] says Snodgrass, even in his earliest and most personal poems, and as he developed so did his use of many voices. Strongly influenced by Browning's dramatic monologues, Snodgrass came to feel that "the most interesting poems of the last fifteen years have all been poly-voiced poems,"[14] and that all voices are, in a sense, "angles of yourself."[15] So even the characters of *The Führer Bunker*, far removed as they seem from the personal voice that speaks in Snodgrass's early poems, are in some sense "a distillation of one's self."[16] In fashioning these characters on the basis of historical knowledge the poet conceives them truly only through faithfulness to his own experience and the truth of his own imagination.

Understanding these convictions and these purposes enables us to understand the apparently divergent directions Snodgrass's poetry has taken. *Heart's Needle*, *After Experience*, and *Remains* are poems of discovery: efforts to understand, evaluate, and come to terms with often agonizing personal experience. The voice that speaks in them was described by a critic as "urgent but controlled, muted but passionate, unassuming but instructive."[17] Snodgrass himself speaks of "a humanity of tone" characteristic of the better poems produced in recent years: "common-sensical, stylistically almost ordinary—such a voice as you might hear in this world, not a voice meant to lift you out of this world."[18] Their verse forms are varied but always tight and controlled, the emotion present in image, in rhythm, in tone—not in assertion. Their subjects—alienation, failure, loss and grief, guilt, bitterness, anger, survival—poignant in themselves, gain emotional power through both the precision and the restraint of language and form. And, finally, all qualities work together to achieve astonishing moral power. As one of his critics remarks, "Snodgrass's mild, reflective art has specialized in a depth of experience few poets have dared to reveal, few men risked feeling so completely."[19]

To turn from these volumes to the *Six Troubadour Songs* and the *Traditional Hungarian Songs* is to enter a different world. Strongly influenced by music, by German lieder, and Spanish and Italian songs of the sixteenth and seventeenth centuries, Snodgrass says of the latter: "I still remember the first day I heard them—my hair simply stood on end. And I wanted to do something as directly and stridently passionate."[20] These translations of the troubadours of Provençal and of Hungarian folk songs are not explorations, poems of probing and discovery, but celebrations, simple, sensuous, and passionate, as Milton said poetry should be. They are joyous poems, plain and vigorous in speech and racy in situation, or bawling and striding along with swinging meters, or singing sweetly of the ineffable sweetness of love. They are full of the drama of human relationships, of the concreteness of the physical world, of the joy of living. Variable in scene, in mood, in voice, they are alike in the passion, the energy with which they proclaim the glory of life.

"Ladies with Cats," from the *Troubadour Songs,* should be compared with "Leaving the Motel" from *After Experience,* for an unforgettable lesson in the importance of tone and rhythm. The voice that speaks in the former, an amused, self-mocking, cock-o'-the-walk boasting of the bawdy pleasures of illicit sex, is a marvelous contrast and antidote to the tentative, melancholy voice of the modern lover and his cramped, wistful lovemaking. This voice gives us the wry pleasure of recognition:

> Check: is the second bed
> Unrumpled, as agreed?
> Landlords have to think ahead
> In case of need,
>
> Too. Keep things straight: don't take
> The matches, the wrong keyrings—
> We've nowhere we could keep a keepsake—
> Ashtrays, combs, things . . .

This one, recounting the end of an adventure with the errant wives of two knights, releases us from respectability and convention into the anarchic world of forbidden pleasures and robust self-assertion, and we smile at the rogue's "distress and pains" half because of the situation and half because it is contradicted so lustily by the rhythm:

I screwed them, fairly to relate,
A full one hundred eighty eight.
My breech-strap near broke at that rate.
    Also my reins
I can't recount all my distress
    Or half my pains.

"New Songs for New Days" is in a very different mood. Here a true lover rejoices in the sweetness, the grace, the beauty of the beloved and the peace that comes after the war of love. The direct physical lust of its close does not clash with but rather emphasizes the ecstasy of this singing voice:

That morning comes to mind once more
We two made peace in our long war;
She, in good grace, was moved to give
Her ring to me with true love's oaths.
God grant me only that I live
To get my hands beneath her clothes!

"Love Can't," on the contrary, rejects passion, romance, and the slavery they impose and asserts the dignity of him "who's conquered his heart's treach'ry." Altogether the *Six Troubadour Songs* are a mixture of lyric celebration, spicy dialogue or elevated diction, and slangy, rollicking song.

The *Traditional Hungarian Songs* have an equal gaiety of mood and rhythm but a more down-to-earth, commonplace tone of voice and a rueful humor on the subject of love and other frailties of humanity. These lovers refuse to take either themselves or love very seriously. "The Bad Wife" is a splendidly cynical dialogue in a comic mode between the lady of the title and her distressed daughter imploring her to hurry home to her husband's deathbed.

Hurry home, now, dearest mother;
We just called the holy father.
    Wait, daughter, wait a bit;
    I'll just dance a little bit;
    I'll come home directly.
    Just another turn or so
    Then you can expect me.

"Crying Johnny" gives an insinuating, whining, would-be seducer his proper vigorous comeuppance.

> Crying on the bedstead, still, lies Johnny—
> So his master's lady asks him,
> What's your trouble, Johnny?
> Would my mistress maybe let me
> Lie down on her daughter only?
> Would I, dearest Johnny?—
> Devil take you, Johnny!

"All Sorts of Drunkards," with its vivid details, comic rhetoric, and long, heavily stressed trochaic lines and triply rhyming stanzas is a wonderfully high-spirited description of the abuses and pleasures of wine:

> Hearken, all you drunkards, while I sing your wickedness,
> All the sins committed in your raging drunkenness;
> Time and time again forgetting all God's righteousness. . . .
>
> Soon as Noah sampled that, he fell down stinking drunk,
> Fell asleep, incontinently, naked on his bunk;
> Ham, his son, laughed right out loud to see his naked trunk. . . .
>
> Come now, all you drunkards grown so riotous and bold,
> Think on all these sins against the Lord that I've just told;
> End this drunken life; reform; come back into the fold.

Simplicity of emotion and relationship after complexity and ambiguity; release after restraint; passion and joy after pain; drama after analysis; song after speech: these translations and their settings must have been a restorative and therapeutic experience for this passionately honest, painfully scrupulous poet.

As these songs are a contrast to the world of the earlier poetry, so *The Führer Bunker* contrasts with both. In this series of dramatic monologues Snodgrass comes closest to achieving his own statement of the aim of a work of art. "The aim of a work of art surely is to stretch the reader's psyche, to help him to identify with more people, with more life than he normally does. He is only going to be able to do that if you get him past his beliefs about right and wrong . . . if the work of art doesn't bring the observer to see more of himself than he was aware of before, what use does it have to exist?"[21] So in these poems we are overhearing people talking to themselves, each character speaking in a verse form expressive of his or her personality, revealing who and what they are with a dramatic power that carries conviction almost against our will. For these are monsters; we know that; some of us, at least, have lived through the times they triumphed over before their defeat. And it is Snodgrass's triumph that he makes us understand and—almost—sympathize with them.

"My aim is to investigate the thoughts and feelings behind the public facade which made these actions necessary or even possible. My poems, then, must include voices they would hide from others, even from themselves."[22] The voices speak of a monstrous world of cruelty, power, perversion, illusion, but the voices that speak are not those of monsters but of human beings "not so different from you." "I am sure," says Snodgrass, "that being willing to identify with what you think is evil is perhaps what is most crucial to the making of a work of art that has some kind of breadth."[23]

Of these poems those which Goebbels speaks seem to me most successful, both in their imaginative realization of character and in their astonishing wit. Wit is not the most outstanding feature of that sort of verse called confessional; Snodgrass's wit is one of the qualities that separates him from his fellows. "April Inventory" is witty in a wry, self-deprecatory sort of way.

> I haven't read one book about
> A book or memorized one plot.
> Or found a mind I did not doubt.
> I learned one date. And then forgot.
> And one by one the solid scholars
> Get the degrees, the jobs, the dollars.

Goebbels's speech, 22 April 1945, with its tight octosyllabic couplets and six-line stanzas, is witty in its terrifying, icy, demonic glee:

> I am that spirit that denies
> High Priest of Laymen, Prince of Lies.
> Your house is founded on my rock;
> Truth crows; now I deny my cock.
> Jock of this walk, I turn down all,
> Robbing my Peter to play Paul.

Aristotle said that poetry was truer than history. If Goebbels wasn't the kind of voice that speaks through his poem, he should have been. Magda Goebbels, in her all-consuming vanity and self-deception, beautifully conveyed by the taut repetition of the villanelle form, Eva Braun's emptiness to the accompaniment of "Tea for Two," her favorite song, and Hitler himself in his crude, brutal, self-colloquies are almost as convincing.

"The truth is," says Snodgrass, "that most of the time we don't see the horrors that are going on in family life all around us. As a matter of fact, *The Führer Bunker* is a kind of reflection on family life. When I was writing the poems about family life itself, I made some references to the Nazis, I believe. I compared the family to a concentration camp. . . . These poems are in many ways making such comparisons the other way around."[24]

Well! Few of us, perhaps, would go so far as to agree to any great likeness between *The Führer Bunker* and home sweet home. But it is clear enough that the poet who began by trying to understand himself, and through himself the world, has arrived at the point where he has earned the right to say, "I am a man; nothing human is alien to me." And, by moving from the self out into the world, he has become more fully both a man and a poet.[25]

NOTES

1. W. D. Snodgrass, *In Radical Pursuit* (New York: Harper and Row, 1975), 14.
2. Snodgrass, *In Radical Pursuit*, 32.
3. Snodgrass, *In Radical Pursuit*, 32.
4. Paul L. Gaston, "W. D. Snodgrass and *The Führer Bunker:* An Interview," *Papers on Language and Literature* 13 (Fall 1979): 296.
5. Gaston, "W. D. Snodgrass," 296.
6. Gaston, "W. D. Snodgrass," 298.
7. W. D. Snodgrass, *Heart's Needle* (New York: Alfred A. Knopf, 1959), 51.
8. Gaston, "W. D. Snodgrass," 302.
9. Gaston, "W. D. Snodgrass," 297.
10. Snodgrass, *In Radical Pursuit*, 18.
11. J. D. McClatchy, "W. D. Snodgrass: The Mild, Reflective Art," *Massachusetts Review* 16 (Spring 1975): 282.
12. Snodgrass, *In Radical Pursuit*, 18–21.
13. Gaston, "W. D. Snodgrass," 299.
14. Gaston, "W. D. Snodgrass," 299.
15. Gaston, "W. D. Snodgrass," 299.

16. Gaston, "W. D. Snodgrass," 299.
17. McClatchy, "W. D. Snodgrass," 297.
18. Snodgrass, *In Radical Pursuit,* 55.
19. McClatchy, "W. D. Snodgrass," 314.
20. McClatchy, "W. D. Snodgrass," 285.
21. Gaston, "W. D. Snodgrass," 303
22. Gaston, "W. D. Snodgrass," 401.
23. Gaston, "W. D. Snodgrass," 408.
24. Gaston, "W. D. Snodgrass," 403.
25. In addition to *In Radical Pursuit* and *Heart's Needle,* Snodgrass's other books cited in this paper are: Christian Morgenstern, *Gallows Songs,* translated by W. D. Snodgrass and Lore Segal (Ann Arbor: University of Michigan Press, 1967); *After Experience* (New York, Evanston, London: Harper and Row, 1968); *Remains* (by S. S. Gardons [W. D. Snodgrass]) (Mount Horeb, Wis.: The Perishable Press, 1970); *Six Troubadour Songs* (Providence: Burning Deck, 1977); *The Führer Bunker: A Cycle of Poems in Progress* (Brockport, N.Y.: BOA Editions, 1977 [97 Park Avenue, 14420]); and *Traditional Hungarian Songs* (Newark, Vt.: The Janus Press for Charles Seluzicki, Poetry Bookseller at 3012 Greenmount Avenue, Baltimore, Maryland 21218, 1978). I am grateful to Mr. A. Poulin, Jr., of BOA Editions, to Mr. Seluzicki for supplying copies of *The Führer Bunker* and *Traditional Hungarian Songs,* and to Burning Deck for *Six Troubadour Songs.*

DAVID WOJAHN

Snodgrass's Borrowed Dog
S. S. Gardons and Remains

In a canny essay about portraiture and self-portraiture entitled
"Borrowed Dogs" the photographer Richard Avedon begins
with the tale of how his family took snapshots of themselves
when he was a child. Photographs were meticulously planned,
almost to the point of absurdity: "We dressed up. We posed in
front of expensive cars, homes that weren't ours. We borrowed
dogs. . . . It seemed a necessary fiction that the Avedons owned
dogs. . . . I found eleven different dogs in one year of our family
album. There we were in front of canopies and Packards with
borrowed dogs, and always, forever, smiling."[1] This anecdote is
a deft introduction to Avedon's thesis, a point that should be
obvious to all of us—that all self-portraits are really a form of
performance. Revelation is imparted not so much by disclosure
as it is by the subtle mingling of disclosure with the smoke-and-
mirror props the artist selects, and such props can range from the
stylized hand gestures of Egon Schiele's numerous self-portraits
to the costume-shop burnooses and turbans that Rembrandt
sports in certain of his. Schiele, Rembrandt, and the Avedon
family—all but the appropriated Spots and Fidos—are *acting*. So
I have begun by reiterating what is self-evident, that the artist
varnishes the truth, distorts it for the sake of what is (we hope)
some high aesthetic purpose. He reveals himself, surely, but only
through a scrim of "necessary fiction."

And yet, as anyone who has taught undergraduates the work
of the so-called confessional poets knows, such a distinction be-
tween literal truth and performance is one that the unsophisti-
cated can often fail to grasp. Thus, during a class discussion of
Lowell's "Skunk Hour" I once had a student wonder aloud why
the Castine, Maine police hadn't arrested Cal Lowell for peeping
into the "love-cars" parked on the hill above the town. Weren't
the cops vigilant enough to keep an eye on the visiting crazy poet
and peeping tom? After all, Lowell himself confesses that his
"mind's not right." On another occasion I received an essay on

Plath's "Daddy," which began, "Sylvia Plath, a Jewish woman born in Germany to a Nazi father. . . ." These students may not have been very informed, nor did they apparently pay much attention to what was going on in class, but in a certain sense their assumptions were logical, if not *sensible.* If confessional poetry emphasizes a stance of intimate personal disclosure, then shouldn't we assume that the poet is telling the literal truth about himself? No wonder college students voted overwhelmingly for Reagan in 1980 and 1984.

There's little excuse for this sort of gullibility among college literature students and even less of an excuse for a sadly similar sort of gullibility on the part of critics who have written about the confessional group, for the prevailing tendency in their writings is to see autobiographical poems *as* autobiography. For whatever the reasons the confessional poets have attracted the sorts of critics who have regarded Lowell, Berryman, Plath, and related figures such as Sexton and Snodgrass as rather helpless chroniclers of their personal lives' traumas and miseries. Dabbling just a bit in psychoanalytical criticism, suspicious of the new critical methods of literary analysis which the confessional poets rebelled so strongly against, and generally indifferent to other current modes of literary theory, these critics have come to regard the poems of the confessional school as simply more compressed versions of the self-accusations and troubled meditations, which occur in many writers' entries. As a consequence of this tendency, we have gloating, gossipy, and histrionic treatises such as Jeffrey Meyers's recent *Manic Power: Robert Lowell and His Circle.* Although he purports to be writing a serious study, Meyers is instead engaged in a *New York Post*–style sensationalizing of the lives of the Lowell circle. Such *tabloidization* by Meyers and other critics is often accompanied by a similarly simplistic reading of the poems. Meyers's appraisal of confessional poetry is usually limited to remarks such as these:

> They helped to establish the dangerously fashionable notion that living on the edge of suicide—or falling over—was the most authentic stance, almost an absolute requirement of the modern sensibility. John Bayley observed that their menacing, morbid verse is "almost wholly interior-ized, the soul hung up in chains of nerves and arteries and veins." Their poems are arrested in their own finality, "like a suicide hitting the pavement."[2]

What critics such as Meyers seem not to notice is that there are borrowed dogs aplenty in the self-portraits that constitute confessional verse. Although the borrowed dogs have, perhaps, moved a bit into the background of the photograph, they remain integral to its composition. Granted, there are times when the poet tries slyly to conceal his borrowed dogs. Lowell's insertion of his prose memoir "91 Revere Street" exactly in the middle of *Life Studies* is on one level meant to validate the "truthfulness" of the poems that follow it, but does this mean that Lowell has tethered himself to the literal truth? Hardly. And it is, needless to say, the robust and picaresque character of Henry that makes *The Dream Songs* great. While the introspective and deeply neurotic John Berryman is the puppeteer who commands the quixotic Henry, *The Dream Songs* belong to their performer, not to the man who toils with the strings of the marionette. In sum, the author of the confessional poem identifies with his speaker, but it is simplistic to regard author and speaker as always one and the same. The costume of the speaker and the borrowed dogs he employs do not often flatter the performer of the poem, but they frequently serve to enhance the poem's tension, complexity, and ultimate artistic success. This can be seen in the sequence that is one of the most interesting of all the "borrowed dog acts" of the confessional movement, S. S. Gardons's *Remains*. It's not a secret—as it was meant in some degree to be in the 1950s and early 1960s— that the author of Gardons's poems is W. D. Snodgrass, who, as Gardons, wrote some of his most harrowing and memorable verse.

Gardons's poems began appearing in journals in the late 1950s at roughly the same time that Snodgrass's own early poems surfaced, those that were eventually gathered in his first volume, *Heart's Needle*. Only a handful of Gardons's efforts were published, but they appeared in respected places, most notably in Hall, Pack, and Simpson's influential formalist anthology, *New Poets of England and America,* which featured the first anthology appearances of James Wright, Robert Bly, and, near the end of the alphabetically arranged sections, far removed from G men such as Gardons and W. S. Graham, one W. D. Snodgrass. We're told in Gardons's contributor's note that he is a Texan, had attended Rice University, and now works in a gas station: quite a significant contrast to the information given about the other contributors, who are bejeweled with the 1950s' most prestigious vitae—Prix de Romes, Guggies and Fulbrights, teaching gigs at East Coast universities. Gardons, then, is not a typical

1950s academic formalist, is not, in fact, an academic at all. Perhaps this is why, unsullied by the need to goose-step to some English departments publish-or-perish marching orders, Gardons chose not to be a terribly prolific writer, and certainly not a very public one. In fact, his single slim volume of poetry was probably published posthumously, in a fine press edition of two hundred copies, in 1970. The collection, entitled *Remains,* contains a prefatory note that elaborates on the earlier information given about Gardons and relates a mysterious disappearance that is at least as interesting as those of Weldon Kees and Jimmy Hoffa:

> S. S. Gardons lived most of his life in and near Red Creek, Texas. For years he worked as a gas station attendant, though he took a few university classes in Houston, and later became an owner of a cycle shop. Also a musician, he played lead guitar in a well-known rock group, Chicken Gumbo. This sequence of poems was collected by his friends after his disappearance on a hunting trip in the mountains. From the condition of his abandoned motorcycle, it was impossible to determine whether he suffered foul play, was attacked by animals, or merely became confused and lost, or perhaps fell victim to amnesia. At present the case is listed as unsolved.[3]

Of course, the identity of the true author of the Gardons poems was never, as A. Poulin, Jr., reminds us in his foreword to the second edition of *Remains,* "a very well-kept secret along the literary grapevine."[4] Poulin's BOA Editions released *Remains* under Snodgrass's own name in 1985, and in Snodgrass's recent *Selected Poems* the Gardons oeuvre appears in its entirety. In Snodgrass's backnotes to this volume we are given the ostensible reason for the abandonment of the Gardons disguise: after the death of Snodgrass's parents he was able to release the poems under his own name. And, indeed, the portraits of the mother and father who figure in *Remains* are mercilous ones, hardly the sort of characterizations that even the most estranged of sons would want his parents to see.

So there we have it. Gardons was created in part to perpetrate a "po-biz" hoax or in-joke, and in part to shield Snodgrass's parents from hurt. Now that Gardons is out of the way (perhaps even eaten by wolves), can we simply, though belatedly, add an intriguing sequence of poems to the Snodgrass canon and forget about the subterfuges their author employed in originally bringing the poems to print? The new critic lurking in us all would, of course, say yes, and ask that we see *Remains* as a sequence of eight *very* well-wrought urns, and that we leave issues that speculate upon the identity and intentions of the poems' author to bad-boy dabblers in deconstruction. But the fact remains that *Remains* presents us with some vexing problems pertaining to the interrelationship between Gardons and Snodgrass, problems that must be solved if we are to truly understand the poems. Why, for example, does Gardons often seem to be a better writer than Snodgrass? And why is it that the poems of *Heart's Needle*—especially its famous title sequence upon which much of Snodgrass's reputation rests—are in many ways less engaging than the more forceful and dramatically complex poems of *Remains?*

That a writer's best work can result from a kind of literary hoax is not as surprising as it may initially seem. There is, as the psychologist Louise J. Kaplan points out in her recent study of Thomas Chatterton, a long tradition of "imposter-poets," whose literary production reaches its fullest expression in what might at first seem elaborate practical jokes.[5] Kaplan argues that the fatherless teenager Chatterton had no benevolent authority figure in his life and therefore chose to create one in the form of his bogus fourteenth-century monk, Thomas Rowley; Kaplan further contends that the poems of Rowley are far more significant and expressive than the satiric poems that Chatterton published under his own name after his Rowley hoax had been exposed.[6] Surely the twentieth century's best-known imposter-poet is the Portuguese writer Fernando Pessoa, who referred to his three extremely distinct alter egos—Alberto Cariero, Alvaro de Campos, and Ricardo Reyes—not merely as pseudonyms, but as *heteronyms.* He concocted elaborate biographies for each and even confessed that one of the trio, Cariero, wrote better Portuguese than could Pessoa himself—a claim that is borne out when comparing the lackluster poems that appeared under Pessoa's own name with the dazzling productions of Cariero and his heteronymic brothers. The imposter-poet not only borrows dogs for his self-portraits but also goes to elaborate lengths in order to make us think the borrowed dogs are his; he fakes their pedigrees, gives them new names, and somehow, in the act of borrowing, creates something of depth, a joke of deadly seriousness.

Perhaps it is this very seriousness that most distinguishes Gardons from Snodgrass. Although the persona of *Heart's Needle* confronts some very troubling personal issues—divorce, separation from a beloved young daughter, and the speaker's own aging—his approach to these subjects never strays too far afield from the elegance and wit that characterize so much of the poetry of the 1950s. The Snodgrass of *Heart's Needle* is prone to melancholy but is finally more interested in *checking* his sorrow through self-deprecating humor than he is in straightforwardly expressing his grief. Thus, we have the tone of "April Inventory," perhaps Snodgrass's best-known poem. It's all there in the opening stanzas:

> The green catalpa tree has turned
> All white; the cherry blooms once more.
> In one whole year I haven't learned
> A blessed thing they pay you for.
> The blossoms snow down in my hair;
> The trees and I will soon be bare.
>
> The trees have more than I to spare.
> The sleek, expensive girls I teach,
> Younger and pinker every year,
> Bloom gradually out of reach.
> The pear tree lets its petals drop
> Like dandruff on a tabletop.[7]

This is wonderfully modulated phrasing, of course, but the net effect is as if Richard Wilbur had rewritten one of the anxiety-ridden comic soliloquies we encounter in Woody Allen films. Somehow the tone and the form of the poem are at odds: Is the speaker telling us that things are much worse than they seem, or is he simply exhorting himself to "lighten up"? Although Hayden Carruth greeted *Heart's Needle* with praise for its "genuine feeling," and Donald Hall spoke of the book's "true feeling,"[8] "April Inventory"'s *feelings* are, in fact, expressed in a rather muddled fashion—as a catalog of somewhat wimpy ironies masquerading as a record of the poet's struggle toward wisdom. Yes, I know I'm being unduly harsh toward the poem, but to contrast it with the terse eloquence of "Viewing the Body," a short lyric at the center of *Remains,* shows that my characterizations are not wholly groundless. Gardons, too, has a capacity for irony, but irony of a much more brutal sort. One doesn't even need to know that it is Gardons's sister in the casket to see that the Hardyesque snarl of the tone arises from a very immediate sense of grief and pain:

Flowers like a gangster's funeral;
   Eyeshadow like a whore.
They all say isn't she beautiful.
   She, who never wore

Lipstick or such a dress,
   Never got taken out,
Was scarcely looked at, much less
   Wanted or talked about;

Who, gray as a mouse, crept
   The dark halls at her mother's
Or snuggled, soft, and slept
   Alone in the dim bedcovers.

Today at last she holds
   All eyes and a place of honor
Till the obscene red folds
   Of satin close down upon her.

Instead of the posh tetrameters we find in "April Inventory," Gardons employs a stuttering but brilliantly effective trimeter: spondaic and trochaic substitutions are everywhere, and they help to give the poem its gruff dignity. The strained effort to pepper "April Inventory" with the occasional colloquialism ("In one whole year I haven't learned / A blessed thing they pay you for") contrasts sharply with the blistering conversational bite of a passage such as Gardons's "Never got taken out, / Was scarcely looked at, much less / Wanted or talked about." (It's worth remembering here that Gardons went to the "college of life" and not the Iowa Writers' Workshop.)

"Viewing the Body" should not be seen as Gardons's best poem, no more than "April Inventory" should be regarded as Snodgrass's worst. Yet the two poems are very typical of their respective authors' tones and concerns. Gardons tells it like it is; he has a fine eye for the right, dramatic detail and is always the outraged, impulsive witness to human cruelty and suffering. Snodgrass is introspective, analytical, discursive. Gardons's principal creation is a sequence of poems that explore the grisly dynamics of a pathological family unit; there are six main characters. *Remains* reads like a novella or one-act; it could be turned into a marvelous opera libretto. The principal effort of Snodgrass's *Heart's Needle* adopts a different kind of model; the title sequence is a poetic diary, unfolding over the course of a year. Only two figures are involved, the speaker and his young daughter, to whom he addresses the poems. "Heart's Needle" is meditative and rangy; its reader is meant to be a kind of eavesdropper. In *Remains,* however, the reader is led to a seat in the audience; the houselights dim, and before him the Gardons clan struts their stuff. They are not a happy family; the playlet reminds us not of the Waltons but of O'Neill's tortured Tyrones.

Gardons and Snodgrass, then, are not one and the same, and the other differences between the author of *Remains* and the poet of *Heart's Needle* could easily be brought forth. But my purpose in the following pages will instead be to talk of Gardons's poems themselves. Gardons does, after all, deserve to be better known. Although I don't think Gardons would have begrudged Snodgrass and other poets their Pulitzers and writing fellowships, one sometimes wonders if Gardons would have welcomed a *little* more attention: to be a cult figure within today's already miniscule poetry audience is to have a very small readership indeed.

Gardons would certainly agree with Snodgrass's contention, expressed in his essay "Tact and the Poet's Force," that "the poet faces the same problem faced daily by the individual conscience. We know that we must restrain some part of our energies or we destroy ourselves. Yet, as we turn these energies back against ourselves, they too may destroy us."[9] This statement could serve as the thesis of *Remains.* Gardons confronts a world in which the Middle American virtues and restraint and tactfulness are almost invariably perverted into forces of repression and destruction. The effects of such a transformation are studied in excruciatingly vivid detail, and, try as he might, Gardons seems ill-equipped to offer alternatives to the pattern. All of the family members who populate Gardons's poems are victims of this process. Gardons and his parents are psychologically maimed by it, and his sister, who had never left home, has died from its effects, from an asthmatic condition that is interpreted by Gardons as psychosomatically induced. The results of this process are so crippling that Gardons repeatedly wonders if his sister is not, in fact, better off dead. In "The Survivors" he addresses the dead sister during a visit to his parents' home. "Nothing is different here," he concludes. Perhaps not: in an earlier poem he imagines his sister in a gray and Attic sort of afterlife. Its TV set notwithstanding, the parents' house is a similar sort of underworld.

The Venetian blinds are drawn;
Inside, it is dark and still.
Always upon some errand, one by one,
They go from room to room, vaguely, in the wan
Half-light, deprived of will.

Mostly they hunt for some-
thing they've misplaced; otherwise
They turn the pages of magazines and hum
Tunelessly. At any time they come
To pass, they drop their eyes.

Only at night they meet.
By voiceless summoning
They come to the living room; each repeats
Some words he has memorized; each takes his seat
In the hushed, expectant ring

By the television set.
No one can draw his eyes
From that unnatural, cold light. They wait. . . .

How did the Gardons family come to be this way? By looking
at the sequence's structure some explanation can be arrived at, and
we can see what efforts Gardons makes at coping with these hor-
rors. Much of the blame is placed upon the parents. In the diptych
portrait that opens the sequence we are introduced to "The
Mother" and to the subject of "Diplomacy: The Father." The two
poems bristle with mercilous invective. The mother is portrayed
as domineering, unforgiving, and silently vengeful. Although the
father is, as the title of the poem implies, diplomatic and deferen-
tial, these qualities are seen as flaws: conflict avoidance pursued to
the point of cowardice. Need it be added that opposites attract and
that a sort of perverse symbiosis has been created by this union?

Still, it is the mother who controls the Gardons home. The
metaphors employed to describe her are celestial but also dark
and brooding. Such a combination makes for some very un-
settling writing, as in the poem's opening stanzas:

She stands in the dead center like a star;
They form around her like satellites
Taking her energies, her heat, light
And massive attraction on their paths, however far.

Born of her own flesh; still, she feels them drawn
Into the outer cold by dark forces;
They are in love with suffering and perversion,
With the community of pain. Thinking them gone,

Out of her reach, she is consoled by evil
In neighbors, children, the world she cannot change,
That lightless universe where they range
Out of the comforts of her disproval.

Rather churned-up rhetoric, but we ain't seen nothin' yet. In the stanzas that follow the rhetorical flourishes continue to crescendo:

If evil did not exist, she would create it
To die in righteousness, her martyrdom
To that sweet domain they have bolted from.
Then, at last, she can think that she is hated

And is content. Things can decay, break,
Spoil themselves; who cares? She'll gather the debris
With loving tenderness to give them; she
Will weave a labyrinth of waste, wreckage

And hocus-pocus; leave free no fault
Or cornerhole outside those lines of force
Where she and only she can thread a course.
All else in her grasp grows clogged and halts.

This goes on for two more stanzas. If the Gardons household is a kind of underworld, then the mother has been selected to play Satan—a distinctly Miltonic Satan, in fact, for the Latinate phrasing and rhetorical flourishes turn the poem into a sort of pastiche of the infernal councils that open *Paradise Lost*. Compare the above descriptions to Satan's scheming in book 1:

And all is not lost—the unconquerable will,
And study of revenge, immortal hate,
And courage never to submit or yield—
And what is else not to be overcome.

It's an outrageous scheme that Gardons pursues in the poem, but he is too purposeful, too angry, to let the writing become merely an outlandish tour de force. Gardons believes in the integrity of his project, however unfair and unflattering a portrait "The Mother" may seem to us.

Regrettably, the father's poem is not nearly as powerful; perhaps it is not intended to be. The problems of style Gardons chooses to confront in the poem are tricky ones; if cosmic-sounding Miltonisms are the proper style for describing the vampirish mother, then a kind of jargon-polluted gassiness is the language sought for the evocation of the father, who is not simply the henpecked husband. His adamant neutrality, his pose of diplomacy, is seen as just as blameworthy and manipulative as any of the mother's stratagems, for it is the source of *his* misuse of power:

> Your fixed aim,
> whatever it costs, must still be for a balance
> of power in the family, the firm, the whole world through.
> Exactly the same
>
> as a balance of impotence—in any group or nation
> as in yourself.
> Suppose some one of them rose up and could succeed
> your foe—he'd *be* your foe. To underlings, dispense
> all they can ask, but don't need; give till they need
> your giving. One gift could free them: confidence.
> They'd never dare ask. Betray no dedication
> to any creed
>
> or person—talk high ideals; then you'll be known
> as, in yourself,
> harmless. . . .

The father may not dwell in Milton's hell, but he certainly would be assured a place in Dante's, probably in circle eight, with the Hypocrites, Flatterers, and Fradulent Counselors. The Flatterers, you'll recall, are condemned to swim in bullshit for eternity. Unfortunately, although bullshit may be the essential weapon that the father employs in maintaining a balance of power within the family and within his professional life, it is not poetry's most effective stylistic device. The workings of the father's mind are evoked through an impossibly intricate verse form, an eight-line stanza rhyming *a/b/c/d/c/d/a/c*. Generally, lines 1, 4, 5, and 6 are written in pentameter, lines 3 and 7 in hexameter, and lines 2 and 8 in dimeter, with line two comprising a refrain that is repeated in every stanza, "as in yourself." The poem is *Remains'* longest effort, and it is apparently one that has always given Gardons trouble: between the 1970 and 1985 editions of the sequence he substantially revised the poem. Yet even in its latest version the problem persists: How does one write an interesting poem about garrulousness and evasiveness without the poem itself becoming garrulous and evasive? Gardons's colleague Snodgrass confronts similar problems in testing the prosodic limits of the imitative fallacy in the monologues of his *The Führer Bunker*—the poems of the inhumanly analytical Himmler appear on graph paper; Magda Goebbels poisons her children while reciting a kind of nursery rhyme—and yet these later efforts are considerably more successful than is the father's poem.

In the sequence's next three poems there is a marked change of approach. The ironic grandiosity and pyrotechnical displays of the portraits of the parents are replaced by a hardboiled realism and a more businesslike use of form. The earlier poems' invective turns to pathos as we are introduced to Gardons himself and to his sister. "A Mouse" begins with a memory from childhood. The tone is saved from bathos by Gardons's barely suppressed anger:

> I remember one evening—we were small—
> Playing outdoors, we found a mouse,
> A dusty little gray one, lying
> By the side steps. Afraid he might be dead,
> We carried him all around the house
> On a piece of tinfoil, crying.
>
> Ridiculous children; we could bawl
> Our eyes out about nothing. Still,
> How much violence had we seen?
> They teach you—quick—you have to be well-bred
> In all events. We can't all win. . . .

The poem then takes a rather preposterous turn, equating the sister with the wounded field mouse and the "old insatiable loves" of the parents with the predatory games of a cat, who "pats at you, wants to see you crawl / Some, then picks you back alive; / That needs you just a little hurt." Still, we feel that Gardons has earned this garish conceit. He even seems to get away with the tricky business of implying that he, too, can be identified with the figure of the tortured mouse:

> And then the little animal
> Plays out; the dulled heart year by year
> Turns from its own needs, forgets its grief.
> Asthmatic, timid, twenty-five, unwed—
> The day we left you by your grave,
> I wouldn't spare one tear.

This sort of corrosive deadpan continues in the previously quoted "Viewing the Body" and in "Disposal." The latter achieves its power by simply listing some of the dead sister's personal effects and has the tone and structure of certain poems of Larkin's such as "Mr. Bleaney." Snodgrass has written admiringly of Larkin's work, and Gardons too seems to have studied him. In fact, the ending of "Disposal" is one of the few poems I can think of that actually *outdoes* Larkin in the dyspeptic hiss of its closure:

> Spared all need, all passion,
> Saved from loss, she lies boxed in satins
>
> Like a pair of party shoes
> That seemed to never find a taker;
> We send back to its maker
> A life somehow gone out of fashion
> But still too good to use.

The method of sequence changes again in the following poem, "The Fourth of July." More dramatically and narratively complex than the previous poems, its ironies are enacted upon a much larger stage than before. Gardons and his second wife are on a visit home to his family's rustbelt mill town, a place Gardons conjures up through the use of by now familiar imagery of the infernal. It's no wonder the sister could not breathe in this environment, for, as Gardons tells us, "the sulphurous smoke / That is my father's world" has permeated everything. Although its steel mills are closed because of a workers' strike, the town remains "stifling," "smoke-filled," and after the evening's fireworks display a politician "fumes." When a "blonde schoolgirl" is crowned "Queen of this war-contract factory town," Gardons imagines his sister, dead now for a year, as celebrating the anniversary of her death in the underworld, "a tinsel wreathe on her dark head." Yet these lavishly macabre descriptions serve merely as the backdrop to the more dreadful ironies that are presented to us in the Gardons home. Gardons himself is smoldering, fuming in a silent rage. He and his wife are sleeping in his sister's old room, still furnished with her possessions. To express his anger is his only hope for defeating this domestic hell, but silence is a Gardons family tradition. And besides,

> What can anybody say?
>
> In her room, nights, we lie awake
> By racks of unworn party dresses, shoes,
> Her bedside asthma pipe, the glasses whose
> Correction no one else will take.
>
> Stuffed dogs look at us from the shelf
> When we sit down together at the table.
> You put a face on things the best you're able
> And keep your comments to yourself.

Furthermore, Gardons bears the burden of his guilt for having brought his pregnant wife into this clapboard isle of the dead. Her birthday is less a celebration than it is a rite of initiation into the Gardons family's underworld:

> It is a hideous mistake.
> My young wife, unforgivably alive,
> Takes a deep breath and blows out twenty-five
> Candles on her birthday cake.
>
> It is agreed she'll get her wish.
> The candles smell; smoke settles through the room
> Like a cheap stage set for Juliet's tomb.
> I leave my meal cold on the dish.

By the conclusion of the poem nothing is resolved. Gardons's grim observations have become a kind of litany:

> It is an evil, stupid joke:
> My wife is pregnant; my sister's in her grave.
> We live in the home of the free and of the brave.
> No one would hear me, even if I spoke.

"The Survivors," the poem that follows "The Fourth of July,"
continues to explore the same sorts of concerns. But by address-
ing the poem to his sister, Gardons is able to overcome to some
extent his misanthropic rage. The ending of the poem, although
it is no less ironic than the conclusion of "The Fourth of July," is
suffused with regret. The purpose of the sequence's previous
poems has been as much to condemn the family's twisted values
as it has been to elegize the sister. Yet "The Survivors," despite
its title, ends by belonging to the sister. Gardons's rage and
obsession with decay turn—almost involuntarily—into a poi-
gnant farewell:

> In the cellar where the sewers
> Rise, unseen, the pale white
> Ants grow in decaying stacks of old newspapers.
> Outside, street lamps appear, and friends of yours
> Call children in for the night.
>
> And you have been dead one year.
> Nothing is different here.

In its tentative way "The Survivors" also introduces the
theme that concerns Gardons in *Remains'* final poem, "To a
Child." Although Gardons's sister could not escape her suffocat-
ing fate, and although Gardons himself believes he shall never
recover from the apparent cruelty he suffered as his parents'
child, it is possible that other children will grow up to be normal
and healthy. Although Gardons cannot save himself, perhaps he
can save his own daughter, and in attempting to do so change
Remains' bleak expressions of blame and betrayal into something
more nurturing than stark pathos and anger. Although "To a
Child" concerns itself with renewal, it is less an arrival at redemp-
tion than it is a coda for the previous poems; it asks us to read the
sequence as a grim cautionary tale. The epistolary mode recalls
"Heart's Needle," but "To a Child" is a far more turbulent
poem. *Don't let this happen to you,* Gardons seems to plead to the
daughter. Yet at the same time he fears that perhaps the die has
already been cast because of his own inadequacies as a father and
husband. He begins his lecture with the intention to discuss with
his daughter "the birds and the bees," but the poem soon be-
comes an account of his own sexual anxieties, a meditation on
death, and an attempt to put his divorce into some perspective.
The structure of the poem, however, is a sly one, anything but

rambling. Although we at first suspect that the poem's circuitousness is caused by a self-conscious father's reluctance to get to his point about sex, we eventually see that Gardons is striving for catharsis. He wants, more than anything else, *forgiveness* from his daughter and admits to his own role in his poisonous family history:

> We have walked through living rooms
>
> And seen the way the dodder,
> That pale white parasitic love-vine, thrives
> Coiling the zinnias in the ardor
> Of its close embrace.
> We have watched grown men debase
> Themselves for their embittered wives . . .

The line about grown men "debasing themselves," with its ambiguous reference, comes shortly after a passage describing the effects of Gardons's divorce and separation from his daughter: it indicts himself as well as his father, and Gardons's own admission of guilt might to some degree help to justify the horrific allusion to the mother which immediately follows it:

> And we have seen an old sow that could smother
> The sucklings in her stye,
> That could devour her own farrow.
> We have seen my sister in her narrow
> Casket. Without love we die;
> With love we kill each other.

A dizzying tour de force, this passage. Before we are able to recover from the shocking characterization of the mother as a sow who smothers her offspring—a comparison that has already been made, but in a much less blatant fashion, near the end of "The Mother"—we are again reminded that Gardons feels he has a reason for his wrath: his vicious hyperbole is followed by an abrupt "jumpcut" to the figure of the sister in her coffin. Then Gardons sums it all up with a glib perversion of the ending of "September 1, 1939." And yet this statement's grim conundrum, its terrible double bind, has been the theme of all of *Remains'* poems thus far. But, as *Remains* ends, in Gardons's most notable lines, he chooses to rebel against this belief. He asks that his daughter see the world with a vision that is different from his own. His phrasing is cautious, his rhetoric tentative, and yet the sequence ends with a flourish of genuine grandeur:

> You are afraid, now, of dying;
> Sick with change and loss;
> You think of your own self lying
> Still in the ground while someone takes your room.
> Today, you felt the small life toss
> In your stepmother's womb.
>
> I sit here by you in the summer's lull
> Near the lost handkerchiefs of lovers
> To tell you when your brother
> Will be born; how, and why.
> I tell you love is possible.
> We have to try.

And, thus, S. S. Gardons disappears, though surely his influence lives on in certain of Snodgrass's later works—in the monologues of *The Führer Bunker* and in the character of "W. D.," the alter ego who ambles about in many of Snodgrass's most recent poems. Such creations are merely borrowed dogs of a different color. Snodgrass and Gardons would both concur, I'm sure, with a remark of Machado's. "In order to write poetry," he said, "one must first invent the poet who will write it." From necessity, from what could only have been a deep inner need that could not find expression in the poems of W. D. Snodgrass, the poet S. S. Gardons was born. And Gardons was a powerful and original writer, superbly capable. In fact, if W. D. Snodgrass had never existed, then S. S. Gardons would surely have invented him.

NOTES

1. Richard Avedon, "Borrowed Dogs," *Grand Street* 7, no. 1 (Autumn 1987): 53.

2. Jeffrey Meyers, *Manic Power: Robert Lowell and His Circle* (New York: Arbor House, 1987), 23.

3. A. Poulin, Jr., Foreword to W. D. Snodgrass, *Remains: A Sequence of Poems* (Brockport, N.Y.: BOA Editions, 1985), n.p.

4. Poulin, Foreword.

5. Louise J. Kaplan, *The Family Romance of the Imposter Poet Thomas Chatterton* (New York: Atheneum, 1988), 75.

6. Kaplan, *Family Romance*, 115–16.

7. W. D. Snodgrass, *Selected Poems, 1957–1987* (New York: Soho Press, 1987), 28. All subsequent quotations from the poetry have been taken from this volume.

8. Donald Hall, Hayden Carruth, jacket notes to 1983 ed. of W. D. Snodgrass, *Heart's Needle* (New York: Alfred A. Knopf, 1959).

9. W. D. Snodgrass, "Tact and the Poet's Force," *In Radical Pursuit: Critical Essays and Lectures* (New York: Harper and Row, 1975), 22.

RICHARD JACKSON

The Heart and the House
The Early and Late Poems of W. D. Snodgrass

It was Hayden Carruth, in his typically self-righteous manner, who first raised doubts about the poetry of W. D. Snodgrass in his 1959 *Poetry* review of *Heart's Needle*, doubts as to "whether the poems should have been published at all." Carruth's objections, like several at the time, were about the appropriateness of the very personal and autobiographical subject matter, objections that seem ill conceived after Berryman, Lowell, Plath, Sexton, and most of the poets of the past three decades. What Carruth fails to see is that the focus on the self is counterpointed by a language so jarring that it questions and prevents solipsism and by a symbolism that balances two of Snodgrass's major symbols, the inner world of the heart and the outer world of the house. Snodgrass's far-ranging metaphysical conceits also substitute for any lack of poetic range or vision in the poems. But something does happen to Snodgrass's later poetry, for, while the pseudonymous *Remains* (1970) contains stunning work, probably the poet's best, and while *After Experience* (1967) contains many superb poems, one later book, *The Führer Bunker* (1977), spoken by members of that sinister bastion, seems limited in what it can accomplish. Despite a number of very interesting and powerful poems, *The Führer Bunker* has speakers who simply are not as imaginatively daring as, say, Browning's misfits, or as emotionally complex as Norman Dubie's characters, and they are not balanced against larger worldviews like Milton's Satan or Hardy's despairing creatures. More recently, the poetry of the last decade or so contains two books (*If Birds Build with Your Hair* [1979] and *A Locked House* [1986]) that mainly return to the concerns and mode of *Heart's Needle* but without as much verve and tension. One other cycle of poems, "Kinder Capers" (1986), declines into a private mythology of parody and self-irony. The situation of the later work may reflect the dictum that the greatest strengths of any poet or poem also contain the potential for the greatest weaknesses. "We need the landscape to repeat us," Snodgrass says in the sixth section of

"Heart's Needle," but the danger in that stirring statement is that it will *only* repeat, not act as a further catalyst, or allow us to add to it—that the house will be merely a reflection of the heart and not built from it. But this is an overgeneralization and in some ways an unfair evaluation, for it measures later work against earlier work that is, arguably, among the best of our age. And it ignores the fact that there are several interesting poems in *A Locked House* and *If Birds Build*. . . . It will be useful, then, in addressing these issues, to focus on *Heart's Needle,* "Kinder Capers," and these two relatively recent books.

Typically, an early poem by Snodgrass is written in a very colloquial and straightforward style, often clanging in creative ways against rhyme and meter. The speaker generally begins at some distance from his subject and then gradually reveals a more intimate connection, pulling the external descriptions, often of nature, and the internal symbolic meanings together. When the poems work best the metaphoric relationship functions something like a metaphysical conceit. One good example is the relationship between the Korean War and divorce, introduced in the opening sections of the masterful "Heart's Needle" and developed variously throughout the sequence so that the emotions of separation are given resonant and unpredictable dimensions. When they fail the conceits tend to become simple one-tone correspondences. In "Kinder Capers," for example, the poems are related to paintings by DeLoss McGraw that deal with the death of Cock Robin and also have Snodgrass, called W. D., as a main subject. The paintings are rather playful and perhaps show an influence of Miro and others, but the poems are basically only coda for the paintings, and their own playful mode serves only to diminish the subjects even more. I'm not trying to suggest that all poems must have some sort of Rilkean seriousness to them, for we have Roethke's great and oddly conceived comic poems like "The Sloth" to warn us against that. But metaphors and analogies in a poem can either raise the subject, comic or serious, giving it a kind of resonance, as in Byron, Pope, Auden, or in our own day William Matthews and James Tate, or they can undercut it so much that the focus of the vision narrows.

The titles of the poems in "Kinder Capers" suggest something of their bemused tone but also suggest the narrow confinement, ultimately, to the self as self. I have in mind titles such as "W. D. Lifts Ten Times the Weight of His Own Body," "W. D. Meets Mr. Evil while Removing the Record of Bartok and Replacing It with a Recent Recording by the Everly Brothers in Order to

Create a Mood Conducive to Searching for Cock Robin," "Disguised as Humpty Dumpty, W. D. Practices Tumbling," and "The Poet Ridiculed by Hysterical Academics." In this latest poem the academics do their tiny best in *abab* quatrains, but the speaker never rises above citing them, unless we take the last quatrain as his own voice, ironically parodying theirs—but then he still hasn't risen above their vision:

> Ah, what avails the tenure race,
> Ah, what the Ph.D.,
> When all departments have a place
> For nincompoops like thee?

In essence the poem, like most in this cycle, is a one-joke or a one-line poem, the whole thing existing for that one effect, and the single effect mentioned over and over again. All too often the poems end with a moral that is both obvious and tacked on, as if the speaker were striving for the lowest common denominator. In "Disguised as Humpty Dumpty, W. D. Practices Tumbling," the tone seems a bit more "serious," and the poem ends:

> We hope to build this to a smash
> Hit sport just like the Fender Bash,
> The Fall from Grace, the Market Crash.
>   The real point isn't winning; what's
>   Important is to show some guts.

The pun in the last line leads nowhere except to a winced chuckle, and the links between the character's fall and the edenic fall and economic collapse are brushed over with a tone that belies their importance. A poem about a Kafka character ends simply by repeating the kinds of questions one might find in *The Trial* and takes us to no deeper insights or ironies, does not even use a comic mode to underscore our sense of self-importance and security. What is so odd about this book is that the speaker has numerous opportunities to play off childhood, off literary and adult mythologies, and, in everyday experiences, off our failings and our necessary, comic self-irony, but in nearly every case the poems take a reductive stance. One exception might be "The House the Poet Built," with its deflating and bemused sense of "the dotty old bard" that grows even as the poem incrementally builds in this traditional format. And a number of letters in the compelling "A Darkling Alphabet," though sometimes predictable, have moments of power. Here is "Z"—

> **Z** is for Zero, the last
> numeral and, in a blast,
> the last place to be on the ground.
> It's infinite, since round,
> and devoid of any contrast.
> All things on earth have passed,
> or will, through this small, profound
> hole to enter the vast
> and the vacuum. It closes fast.

There are some interesting word plays here, on *ground* and *passed* and between *devoid* and *vacuum,* for instance. Each of the letters works this way, reminiscent of the way riddle poems behave. The problem with "Kinder Capers" on the whole, though, is that the stakes are rarely this high.

What are some of the early strengths that contain the seeds of these later problems? In *Heart's Needle* the ability to change linguistic gears quickly, the stunning use of seemingly inappropriate metaphors, details, and expressions, and the clunky, end-stopped rhythms working against sentence structure all keep the reader off guard so that the basic symbolism evolves almost as an afterthought and hardly seems obtrusive. In "Orpheus," for example, the interest is hardly in the character of Orpheus himself, for hardly any energy in the poem goes into exploring the inner complexities of his philosophical and ethical stance. The theme is rather simple: the inability to bring things back yet the endless task of trying to do so. Orpheus becomes the symbol for that ongoing act and for the irony of not knowing what he should have known. Snodgrass chooses to explore neither the psychology of the individuals involved nor the larger issues of the relationship of the dead to the afterlife, of the pathos of love, of fulfillment and rest, or even the drama of the situation—all things that Rilke goes after in his "Orpheus. Eurydice. Hermes." Instead, Snodgrass's Orpheus begins by focusing on the world around him, a world that is shockingly like ours—"the charred rail and windowsill, / Windows hunched with fusty shawls"— and on a landscape so alive it immediately becomes internalized. The speaker develops references to Tantalus, Sisyphus, and Juno to suggest a mythic and allegorical dimension—and then Orpheus makes his revelation:

Yet where the dawn first edged my mind
In one white flashing of mistrust
I turned and she, she was not there.
My hands closed on the high, thin air.

It was the nature of the thing:
No moon outlives its leaving night,
No sun its day. And I went on
Rich in the loss of all I sing
To the threshold of waking light,
To larksong and the live, gray dawn.
So night by night, my life has gone.

There is a fine turn here, and Orpheus's accepting philosophy in the opening of the last stanza, stated in such inadequate terms as opposed to the rest of the poem, underscores his helplessness, his lack of understanding. But he is not supposed to be such a deep character. The point is that his situation becomes a symbolic loss for all of us, repeating itself in our lives as it does in the poem, as it does night after night. Snodgrass achieves a fine balance here between the lesser demands of character and the greater needs of symbolism.

A poem like "Ten Days Leave" succeeds by its sense of abandon in language. There's a kind of crotchety fumbling, a use of colloquialisms, which makes the situation come alive. The character seems as out of place at home as the verse does in poetry. At one point the narrator says:

He is like days when you've gone some place new
To deal with certain strangers, though you never
Escape the sense in everything you do,
"We've done this all once. Have I been here, ever?"

And then he counters with:

But no; he thinks it must recall some old film, lit
By lives you want to touch; as if he'd slept
And must have dreamed this setting, peopled it,
And wakened out of it. . . .

The poem ends with his desiring to return to sleep, ironically in the present world.

"September in the Park" is one of the loveliest poems in the book. For most of the poem there is a description of the natural world. The moon at dusk seems to recall the sun; the drunk (a deftly surprising touch) seems to echo the ducks; the oak tree is bare. Here is a landscape of loss and emptiness. And its mood is supported by a startling metaphor:

> This world is going
> to leave the furnitures
> of its unsheltering house
> in snow's dustcovers.

With this figure the external world, even with its drunk, is moved metaphorically indoors, or to what was once indoors, a burned-out mansion. The focus shifts to the abstract, to the "iron cage" of "age" before returning to nature, to the gray squirrels. Finally, the poem ends:

> And I, dear girl,
> remember I have gathered
> my hand upon your breast.

Now we realize that the movement of the poem, with its abstract natural and domestic realms, is meant to set up the symbolic gesture that counters the impulses up until that point. It is a sudden and masterful ending. A whole world is brought to bear upon that final gesture. Its power and resonance make it one of the more memorable moments in contemporary poetry.

But there are several potential weaknesses in these poems that *Heart's Needle* carefully avoids and which reveal just how skillful a book it is. From a slightly askew perspective we can imagine that "September in the Park" could become a one-effect poem because of the focus on the last sentence. "Orpheus" runs the risk of a pretentious moralizing because the philosophy is so simple: he does not stun us with his deep thinking and is almost too unaware to feel very deeply. And "Ten Days Leave" could easily have slipped into a simple analogy, so close do subject and technique match.

Granted, these seem almost bizarre issues to raise, but there are poems in *Heart's Needle* that are more limited for similar reasons. "At the Park Dance" is a delightful but confined description with another stunning conclusion:

> Beyond, jagged stars
> are glinting like jacks hurled
> farther than eyes can gather;

> on the dancefloor, girls
> turn, vague as milkweed floats
> bobbing from childish fingers.

The intriguing relationship between jacks and milkweed is so startling as to overwhelm the more conventional comparisons between stars and jacks. Likewise, the relationship between milkweed and girls, which is the central analogy the poem has worked toward. It is *almost* as if the main theme by itself needs to be dressed up and disguised rhetorically in order to create the illusion of an acceptable complexity.

"A Cardinal" has a dramatic turn that seems all too set up— "Go to hell!" the narrator exclaims in the middle—and it contains truisms ("Each trade has its way of speaking, / each bird its name to say") that seem trite. This is a poem, as Snodgrass explains in *In Radical Pursuit,* that he revised by adding significantly. The need to expand might be a symptom of how much more he subconsciously felt the poem had to work to integrate inner and outer, but it was not a problem solved quantitatively. And the poem's final concern is very narrowly the self, for the outer world is not integrated, only mechanically linked to the poet's predicament. The poem ends in a kind of self-pity:

> All bugs, now, and the birds
> witness once more their voices
> though I'm still in their weeds
> tracking my specimen words,
> replenishing the verses
> of nobody else's world.

Even the much anthologized "April Inventory"—which doesn't seem nearly as complex and powerful as many of the other poems in the book—sets its sights, like the later "The Poet Ridiculed by Hysterical Academics," only on the academic world, a setting for several of Snodgrass's poems throughout his career, where so little seems at stake. The problem is that the psychology of the situation isn't linked to anything larger, and the poem makes no symbol of the predicament. In this respect it is in marked contrast to "Orpheus." Here is the ending:

> Though trees turn bare and girls turn wives,
> We shall afford our costly seasons;
> There is a gentleness survives

That will outspeak and has its reasons.
There is a loveliness exists,
Preserves us, not for specialists.

It would be foolish to criticize the sentiments here, but it is
important to realize that left there at the end of the poem they
comprise a sort of tacked-on moralizing.

If we turn to *If Birds Build with Your Hair* and *A Locked House*,
we can see some of these problems resurfacing on a more serious
level. The point is that these are not weak books but that they
needlessly limit themselves by having developed the weaknesses
marvelously avoided earlier, and that they lead to the seriously
limited poems of "Kinder Capers." "Phoebe's Nest," from
which the book gets its title, is a poem that counterpoints descrip-
tions of birds nesting in several places against a sort of commen-
tary. The descriptions run in regular quatrains in a plain style,
and the commentary borrows from a Roethke-like satiric, lilting
rhythm and is set off in indented and variable stanzas. Gradually,
the descriptions of nest building, an obvious analogy to house
and relationship building, becomes ominous—"Ones that stay
faithfulest to their nest / Just somehow never got fed." The
commentary delivers sterner warnings and the second-to-last
section becomes savage:

> Polish ciocias, toothless flirts
> Whose breasts dangle down to there,
> Triple sea-hags say: headaches if
> Birds build with your hair.

The poem ends with an ambiguous "we" talking about "my
lady": "We loop loose strands of her hair." The two parallel
halves of the poem, though, never really mesh, and there are no
startling conceits to carry the language over that chasm. The
poem, then, has to rely on more conventional strategies. But the
only development is between the ambivalent idea of nesting and
the turn in the last line that implicates the speaker. The poem
goes on for sixty-six lines more or less repeating its premises,
trying to set up the basic allegory and its single turn. This is a
strategy that we saw work earlier, but here Snodgrass disregards
his usual complexities of psychology (the guilt of the narrator
only surfaces in the end, the lines about faithfulness are never
followed up), disregards any varying relationship between the
couple and the image of the birds, and disregards the whole

dramatic situation and the rich tradition of folklore behind the saying that generated the poem. Finally, the occasional rhymes themselves are not nearly as jarring and startling as in the earlier books. What seems to have happened—and we can almost sense this in the rationalizing way Snodgrass talks about his poems in the first part of *In Radical Pursuit*—is that the poem is too predetermined, too planned, too set up.

"Old Apple Trees" presents another basic analogy, this time between trees and people. It opens, for instance, with:

> Like battered old millhands, they stand in the orchard—
> Like drunk legionnaires, heaving themselves up,
> Lurching to attention. Not one of them wobbles
> The same way as another. Uniforms won't fit them—
> All those cramps, humps, bulges. Here, a limb's gone;
> There, rain and corruption have eaten the whole core.
> They've all grown too tall, too thick, or too something.
> Like men bent too long over desks, engines, benches,
> Or bent under mailsacks, under loss.
> They've seen too much history and bad weather, grown
> Around rocks, into high winds, diseases, grown
> Too long to be willful, too long to be changed.

The problem is that the analogy is too neat, going on long after the point is made and showing none of the creative strain of the more metaphysical conceits of the earlier poems. This leads to a series of typecast and expected figures that don't progress the theme. So, after adding quantitatively to the analogy, taking a couple of easy shots at "an adman" and "executives' children," the poem focuses for a moment on the trees, then on the bar the protagonists will travel to. There they will meet more character types—Hungarian, Polish, or Greek "meatcutters and laborers" (the good guys, obviously, as opposed to the "executives' children"). Snodgrass's method—and we saw this in the way he couldn't or wouldn't treat Orpheus as a unique individual—is that the poem, like most of the later ones, is not interested in people but in symbols. This leads to the problem of the ending of this poem: there is not enough complexity of relationship in the poem—on the verbal, analogic, or psychological level—for the poem to raise the ending beyond trite moralizing:

> We'll drive back, lushed and vacant, in the first dawn;
> Out of the light gray mists may rise our flowering

Orchard, the rough trunks holding their formations
Like elders of Colonus, the old men of Thebes
Tossing their white hair, almost whispering,
Soon, each one of us will be taken
By dark powers under this ground
That drove us here, that warped us.
Not one of us got it his own way.
Nothing like any one of us
Will be seen again, forever.
Each of us held some noble shape in mind.
It seemed better that we kept alive.

This is a poem, then, that, despite its admirable sentiment, strives too hard, in an attempt to be wise, to incorporate a gratuitous classical context (not develop it as in the earlier poems), and to offer a bit of homespun philosophy, rather than, as one of Frost's poems might have, a dramatization of that philosophy. Yet it is a poem, I might add, that many poets of lesser stature than Snodgrass might be happy with—and, in fact, is really an accomplished poem in its own way.

This lack of energy is a problem that affects the rest of *If Birds Build with Your Hair*. "Cherry Saplings" adds a historical dimension: After we cut down the trees, "what will we leave here still worth our hate?" "Owls" suggests the isolation and distances between each of us by their night calls. And "Seasoning Barn" focuses on the way the wood reveals a past, "the crimes and follies, the beliefs and lies. . . ." Here, though, there is a more fully drawn character than in the other poems. This is one of the better new poems that recaptures, in a new way, the energy of the earlier work. In this piece there is an old man who is "searching / For the sworls and twists, for those deep flaws that mean / Character in the finished work. . . ." But here the poem ends not with a truism about him but, rather, follows him as a symbol, like Orpheus, to pull the impulses of the poem together. The poem ends enigmatically, a kind of ending the later Snodgrass prefers over the startling endings of the earlier poems:

When he has shaped and planed these, he will sand
And rub by hand, building a finish, hour after hour.

And the old man sits down, rubbing the cat's ears,
Or hikes up his suspenders and walks home.

The enigma of the ending allows the poem to avoid a weak one-to-one correspondence, allows the symbolic value of the man to gain stock: he can take or leave the history he himself is involved in, and his simple leaving would not be a simple statement of avoidance, for it is just as much a new beginning, an assertion of freedom from history as his sitting down would be an understanding of its weight. The two actions are equal, joined by the "or" because they are so intimately linked in consciousness.

A Locked House continues in the same mode as *If Birds. . . .* "Silver Poplars," for instance, "stand / for us. For what stands." The basic analogy is between surface and what "lies beneath," between "enchantment" and reality. It ends by oddly throwing away any further development in favor of an ironic and askance undercutting of our own selves:

> Not much you can do with it; tends to splinter
> on you, check or twist, suppose it's been left
> years to season. Chainsaw; stack the leavings
> against chill mornings, what with winter
> coming on. For all that figured grain, too soft
> to last long; to soft for much real heating.

But this poem, too, starts to generate some of the energy of the earlier poems. After a storm, one tree seems "torn / out like a mind from its own ground / of understanding. . . ." This sort of startling metaphor, which could serve to set off a number of diverging associations, is, however, not developed any further. Similar comments might be made about the title poem, where the house being robbed was the worry of the protagonists when they should have been worrying about what it symbolized, their relationship. And "A Seashell" describes, as we might expect, the shell of a relationship, which is all that's left for the speaker.

I have tried to suggest here the ways in which some tendencies in Snodgrass's earlier books, which were hardly important because of the language, conceits, and symbolic charge of the poems, surface in the later poems when these other things begin to abate. Almost every strong poetic style, I suggest, has elements in it that are potentially its weakest and most self-destructive forces. Wordsworth's great power to paint characters in philosophical descriptions turns, in 80 percent of his work, into washed-out truisms spoken by or about dull characters. Hardy's ability to focus quickly on the terrible ironies of fate and circumstance can quickly become unsubtle and result in trite reversals. In Snodgrass's case the problem of some of the later poems is so apparent because of the promise of the earlier ones: it is almost as if the poems were written according to some unspoken formula, some hidden program, as if there were no heart left in the plans for the poetic houses he constructs. The final limitation of the later poems is their tendency, say in the self-reflexive poems of "Kinder Capers," to see the self, despite outside references, only in the context of the self, without the techniques of the earlier poems, which always seemed to push the context to a more resonant and expansive vision. The subject in those earlier poems was never really the self, but the self seeing something else.

LESLIE ULLMAN

"A Darkling Alphabet"
A Song of Bleak Radiance

A pervasive cynicism, oddly combined with a generous impulse to heal or make whole, seems to have fueled Snodgrass's most innovative work at every turn. *Heart's Needle* in 1959, *The Führer Bunker* in 1977 (his fourth volume), and now this long, relatively recent poem, which appeared in his *Selected Poems* in 1987, differ considerably from one another, but they offer a similar jolt as they work against what had or has been comfortable and fashionable at the time of their publication. That Snodgrass himself has helped to set levels of comfort and fashion over the years makes his occasional upheavals particularly courageous. Courage, however, seems a by-product of other traits: honesty, as expressed in his persistent confrontation of the dark needs and motives behind the self's gestures in the world, and defiance, which comes from his wariness of success.

Snodgrass's first bold move in the 1950s, away from the pristine realm of new critical aesthetic and into the more unpredictable territory of personality and personal history, earned him rejection and then emulation from his teachers at Iowa. Ultimately, it helped open the way for a generation of younger writers to explore ways in which large subjects might be evoked from the seemingly small realm of the self. To his own mind Snodgrass, who was engaged in psychotherapy at the time, achieved exactly what he wanted: to highlight threads in the pattern of his own life that might illuminate the questions of will, choice, guilt, and betrayal faced by an individual listening honestly to himself during the course of his life. This was a radical and salutary stance at a time when smugness seemed to pervade established (as opposed to underground) poetic aesthetic, as it did most other aspects of our culture. Until the appearance of *Heart's Needle,* intellect and artifice, shaped into poetic intent, encouraged the poet to step away from the real self into the self posing as sovereign, skilled at formal devices, a step or two above his material. This grounding within the self as a fallible entity is a stance Snodgrass has maintained throughout his career and which he defined clearly in the early essay "Finding a Poem": "the only reality which a man can ever surely know is the self he cannot help being. . . . If he pretties it up, if he changes its meaning, if he gives it the voice of any borrowed authority, if in short he rejects this reality, his mind will be less than alive. So will his words."[1]

In the late 1970s, after the publication of two more confessional volumes, and after the turmoil of the late 1960s had subsided to leave American culture on the verge of a resigned self-righteousness, Snodgrass published the startling dramatic monologues of *The Führer Bunker,* where key members of the Third Reich are depicted through their most private thoughts during their last days, then moments, of life. This collection offers an intimate view of people who dramatically are "other" than Snodgrass and, we'd like to think, other than all of us. Disturbingly, it manages to make its subjects comprehensible without diminishing the force of their monstrous singlemindedness. Joseph Goebbels, burning the mementos of his life of pillaging and womanizing, bluntly reminds us that "Only a man / who has no possessions can / Afford ideals." And Magda Goebbels reveals something terrible yet familiar behind maternal love in her last thoughts, set in villanelle form, just before killing her six children:

> You try to spare them the worst misery
>
> But they'd still want to live. What if they'd be
> Happy—they could prove all we thought untrue.
> How could we let them fall to treachery
> And their own faults? You end their misery.[2]

In giving these people real voices and making their most private thoughts understandable, Snodgrass forces the reader to suspend judgment, to slip into comprehension and empathy despite conventional scruples, and finally to confront the possibility of such forces in him- or herself. This identification with the darker sides of human nature, Snodgrass wrote in another early essay, "Tact and the Poet's Voice," is the only way any of us can gain the knowledge that might enable us to turn around and write about human "dignity and gentleness."[3]

Although both these innovative works oppose each other in their relation to Snodgrass's personal experience, they do share the quality that he has stated many times is vital to the aesthetic of "tact," that of evoking rather than making statements through the specific experience of a specific character or speaker. With Snodgrass's help, concreteness of this sort has become essential to the authority of much of the poetry written in the last three decades and has been perpetuated by writers who teach. Additionally, both works arise from Snodgrass's belief that we can inform and heal ourselves only through confrontation with the concrete aspects of personality and experience, be they our own or those of people we habitually hold at a distance.

It is against this backdrop, the expectation of concreteness, that "A Darkling Alphabet" seems shockingly out of character, as it reveals its speaker apparently stepping onto a soapbox and speaking forcefully as an "I" of the general "we." Snodgrass has written this poem in twenty-six sections, beginning each section with a different letter of the alphabet. His voice in the poem is reminiscent of the way he spoke in interviews conducted with him by Robert Boyers, David Dillon, Paul Gaston, and others, where he revealed some of the extreme opinions that underlie the more specific, more open-ended explorations in his earlier poetry. The O section offers a taste of the blunt didacticism that characterizes much of this poem:

> O is for Others, the one
> thing we can't abide. Comparison
> is odious. We can't endure
> that others seem stronger, more secure,
> more gifted; self-preservation
> and pride
> drive out uncommon sense,
> brilliance or power, try to dispense
> with genius and its cruel pretense
> to difference.
> Lonely, bored, you take a bride
> only in due time to learn
> she has more concern
> with some strange life of hers
> than yours.
> All men may be brothers;
> brothers are known
> for treachery. If you had your druthers
> you'd just as lief be left alone

with your own
looking glass or clone.

Bluntness in this poem becomes a tactic for providing points of contention, each sentence acting as a hammer blow that finally makes the didacticism effective. Before we can decide to disagree with each bleak generality we are caught up in another and so find ourselves seduced forward, our arguments finished. By the end of this passage Snodgrass has moved us not so much by persuasion as by disarmament, an accumulation of insults both to what we would like to believe about ourselves (that we love others and can at least sustain if not admire our differences) and to our expectation of the concreteness and understatement that make for tact in a poem. "A Darkling Alphabet" is a far cry from what J. D. McClatchy, writing of Snodgrass's first two volumes, termed his "mild, reflective art."[4]

Snodgrass does not spare himself from his own sweeping judgments in this poem, speaking always as a participant in its "we-ness." Nor does he leave us or himself any room for equivocation, especially in passages like the following, which closes on a note of pure challenge:

> **G** is for Glamour; once, that meant
> a diabolical enchantment
> gypsies or sorcerers could lay
> over one's eyes; this took away
> all common sense, all will to fight
> their will, all care for wrong or right
> until their power grew absolute.
> Now'days, we'll take no substitute.

No substitute? The line invites recoil, suggesting that we are as single-minded in our need to be drugged or transformed as are the "sorcerers" (an example of which, Snodgrass tells us in the following section, was Hitler) in their need for "absolute" power. If we are not to reject such a statement outright, we are forced instead to give it hard thought, to find a way to exempt ourselves by considering its implications first. This is the process of engagement that "A Darkling Alphabet" forces the reader to undergo in passage after passage. It is also the process Snodgrass has undergone himself by writing confessionally and in the form of dramatic monologue, as a prerequisite to the clarity of vision that has enabled him to make and then live with his choices as a husband, father, and poet.

It is not difficult to imagine Snodgrass sitting down to this poem in a spirit of play, to see what might happen if he ruminated briefly, within the disciplines of different rhyme and metrical patterns, on words arising from each of the alphabet's twenty-six letters. The alphabet offers collagelike possibilities as an ordering device, and it also offers a playful, nursery-rhyme ambience that potentially gives the enterprise a sugar coating. The bitterness that overtakes the poem is partially a product of Snodgrass's choice of words such as *Demand, Family, Hitler, Power, Success, Tyrant,* and *Wrong.* And it is partially a function of the movement of thought within each section, from the apparently neutral attempt to define a word to a dismantling of one of the myths or illusions "we" use to protect ourselves against our dreary egoism and fundamental unimportance. In short, Snodgrass seems to have entered the open-ended framework posed by the alphabet only to find himself up against some of his old concerns, stripped of the particularity that may have softened them in other contexts. Here they become abstractions, larger than life as they echo one another and become increasingly interconnected, ghosts and bogeymen that cannot be banished or even reduced.

Taken in the context of Snodgrass's confessional poems, his statements in interviews and his plausible renditions of the private thoughts of Nazi leaders who embody most purely the concept of evil in our time, this long poem at one level is an earned condensation of subjects he has already explored and discussed thoroughly. The chord restruck most often is the theme of power and how it relates in various ways to what is unfaced and unfinished in us. *Power* resonates with other objects such as the blindness fostered by ego, family as political force, fear of weakness, fear of the nonconformist, the dangers of success, the magnetism of the dictator, and the fundamental isolation we suffer in our unwitting search for our own "looking glass or clone."

The family, as Snodgrass has depicted it many times, provides a hothouse environment for humanity's original sense of weakness and consequent need for power. He evoked its destructiveness most forcefully and specifically through the portrait of his own family in *Remains,* the collection he published after *Heart's Needle* and *After Experience* under the pseudonym S. S. Gardons. There the mother exerts totalitarian power through an obsessive and impoverished love that actually feeds off of, rather than nourishes, her family. Under her regime her husband takes the role of the submissive citizen with no desires of his own save those of coping, and her daughter becomes so dependent, so incapable of breaking away into a sense of self, that she finally loses the will to live.

Clearly, Snodgrass's own experience of mother love illuminated for him the sentiments he later magnified through Magda Goebbels, quoted earlier from *The Führer Bunker*. In that same volume it enabled him to illuminate Hitler's twisted force and frightening effectiveness through a monologue that alternates passages of triumphant review of his purges and betrayals with passages flashing back to his first successful act of manipulation, that of conspiring with his mother to slander his stepbrother and thereby persuade her to have the brother driven from the house:

> With her, it was all my way.
> Talk; talk to her. Her thoughts lay
> Open. My voice soaked into her,
> All sides, like a showerspray. She
> Rammed it down the old man's throat. [5]

This passage prefigures the *F* section of "A Darkling Alphabet," where *Family* is defined as the place in which:

> we first learn we must share
> a world with others, bear
> their being, spare, or care
> for, what we want to drive
> away. In its snug hive
> we also learn to lie, connive,
> blame, betray, and to survive.

Under *L* Snodgrass succinctly captures the power weakness dynamic in families by defining *Love* as synonymous with mothers' "care," which he reveals not as tenderness but as the practical means of our survival and, paradoxically, as destructive as it creates in us an innate dependence on others. Thereafter, he writes:

> we are torn
> by our relentless needs
> and our conspicuous scorn
> for anything that feeds
> and so betrays our weakness.

Having left us in a no-win situation, Snodgrass adds:

> If that sounds like sickness,
> think: we also admire and emulate
> those we hate.

This paradoxical definition of *Love* as it originates in the family echoes the principle of perverse attraction, which appears in other of the poem's sections devoted more explicitly to the political uses of power. Under "*T* is for Tyrant," for instance, Snodgrass ends a catalog of the tyrant's acts of "force and terror" with secrets of his success:

> By those who see him at his worst,
> sweat cold beneath his sword,
> he'll be adored.

And in the "Glamour" section already quoted, he depicts us seeking what amounts to obliteration by forces that override our will and judgment.

A thread that strongly binds sections of this poem, then, is the fact we perversely love what power represents as it oppresses us under its guise of love. This causes us to seek power as adults wherever we can, which we manage at least in the kingdom of the home. "Key," Snodgrass tells us, "confers mastery of space / by setting bounds. . . ." It lets us not into home-as-shelter, but into home-as-jail where we can "shut out . . . possibilities we choose / to miss—murder, rape and theft," only to leave ourselves with "three chairs that match, one wife." In order to be "sovereign," then, we etch out for ourselves a territory whose pettiness we don't even recognize; *Key* represents an illusion, the means to "the exclusive place / where we think we belong." Snodgrass ends this section with another of his blunt closures, "It does as much for Song," establishing a point he takes up later in the poem, that the need to purge or avoid impure "possibilities" kills off creativity.

In the "*W* is for Wrong" section Snodgrass states that even political dictators with seemingly real power are only promoting illusion on a grander scale; "hedged in might," he writes, "they prolong / the time before humanity / proves what mortal fools we be," and then he refers to the self-righteous Achilles ultimately bending his head "along / with the vast throng / of those who'd been, and who'd done, wrong."

In the *S* section Snodgrass links illusion with Success, a form of power he experienced after the enthusiastic reception of *Heart's Needle,* which he came to view as an affliction that put him at odds both with his culture and with himself. "Suddenly if it becomes apparent that you are . . . one of the stronger ones, you hear your own past curses ready to strike you down any minute," he said in a 1973 interview with Robert Boyers. "You feel your whole culture closing down on you. Who goes to an analyst? . . . It isn't the failures."[6] In "A Darkling Alphabet" Snodgrass makes clear that success either forces us to confront our need for the illusion of helplessness or to falsely believe ourselves omnipotent, as in the "wrong" of section *W;* either way, it seems, success is a form of power that throws us off-center:

> . . . one who succeeds
> can't act abused or frail;
> instead,
> he must face others' needs.
> We'd rather fail.
> Yet this can make sense, too:
> conquerors do well to do
> with less
> than everything. Choose
> to win too much
> too soon and you loose touch
> with your wrongheadedness.

Ironically, Snodgrass takes a moderate tack in passages defining *Hitler* and *Power,* words whose immediate connotations rise to meet the harsh observations he makes nearly everywhere else in the poem. Yet Hitler, he reminds us at the end of a brief and accurate description, was "human" and remains "locked in the heart / of every living man or woman." This section condenses the implications of *The Führer Bunker* monologues, and it echoes Snodgrass's oft-stated belief that we can only embrace the good and can only write resonant works, by confronting the potential evil in ourselves. And power, he tells us, "corrupts" no more than does weakness—"All things can / corrupt those born corruptible. . . ." Having blunted the negative definition of *power,* he then redefines it in an uncharacteristically (for this poem) speculative manner, as the means to a creative action:

             . . . rich chances for increased fertility
             lie, often, in impurity,
             corruption and decay.
             Rapists say if you can see
             no possibility to escape
             suffering or committing rape,
             why not . . . ? I don't think I'd agree.
             It *might* pay to avoid hysterics
             and broad theories. Offered powers,
             free time, funds, you could manure flowers
             or write yourself some deathless lyrics.

Here power becomes linked with freedom from restraint, both
aesthetic and financial. It allows for the "impurity" that feeds the
cycle of fertility. And the passage as a whole enriches the texture
of the poem by offering speculation amid the flow of strong
statement and closure, finally making an open question of the
poem's dominant motif.

By now it should be clear that paradox is the effective rhetorical
strategy of "A Darkling Alphabet." The poem challenges not
only through what it states outright but also by subtly subtract-
ing from or changing the course of its apparently sweeping state-
ments, so that we are forced to consider opposites at every turn.
In this sense it engages us, despite its lack of concrete imagery, in
experience. This particular experience resembles a dance, a con-
tinual movement of thought, between three supposedly fixed
points: what we think we know of ourselves, what we think
Snodgrass thinks, and what he actually ends up implying. We are
left feeling as Heisenberg may have felt in determining "un-
certainty" to be a "principle" in modern physics; what fact or
measurement appears to be when fixed in isolation becomes
blurred, slightly unmoored, when viewed simultaneously with
other facts. And here is where we drop the term *soapbox* in
describing Snodgrass's attitude in this poem, since most people
who avail themselves of the soapbox lack the subtlety to seduce
us as Snodgrass does, into a familiar yet only quasidefinable
discomfort, which finally *feels* like the truth.
       Many sections whose definitions seem idiosyncratic in the
poem's larger context nevertheless contribute to its overall effect
by offering isolated nuggets of uncertainty, usually by setting up
and then dismantling the definition of a word. In "*C* is for Cow"
Snodgrass begins with a child's version of cow (". . . when lit-

tle, you / were told that she said, Moo, / and had a crumpled horn"), then touches on the mythical, nursery-rhyme version of the cow jumping over the moon, and finally arrives at the harsh facts, her transformation into unrecognizable forms:

> . . . plastic cartons, wax-
> lined boxes, thin-sliced stacks
> of cheese, ranked steaks or chops
> lining cool butcher shops,
> as catchers' mitts, chairs, shoes,
> purses, things we use
> each day. Still, it's curious how
> you never see one now.

In "*M* is for Mystery" Snodgrass manages to question the notion of mystery not so much by redefining it as by casting it in colloquial language that leaves it sounding unmysterious, even as it persists against the fact that some are "stone blind" to it and others try to hunt it down:

> . . . You've heard the Mystery-mongers say:
> Wait! Wait! Mystery's being driven away!
> Have faith: Mystery can look out
> for itself—from all sides. Mystery
> reads all the papers. Not to worry.

In defining *Nest* Snodgrass casts the word in sexual terms and imagery in order to establish a link between lewdness and religion:

> *N* is for Nest, that's hidden
> far in the arched and bending limbs.
> There, young boys are forbidden
> to get too curious and molest
> songbirds where they take their rest
> or come together in unsuppressed
> vaults of elation—as the blest
> congregation of seraphim's
> spanned cathedral groins attest
> to exalted impulse and, possessed,
> choir forth lascivious hymns.

In this case Snodgrass is only slightly interested in defining *Nest*, using it instead as a means to prod at and finally undermine conventional assumptions about religion.

Passages such as these manage to demythologize certain aspects of the world just as most of the poem's other passages demythologize aspects of the self. In all cases, of course, Snodgrass is really addressing himself to assumptions through which we view both self and world. Thus, we are left questioning the trustworthiness of any individual's point of view, just as Heisenberg, having found uncertainty to be the most provable result of his research, was forced to question his means of measuring the mass and movement of atomic particles. Still, the atom itself emerged as a usable and immensely generative entity, shaping nothing less than the age in which we live, despite or perhaps because of its evasions and contradictions. And in "A Darkling Alphabet" the atom provides Snodgrass with a fitting introductory metaphor for human nature as well as for the themes that resonate in the poem to follow:

> *A* is for Atom, the source
> of the matter. Within it,
> childlike, primal forces
> meet, pivoting their courses
> as unlike poles attract, submit
> to power's laws, commit
> themselves to form and limit.
> For good or evil, it,
> like humans, can be split.

Flux and instability, as physical laws that govern the breakdown and reshaping of form, finally govern the formal as well as thematic resonance of "A Darkling Alphabet." Two more of Snodgrass's abiding interests have been an investigation of Space as opposed to Place, which he introduced in his essay "A Poem's Becoming," and "the transformation of matter into energy," which he discussed at length in "Poems about Paintings," an essay describing four Impressionist painters whose work prompted him to write a series of poems. Both these considerations involved him in the contemplation of modern physics as it mirrors and prompts our increasingly open-ended relation to psychological, moral, and aesthetic questions. With the expansion of perceived space both outside and inside ourselves, he says in the first essay, we lose our sense of operating within fixed limits to a more diffuse "awareness of the self as positioned in space relative to other objects and other selves."[7] In the second essay he discussed his interest in the way the Impressionist painters broke down real objects to see them in terms of light and color, thus in terms of the energy liberated by such an endeavor. This offered him a partial solution to the problem of diffuseness, revealing its valuable by-product. In his discussion of Monet he described this process of breaking down and reseeing as more than an intellectual or aesthetic undertaking, as nothing less than an "effort to break down the armoring of the self and its beliefs and ideas, so that one might become an energy among energies, open to the flux of experience. . . ."[8]

This is the test Snodgrass has put himself through from the beginning of his own career and is also the experience he enacts and himself undergoes again throughout this poem. Its many passages bounce against one another like atomic particles, creating a curiously stable entity out of the unseeings and reseeings they contain within and then create between them. The nature of this achievement is best termed as revelation, as pure awareness. As a single work, "A Darkling Alphabet" is perhaps the closest Snodgrass has come to reenacting for himself what he described as Monet's great accomplishment, that of becoming "an energy moving among other energies, fluid like them and so partaking of them." He added that such an achievement "implies a yielding up of the self and so is terrifying and bleak for all its radiance."[9] It is not surprising, then, that he ends "A Darkling Alphabet" with a definition of *Zero* that evokes the bleakness of the "blast" atoms can lead to, the cancellation that reveals our fundamental unimportance:

> **Z** is for Zero, the last
> numeral and, in a blast,
> the last place to be on the ground.
> It's infinite, since round,
> and devoid of any contrast.
> All things on earth have passed,
> or will, through this small, profound
> hole to enter the vast
> and the vacuum. It closes fast.

The ultimate blunt closure. Yet against this uncompromising backdrop "A Darkling Alphabet" achieves a richness of self-contradiction and empathy that finally works to dramatize the breakdown and redirection of human desire.

Standing by the notion that you can't make an omelet without breaking eggs, Snodgrass has tended to emphasize the breaking stage of the process in his role as a poet. True, the most abrasive aspects of his work manage to effect a healing much as a shaman cures by taking others' illnesses into himself and then wrestling them down, yet at times Snodgrass betrays a curmudgeonly sort of fascination with the illnesses themselves, the bruised or rotten spots in the society he finds himself living in.

When interviewed by Paul Gaston on *The Führer Bunker* Snodgrass mentioned that one of the things that prompted him to write the volume was an accusation made of him by Allen Ginsberg and LeRoi Jones (now Imamu Amiri Baraka) that he was "a rotten fascist" and embodied "what's wrong with American Civilization." His reaction, he reported, was: "What a compliment! That wasn't true. If only it were! If I had that breadth of American society, I'd be a hell of a poet!" He then found himself taken with the question: Was it even possible to "identify with the whole awfulness of American business, of American imperialism, . . . of American lying, above all, of American betrayal?"[10] Thus, *The Führer Bunker* came into being, partially from Snodgrass's knowledge of human nature and partially from the desire to see just how much of its "awfulness" he could embrace.

The second-to-last letter of the alphabet in this poem becomes *Yes*. It stands out as a gathering sort of word, a preparation for an affirmative statement, and Snodgrass gives it a push by calling it "the poet's word." He then bends it toward a curiously negative affirmation, an attitude that amounts to the donning of a hair shirt, when he claims that the poet:

> . . . must affirm
> what makes ideacrats
> and joiners itchy. He can't squirm
>
> out by trying to deny
> what doesn't fit his definition
> of the Good and True. His mission
> is to believe only his eye,
>
> the burning witness of his senses,
> his emotions, passions— . . .

In earlier times such stoicism might have led to a monastery, a life of solitary mortification and contemplation. Or it might have led to prison, where it would have retained a heroic purity. Today it simply requires endurance, the willingness to sustain unpopularity and perhaps ridicule while living in the thick of things. This passage marks the climax of the poem, the culmination of Snodgrass's abiding cynicism and willingness to take blows, before the *Zero* stanza pulls us into its vortex of erasure. He concludes by saying that the poet:

> . . . can't ask things to go away
>
> unsaid. What he'd prefer
> cuts no ice here. He knows his place is
> breadth and his appetite embraces
> victim and executioner.
>
> His job's to celebrate
> what is—now, while it's not too late.
> If all the groupies hate him,
> he's doing *something* right; congratulate him.

This is the stance of a victor, not a martyr. It is the final challenge offered in a poem whose truths are difficult to stomach, by a poet who once again has spoken from long experience of looking faithfully inward and outward and dares now us to do the same.

NOTES

1. "Finding a Poem" (1959), *In Radical Pursuit* (New York: Harper and Row, 1975), 2.
2. "Magda Goebbels (19 April 1945)," *The Führer Bunker* (Brockport, N.Y.: BOA Editions, 1977), 24.
3. "Tact and the Poet's Voice," *In Radical Pursuit*, 15.
4. J. D. McClatchy, "W. D. Snodgrass: The Mild Reflective Art," *Massachusetts Review* 16 (Spring 1975): 281.
5. "Adolf Hitler (1 April 1945)," *The Führer Bunker*, 12.
6. Robert Boyers, "W. D. Snodgrass: An Interview," *Salmagundi*, nos. 22–23 (Spring–Summer 1973): 158–59.
7. "A Poem's Becoming," *In Radical Pursuit*, 56.
8. "Poems about Paintings," *In Radical Pursuit*, 78.
9. "Poems about Paintings," 78.
10. Paul L. Gaston, "W. D. Snodgrass and *The Führer Bunker*," *Papers on Language and Literature* 13 (Summer 1977): 299–300.

LAURENCE GOLDSTEIN

The Führer Bunker and the New Discourse about Nazism

When a book of poetry sets out deliberately to trouble the world, as W. D. Snodgrass's *The Führer Bunker* did a decade ago, it needs to have inscribed into its contents something like the shock of a violent public event. The contents themselves need not be public; indeed, Snodgrass achieved a lasting effect of this kind with his first book, *Heart's Needle* (1959), by dwelling upon entirely private sorrows. The point is to disturb the fixed assumptions about human behavior held by a majority of readers and by doing so create new belief. Yeats noted in *A Vision* that "we desire belief and lack it. Belief comes from shock and is not desired." The aesthetic challenge in this generation is greater than in Yeats's because most readers now seem to desire shock whether it carries belief with it or not. When a poet as skilled in sweet rhetoric as Snodgrass, who can charm and disarm his audience at will, presents twenty dramatic monologues spoken by the most despised Nazis, nothing less than ultimate questions about the enterprise of contemporary poetry loom before us. Is there a shameless sensationalism involved in trying to change belief on *that* dreadful subject? Shouldn't the poet pass by the Medusa head of *that* modern horror lest he petrify, or worse entertain, himself and his readers by staring at vipers? *The Führer Bunker* may carry too much of a charge even for our shockproof sensibilities. Easier to leave it alone, as major publishers and most readers did, than be exposed to revenants as noxious and talkative as Hitler, Goebbels, and Martin Bormann.

Southern Review 24, no. 1 (Winter 1988): 100–114. Copyright © 1988 by Laurence Goldstein. Reprinted by permission. This is the first essay published on *The Führer Bunker* since Paul Gaston devoted a chapter to it in *W. D. Snodgrass* (Twayne, 1978). Like Mr. Gaston, Mr. Goldstein responds to the BOA edition (1977) of the ongoing *Führer Bunker* cycle. Since the BOA edition of *The Führer Bunker* Snodgrass has published two other volumes in the cycle, *Heinrich Himmler: Platoons and Files* (Pterodactyl, 1982) and *Magda Goebbels* (Palaemon, 1983). The cycle is now more than 150 pages long, more than a third of which is uncollected.

I should say at once why I cannot leave it alone. In *Erika: Poems of the Holocaust* (1984) William Heyen recalls being taken as a child to the German *Volksfest* held on Long Island every summer. "All those years," he writes, "there was one word I never heard, / one name never mentioned." My experience was the opposite. If I follow my memory as far back toward my birthdate of 1943 as I can reach, I stall continually at scenes in which I am inquiring of parents and family about the *world war* (the phrase remains resonant, terrifying) recently past. How did it happen? I ask, in the midst of grim, sometimes whispered conversations. "The Germans are monsters" is the usual answer, or sometimes, "The Germans are devils." In our Jewish household the name *Hitler* was more than mentioned; it served as a frequent obscenity, a mysterious fragment of ongoing lamentations over the Jewish condition. For me current events were so thoroughly steeped in the language of folklore that no explanation since of history's dynamics as a political science has seemed credible. What form could my education take, then, but a gradual coming to terms with those monsters and devils in my imagination? Having apprehended the narrative of history as a dark romance, I gravitated toward poetry as a mediator between the chthonic figures of my childhood (Hitler above all) and the postwar realities I read about in newspapers and popular weeklies.

American poets who wrote about World War II tended to read the event by the light of myths as Manichaean as those I received from my family's table talk. Randall Jarrell's intuition that the Brothers Grimm illuminate the European war's shape and origins better than do historians confirmed my own suspicions, and poets like Robert Lowell and Karl Shapiro mobilized biblical and classical sources to argue for an archaic hermeneutics rather than rational, if no less chilling, explanations based on realpolitik. At the same time a majority of the American public, without reading a thimbleful of verse, voted for the devil theory of modern history by reinscribing it in the discourse of the cold war. Stalin and his successors assumed the typological role bequeathed by Hitler. Children since the 1950s have overheard something like the conversations I remember and drunk deep from popular culture diabolizing the Soviet enemies of humanity. One prays that no third world war occurs to call forth from its ashes a retrospective book like *The Führer Bunker*.

I presume that the misgivings of every reader approaching these monologues resemble Snodgrass's own trepidations in engaging the material. Indeed, it's obvious that Snodgrass made the poems as monologues so that their readers would have to undergo the dramatic role of auditor. Like a documentary film in which interviewees make their passionate case before invisible listeners who are also their jurors—I am thinking of relevant examples like *The Sorrow and the Pity* and *Shoah*—*The Führer Bunker* offers a variety of self-defensive testimonies derived, Snodgrass assures us in his "Afterword," from the texts and gossip these Nazis produced during their lives. We listen, we close the book, and that day, that month, that year—for the rest of our lives, perhaps—their discourse becomes a part of our memory of the Third Reich.

The stage directions in the monologues remind us that Snodgrass is writing a theater piece as well as a poetry sequence—and in fact *The Führer Bunker* has been performed off-Broadway and elsewhere. Dramatization of this or any other scenario about the Nazi leaders necessarily complicates our response to the written text. That the Nazis themselves conceived their enterprise on the model of Wagnerian opera and epic theater cannot be doubted, and the historical success of their self-conscious narrative accounts for the uneasiness we feel when confronted with their images and voices on film. Life and art have lost their salutary boundary, we feel, compelling us to judge the Nazis "only" as we would judge the rhetoric and credibility of play actors or the ingenuity of strophic turns in a plot designed for our entertainment. We find ourselves poking fun, as Chaplin and Mel Brooks have done, at Hitler's showy gestures and delusions of grandeur; nevertheless, tens of millions died on his commands. In this century the real effects of the Nazis' *Lehrstücke* are too traumatic for us to preserve the aesthetic distance we now bring to Shakespeare's villains of the War of the Roses or, a more ambiguous case, the French revolutionaries who have had such a vogue in plays and films since the celebrity of *Marat/Sade*. The linguistic authority in Snodgrass's monologues derives from our mental and aural memories of those exhaustively documented policymakers—the fascinating objects of their own propaganda as well as ours. (It is interesting that the least successful monologues, in theme and style, belong to military figures like Gotthard Heinrici and Helmuth Weidling, who are not part of our visceral mythology.) Unlike, say, the faceless speakers of James Schevill's fine sequence *The Stalingrad Elegies* (1964), where the monologues are shaped from actual letters written by doomed Nazi infantrymen at Stalingrad, neither Hitler nor Goebbels, nor Hermann Goering in uncollected monologues from Snodgrass's sequence, can yet be represented without arousing the kind of mediating moral problems belonging to the aesthetics of historical memory.

In the act of silent reading, unlike the theater, we convert the text into our own voice, so that identification with the speaker is automatically guaranteed. For the time it takes to read Hitler's hectic diatribes on his enemies, his words form in the sounding chamber of each reader's consciousness, there to reverberate as the all-too-recognizable sentiments of the reader's own experience. Is Hitler by turns the self-pitying orphan, the low-minded schemer, and the *miles gloriosus?* Who of his auditors has not sympathized with such types, and caught him- or herself acting the role in reality or imagination? (Snodgrass's epigraph for the revised manuscript is this: "Mother Teresa, asked when she first began her work of relief and care for abandoned children, replied, 'On the day I discovered I had a Hitler inside me.' ") Even the extremity of Hitler's speech, which permits us the leverage to judge him, will not be entirely foreign. Here is a selection from the first of Hitler's three monologues in the volume, dated 1 April 1945:

> Who else sold out? Bremen? Magdeburg?
> They would go on in this pisswallow, in
> Disgrace, shame. Who could we send to make
> Their lives worth less to them? In our camps,
> You gas them, shoot, club, strangle them,
> Tramp them down into trenches, thick as leaves.
> Out of the ground at night, they squirm up
> Through the tangled bodies, crawl off in the woods.
> Every side now, traitors, our deserters, native
> Populations, they rise up like vomit, flies
> Out of bad meat, sewers backing up. Up
> There, now, in the bombed-out gardens,
> That sickly, faint film coming over
> The trees again, along the shattered branches
> Buds festering. In shell-holes, trash heaps,
> Some few green leaves, grass spikes thrust
> Up through the ashes, through the cracked cement,
> Shove up into the light again.

A passage so close to blank verse will summon memories of other frenzied dramatic characters on the verge of damnation—Marlowe's Faust, Shakespeare's Richard III, or Macbeth—at the same time as the vituperative imagery, achieving with its dying fall a lyric plangency, reminds us of the metaphors we utilize when faced with those fiends in human form who perpetrate the crimes we find most despicable. Of course, our chief examples will be the Nazis themselves, so that Hitler's paranoia, by a terrible historical irony, ensures our sympathy. He becomes credible by echoing, in a finer tone, the language of abuse we have practiced on figures like himself.

This is dangerous ground to be treading, both for Snodgrass and for any reader who wants to distinguish Hitler from some allegorical devil, in order to bring him to judgment, *and* from oneself, in order to live in this world with a sense of self-esteem. In *Imagining Hitler,* a recent book that does not discuss Snodgrass, Alvin Rosenfeld has complained of postwar representations that "such fictions both exalt the image of Hitler by casting it in terms that intrigue and excite the imagination, and neutralize it by making the man seem so ordinary." If Nazi wickedness is emphasized by the writer, there is the danger that the reader will be inflamed, consciously or not, by fantasies of criminality and corruption, but if Hitler and his cohort are belittled by showing them as ordinary or banal, the authentic historical measure of their evil may be diminished and falsified. A writer is damned if he (and it is almost always a he) strays to one side or the other. Because of "the stakes involved in the attenuation and distortion of historical memory," Rosenfeld concludes that for the time being a moratorium on creative appropriations of the Nazi mystique might be welcome.

Rosenfeld argues that what makes Hitler such a dangerous case is the historical fact of his war against the Jews. Violent abuses of political power have been a common subject in Western literature since Machiavelli spelled out a rational apology for tyrants in *The Prince.* A leader is often obliged, he wrote, "in order to maintain the state, to act against faith, against charity, against humanity, and against religion." Literature is full of ambitious kings or nobles who follow this prescription, killing all perceived enemies before dying themselves at the hands of a saner, more sympathetic rival for the throne. But Hitler's case *is* different. As historians have pointed out, his obsession with solving "the Jewish problem," after its initial usefulness as a scapegoating technique, became counterproductive in the context of a military crusade to Germanize the world. The efforts to identify, round up, and exterminate the Jews drew off supplies and labor needed to "maintain the state" by defending it from *armed* adversaries, so that Hitler's single-minded obsession, infecting the entire hierarchy of the Nazi state, became a psychotic form of self-definition not shared by other dictators in historical drama or historical reality. For this reason, Rosenfeld argues, a cult of Hitler will have the principal consequence of inflaming anti-Semitism with very direct effects in social and political realms (for example, hostility toward Israel). Hitler and his fellow Nazis, then, offer a unique problem of narrative strategy, not only in the profundity of their evil, but in the just representation of their genocidal career.

I have suggested how Snodgrass anticipates this problem in the volume's opening monologue, in which Hitler is necessarily elevated by speaking verse of high quality. In *The Führer Bunker* several of the key characters speak in fixed forms: Goebbels in rhymed couplets and Magda Goebbels in villanelles, for example. Such forms serve a dual function. They bespeak a higher human nature by their orderliness, their more efficient prosodic and linguistic organization, and for that same reason they compel a clearer view into the diseased imagination they expose. Hitler was a spellbinding orator and a monologist whose conversations were preserved by Albert Speer among others. Because he saw himself as a dramatic hero in a cosmic drama of his own authorizing, he is a figure given to what Peter Brooks, in *The Melodramatic Imagination,* describes as acts of "self-nomination." Brooks explains that in melodrama "the villain . . . at some point always bursts forth in a statement of his evil nature and intentions." The function of a fixed-verse form is to make these acts of self-nomination inescapable and definitive, as if the deepest truth will be wrung from the speaker by the demands of a more disciplined medium. (As a formal poet, Snodgrass acts upon this assumption in every poem he writes.) Hitler, like his ventriloquist in this volume, becomes subdued to the literary tradition, compelled to a form of speech act as different from his undisciplined ravings on the platform as meter is from prose. As in verse form, so in general structure: we would expect the progression of Hitler's monologues in *The Führer Bunker* to reproduce in condensed form the *telos* of the Third Reich toward the apocalypse it had formerly imagined for its enemies. If the volume has a viable shape, it ought to answer Rosenfeld's misgivings not only in the totality of its speeches, but in the movement through the three monologues by the first cause of the reich, Hitler himself.

As we have seen, in the volume's first monologue Hitler's obsession with lower nature, with degradation and waste, usurps his public responsibilities as a military commander-in-chief. From his underground perspective every political action contributes to the extermination of his reich and, thus, of his life. The world outside is a "pisswallow," and all the figures on both sides are traitors to a cause he confesses to be indiscriminately murderous. Having failed his vision, they become less than human, all assimilated in his paranoid imagination to resemblances of the Jew who had once seemed an exclusive symbol of the bestial or insectlike in humanity. All of the speakers characterize each other, as well as their former friends and current enemies, by downward comparisons. They constantly describe Germany as a "Hell," a "garbage dump" of "ants," "flies," "leeches," "worms," and excrement. Though we find the ironic rhyme of *Führer* and *purer* in the volume, Hitler's language keeps the impure always before us. Like "flies / out of bad meat," his own armies no less than his enemies disgust him and drive him deeper into the metaphorical bunker of his psyche where his loathing for figures of the alien is compelled to expose its features and origins.

In his second monologue, then, Hitler begins to incorporate the Jew into his self-definition. The dynamics of such an identification had always been an ironic feature of Nazi historiography, beginning with *Mein Kampf* and forming the basis of Hitler's maniacal claims for vengeance against both the capitalist and revolutionary Jews he imagined as Germany's deadly enemies. More recently, this same identification has constituted the most disturbing element of what Saul Friedländer calls "the new discourse about Nazism." The basic terms of this analogy are spelled out clearly in Hans-Jürgen Syberberg's *Hitler: A Film from Germany,* where Hitler declares:

> I believe and avow, at least once, seriously what it was really all about, my struggle, *Mein Kampf,* the program of our final goal. . . . We learned from the practice of the Jewish people how religious racial purity and a sense of mission by a chosen people can help us to achieve world dominion.
>
> Thinking of Jerusalem for two thousand years. In every prayer, every day, until they won. My respects.

Likewise, George Steiner, in *The Portage to San Cristobal of A. H.,* gives Hitler a self-exculpating speech at the very end of the novel (not answered, according to Steiner's intention, except by the reader's shocked response) that draws Jews and Nazis into a conceptual identity. Perhaps, an aged Hitler tells his Israeli abductors, he is the real Messiah of the Jews, since his actions have created an indomitable consciousness among the survivors, resulting in the recovery of Jerusalem. In such works Hitler is imagined in terms of the Romantic-Hegelian myth he nourished for himself even as he denied it to the Jews.

In his second monologue in *The Führer Bunker,* dated 20 April 1945, Hitler reads his endgame reflexively as a dramatic form of his final solution for the Jews:

> I can eat nothing now—only cake.
> Pills and Morrell's injections.
> My cake, chairs, rugs—without them
> There's the bare concrete. Like any
> Jew degenerate at Auschwitz.

In the shorter, plainer verse line Hitler surrenders some of the lyrical confidence of his first speech three weeks earlier. Bereft of everything but his temporary stimulants and sedatives, he regresses to the needs and pleasures of the infant. Alternating with his speeches in verse, a prose commentary describes an act of sexual perversion in which Hitler achieves climax after a woman (presumably Eva Braun) urinates and defecates on him. According to the afterword, "There is [a] film, recently recovered, which records his sexual perversion; Eva Braun had it secretly filmed, fearing that he might abandon her." Whether or not such a film exists, this act serves as a conclusive metaphor of precisely that "degenerate" state projected upon the Jews by Hitler throughout his life. No longer a citizen of the world but its pariah, its evil principle, Hitler regresses further into an oral-anal form of his primal obsession, letting it dominate him to the exclusion of all other satisfactions. In effect, he erases or eliminates the "Jewish problem" from his consciousness by converting the bunker into an *anus mundi,* as the historical Nazis called Auschwitz. If the poetry of the Holocaust insists upon genocide as the definitive feature of Nazism, *The Führer Bunker* drives deep into the psyches that engendered the Holocaust in order to explore the dynamics of anti-Semitism. In Hitler's case, having mortified the entire world, except for his mother's memory, he hardly needs to make a more extended example of the Jew than he does here. Instead, he thinks back to the household arena that preexisted his consciousness of the Jews. It is just when he remembers in verse his mother's favors toward him alone, "Only the two of us together," that the prose commentary announces, "Now he will probably achieve his climax, alone and without assistance." Here is the corrective psycho-analytical version of the heroic romance: the hero revealed as a coddled infant struggling to destroy throughout life the "degener-ate" rivals who frustrate the libidinal pleasure of renewing his original conquest and collapsing at last into the degraded condi-tion he had sought to escape by political action.

If this were Hitler's last chance to speak, we might object to the strict Freudianism of such a conclusion. The image of Hitler wal-lowing in feces juxtaposed to his sentimental reverie of Mama's sweetcakes—this scenario too easily gratifies the reader's vindic-tive feelings by debriding man and ideology alike. However, this scene of degradation is not the last word, but a waystation of Hitler's movement toward his self-glorification ten days later, in his third and final monologue at the end of the volume. This second monologue pushes to an extreme the analysis by Erik H. Erikson in *Childhood and Society,* which traced Hitler's fantasies of power to his domestic upbringing. Erikson pointed out that in *Mein Kampf* Germany is called a "motherland," a term permit-ting Hitler to associate his "pathological attachment to his mother" with his political crusade. Debarred by the extremity of his Oedipus complex from healthy entrance into adult life, Hitler remained fixed in the period of adolescent rebellion, and Ger-many, for a variety of cultural and historical reasons, "surren-der[ed] to the imagery of ideological adolescence." It is precisely this bonding of leader and nation that Snodgrass will develop in Hitler's valedictory statement.

Erikson's study may be said to lie behind the revisionary "new discourse about Nazism." Erikson begins his commentary by asserting that "it is our task to recognize that the black miracle of Nazism was only the German version . . . of a universal con-temporary potential." The terrible notion that Hitler, rather than embodying a nonce perversion of normal human values, some-how represents the Spirit of the Age, as well as its style, has achieved not only notoriety but increasing popularity. Accord-ing to Saul Friedländer, the new discourse is characterized by "the more and more frequent display of a Hitler who is Every-man, himself wrapped in kitsch, and at the same time the image of an almost superhuman power flung into emptiness." Snod-grass's strategy, then, derives from the psychoanalytical situa-tion: he gives the analysand—this putative Everyman—a voice, and more than a voice, a richly wrought rhetorical vehicle for the adolescent anger and defiance shared by the Nazis who formed Hitler's inner circle. What makes *The Führer Bunker* so significant as a contemporary work is that Snodgrass chooses as his model the genre of confessional poetry that has dominated the American scene almost since the end of the war. In effect, *The Führer Bunker* criticizes the mode of self-revelation Snodgrass had indulged in in his own early work before chastening his poetics in *After Experience* (1968) in favor of a more classical practice.

Confessional poetry privileges those acts of self-nomination that characterize the melodramatic imagination. "I myself am hell" is the signature theme of such a mode, a self-laceration that is also a verbal assault upon the reader. Poet and reader agree to share this rite of cleansing, with the understanding that both will find their way to a more well-adjusted mentality by the experience. When the heuristic function of confession is frustrated the weight of damnation must be carried by the poet alone, impairing his or her ability to rejoin the community by means of propitiatory speech. As one of the first practitioners of confessional poetry, Snodgrass knows the chief pitfall of this mode: that the habit of self-nomination can and often does become a self-perpetuating and self-stimulating means of preventing such a happy consummation. Not the Catholic model of speech acts that reunite sinner and congregation, but the more profane one of stripteaser tormenting a prurient audience—that has been the metaphorical fate of this mode. Of course, I am thinking especially of Sylvia Plath's confession about the addictive power of self-regard:

> There is a charge
>
> For the eyeing of my scars, there is a charge
> For the hearing of my heart—
> It really goes.
>
> And there is a charge, a very large charge
> For a word or a touch
> Or a bit of blood
>
> Or a piece of hair or my clothes.
> So, so, Herr Doktor.
> So, Herr Enemy.

In such a rhetorical posture the one who confesses first identifies him- or herself as victim, as Plath does in this poem by comparing her state to that of the murdered Jew ("ash, ash— / . . . A cake of soap, / A wedding ring, / A gold filling") or as Hitler does in Snodgrass's poem ("Like any / Jew degenerate at Auschwitz"), and *then* claims a moral right to destroy the "Enemy" by presumption of his/her terrible suffering. In Plath this is conceived as a vengeance on the male Nazi figure derived from her German father ("Out of the ash / I rise with my red hair / And I eat men like air"), and for Hitler the self-abasement leads in the same way to a savoring, in the third monologue, of the millions he has murdered.

Nor is Hitler the only "victim" of the confessional disease. Goebbels, the broadcaster of the Big Lie in public life, delights in vulgar enumerations of his sexual conquests and his scheming victories over rivals for the Führer's favor. At times there is an uncomfortable (and I suspect deliberate) recall of Snodgrass's mode from *Heart's Needle*. Compare Goebbels—"I never saw one fucking day / So fine I courted it to stay"—with the disgruntled speaker of "April Inventory":

> I haven't read one book about
> A book or memorized one plot.
> Or found a mind I did not doubt.
> I learned one date. And then forgot.

In both speeches the intended effect is to shock the reader by revealing a disfigured human nature. In the early poem the speaker is able to work free of his negative attitude, however, and affirm the value of the world beyond his jealous professional resentment: "There is a loveliness exists, / Preserves us, not for specialists." Goebbels cannot; he taunts the auditor with his death wish: "So; the vile body turns to spirit / That speaks soundlessly. They'll hear it." The remorseless couplet rhyme chimes the fulfillment of the imperious speaker's occult desire. When restraints of the social order cannot be beaten down or declaimed out of existence, the individual must fling himself into emptiness. As in Plath's "Ariel," one's will becomes an arrow "that flies / Suicidal, at one with the drive / Into the red / Eye, the cauldron of morning."

In *The Führer Bunker* Hitler and Goebbels are Mephistophelean figures. Like Marlowe's and Goethe's devils, their gestures of repentance are a knowing travesty of confession, designed to entrap the reader or auditor in a rhetorical and emotional confusion from which there is no escape back to the norms of the community. (Camus' relentless monologist in *The Fall* is another model.) Snodgrass had called attention to the morally ambiguous act of confession in an essay on *Crime and Punishment* published in 1960, shortly after *Heart's Needle*. The essay begins with an epigraph from Simone Weil of considerable relevance to *The Führer Bunker:* "A hurtful act is the transference to others of the degradation which we bear in ourselves. That is why we are inclined to commit such acts as a way of deliverance." Raskolnikov aspires to be a Mephistopheles, but, as Snodgrass points out, his murder of the pawnbroker has the unconscious purpose of securing punishment, the justice of ethical limits and law, as a means of discharging existential guilt. Another confessional work of the early 1960s *seemed* to perform this same therapeutic transaction. "There ought to be a law against Henry. /—Mr Bones: there is." The resounding affirmation of those last two words in John Berryman's Dream Song #4 helps to legitimize the adolescent craving of "horrible Henry" (#9) for deliverance from his persistent consciousness of filial remorse and sexual infidelity. Nevertheless, if one takes Henry as a projection of Berryman's Dostoyevskian ego, the similarity of his and Plath's and Hitler's fate cannot be overlooked. "God's Henry's enemy" (#13) down to the suicidal end, wherein Henry's creator achieves the punishment denied him as a survivor of his father's self-murder. Can any reader of *The Dream Songs* avoid feeling like a Faust in turn, always at the mercy of this spellbinding rhetorician with his honeyed evocation of "the top job of all, / *son fin*" (#46)?

A series of analogies can be posited: Monologist > Reader; Nazi > Jew; Mephistopheles > Faust. In each case the active agent thrives on the opposition of the more passive one, until the weaker is victimized. The receptor may be said to represent the *Bürgerlich* establishment which according to Erikson both desires and fears the adolescent frenzy of the pathological Other. The Jew, for example, founded Judeo-Christian civilization on the basis of being "chosen"; Jews thus symbolize the prevailing rule of law Nazism would annihilate by licentious behavior. Likewise, every Mephistopheles needs a Faust. Snodgrass has chosen Albert Speer for this role. Speer is the guilty coconspirator, given the power to realize his architectural fantasies by the living Word he has no trouble recognizing as a demon. "Yes, we did what humans / could not do. We passed / all limit," he says too plainly, and then quotes Marlowe's Faust to cinch the identification: "Oh, I'll leap up to my / God! Who pulls me down?" Speer is the most troublesome character in *The Führer Bunker* because he must engineer the reader's own judgments of right and wrong; the responsibility of being a talking conscience makes for sententiousness of an undramatic kind. In his confessions Speer is clearly rehearsing for the just punishment he foresees at Nuremberg and for his canny memoirs, which have so influenced contemporary perceptions of Hitler and the Third Reich. He is Hitler's foil and historian, as Goebbels is Hitler's double and executive in both the sexual and political arenas. Goebbels "love[s] only the holes in things" while Speer strives to place lasting erections upon the vacancy his masters increasingly make of the Fatherland.

If Magda Goebbels emerges as the mirror image of her mate, nursing a sexual libido and political absolutism that have no fulfillment but in the scornful purity of death (her children being the last victims of her love of power), Eva Braun manages to make the best case for the *liebestod* motif that informs all the monologues. As with some other Nazis, sexuality is her metaphor for achieved liberation of the personality from the shackles of *Bürgerlichkeit*. But where Goebbels and Fegelein pursue erotic pleasures with the all-consuming possessiveness that characterizes the Nazi enterprise—adolescent bullies to the end—Eva, like her namesake, devotes her favors entirely to her idolized mate. Her first monologue begins, "I ought to feel ashamed / Feeling such joy." Her sense of triumph rises in pitch through the two monologues, culminating in a vision of spiritual consummation as she prepares for the suicide pact.

Eva's satisfactions place her somewhat beyond the confessional mode; she is more like a folkloric princess making the best of her fate in a nasty fairy tale. As Hitler's ruminations are punctuated by exclamations in boldface Gothic script—"***Our men are waiting for their Führer***"—and *Goebbels's ravings are interrupted appropriately with headlines—*"NAZI WHORELORD / COUNTS CONQUESTS"—Eva Braun's first monologue is counterpointed by a favorite American song of hers, "Tea for Two." One notices first the ironic effect, how the sappy lyrics ("Me for you / And you for me") diminish her worship of the führer to the level of schoolgirl sentimentality. But a secondary effect is surely to legitimize the fulfillment of her romantic fantasy as a species of universal need. "Nobody near us / To see us or hear us." This line precedes Eva's exultant cry, "I have it all. They are all gone, the others. /. . . the screaming mobs above all." Hitler never loses his infantile dependence upon the flattery and applause that belong to his self-appointed role as the führer (though he imagines otherwise, his obsession with betrayal in all three monologues gives him away). Eva seems to herself, and intermittently to us, the stronger one, because she needs only him; in the bunker, where he is stripped of admirers, she can possess him on her own terms—the unresisted fantasy encoded in popular song. She forces him to acknowledge his need and affection for her by a public marriage and kiss on the lips, for example. Though she abases herself before him, she does compel him to act the all-too-human role of the husband described in "Tea for Two."

One might say that Eva provides a comic interlude in the midst of this Wagnerian melodrama. If the men are compelled by their extremity to speak in an offensive vocabulary wrought from their lower nature (surely no contemporary book of poems contains so many obscenities), Eva, no less a Nazi, likewise appropriates the "innocent" formulas of a different stage language to serve her fixation. Like the shopgirl or showgirl in countless plays and movies of the 1930s who becomes betrothed to some form of the prince, Eva can exult, "I, above all, am chosen," joining her happy fate to the romance of history predicated since the Old Testament era on divine selection. Unlike the 1930s heroine, however, she cannot guide the reader back to community, to the ongoing cultural traditions that ensure a future. Like some confessional poets (especially Plath and Sexton), she speaks for the feminine fascination with the demon lover. "I am the Black Bride that will be / devoured," she says in her last monologue. She nominates herself a sacrificial figure comparable to Faust dragged down to hell and the Jew murdered in the ovens.

Richard L. Rubenstein has written in *After Auschwitz* that "Nazism was an inverted and demonic transformation of Jewish and Christian values, combined with a Romantic hankering after a paganism it never understood." He compares Hitler to Captain Ahab; both are walking and raving critiques of the Romantic quest for transcendence, characters devoted above all to the annihilation of some hated symbol (the White Whale, the Jews) that resists their absolutist desire for perfect vengeance upon the conditions of mortality and community. As we have seen, Snodgrass's method in *The Führer Bunker* has been to cross this familiar Romantic overreacher with a modern analysand, revealing the neurotic origins and scatological character of the historical obsession. Snodgrass has grafted the habits of identification between speaker and reader implied in the confessional poem onto the narrative of history itself. Hitler never quite turns to the reader to declare, "Hypocrite lecteur, mon semblable, mon frère," but Snodgrass achieves a constant *frisson* by locating the source of identification in the lower nature we have privileged, at least since Freud, as the seat of our being. If we are shocked by this act of familiarity into creating for ourselves some new chastity of spirit, some "new belief," in Yeats's phrase, that allows us to resist more firmly than we already do the imperial intentions of these eloquent villains, Snodgrass has done his work.

Hitler's final monologue, which concludes with his suicide, ought to assist us in measuring the distance between his obsessions and ours. Hitler recounts the previous evening's pornographic events—a film of the would-be assassin Witzleben wriggling on a meat hook in orgasmic frenzy, his secretaries helped to suicide ("to save you / From these Mongolians' greasy hands, / Pricks, the stink of jism")—interspersed with a megalomaniacal counting of his millions of victims. Through these crimes he has bonded to him forever all the executioners of his will, even if they betray him by not killing enough enemies to make Germany triumphant. That the unresolved oedipal condition can culminate in an ecstatic indulgence in the language and performance of mass murder, sexual perversion, and suicide—not to mention the mad delusions indicated by the allusion to *Lohengrin*, "*Once recognized, the Grail Knight must be gone*"—should mortify any desire for identification, not least because Hitler ghoulishly reaches out to the posterity symbolized by the reader as his last hope. As he chews his cyanide capsule he exults:

> once more I
> Am winning,
>   winning,
>   winning

In the next poem, the book's last, Goebbels similarly imagines his survival in the public imagination: "Left like sperm / In a stranger's gut, waiting its term." Like the monologue that concludes George Steiner's fable, these are challenges to the reader to resist the specious empathy enforced by the confessional mode and construct, in Michel Foucault's phrase, a "counter-memory" to the self-made mythology and melodrama of Nazism.

From that sperm left by the potent Goebbels in every stranger's gut has come a monstrous new birth, precisely the new discourse that Erikson, Friedländer, Rosenfeld, Rubenstein, and others have tried to define and warn against—"Fascinating Fascism," as

Susan Sontag titles her essay on Leni Riefenstahl. The victory of Hitler, these writers suggest, comes when he is perceived as a charismatic figure of Everyman, of the perverse acting in history with near absolute power. Such is the ironic fulfillment of our postwar quest to demythologize these "monsters" and "devils" that obsessed our parents. The Nazis could not win on the Wagnerian battlefield, but they found consolation in the notion that their defeat, and the *Götterdämmerung* that resulted, belonged to the Teutonic mythology from which they continuously drew strength. Now their myth is ours, and writers like Snodgrass have been struggling against its power with all the ideological and rhetorical tools at their command. Snodgrass has tried to disinfect our imagination by use of the so-called Jewish science of psychoanalysis, showing how one can apprehend the Nazis as forms of Everyman and yet move beyond such a generous recognition to a mature, and politically urgent, judgment of their twisted natures. The excruciating risk of *The Führer Bunker,* more visible than ever in this decade, was that in intensifying (by exposing) the depravity of the Nazis it would contribute to the "new discourse about Nazism" as *Heart's Needle* unwittingly nourished the pathology of confessional poetry. I think that the volume still has the salutary power to shock and that it braces rather than relaxes the conscience of its readership. But history will have the last word, whether it grinds *The Führer Bunker* down into kitsch or keeps these monologues as a precious countermemory for future generations.

Waiting for the End of the World

Snodgrass and The Führer Bunker

Why won't the Nazis *stay* dead?

I cannot think of the subject at hand without recalling a fugue of voices, each cautionary and emphatic, each a poet's, each in its different way a victim (as all of us are) of the forces of this century. The first is that of Derek Walcott prefacing a poem at a reading by saying: "All empires, including this one, are founded upon genocide." The next is that of Zbigniew Herbert as he sat beside me one day in 1970 in South Pasadena reading the *L.A. Free Press:* "But where is this *revolution?* Hashish, free love. . . . That is *fun.* Revolution is not. I was in only one revolution. Against the Nazis. It was necessary. I hated it. I hated them more." The last voice is Gerald Stern's, with whom I was having lunch one sunny day in San Francisco. I mentioned that I was thinking of writing something about *The Führer Bunker.* He replied in an urgent, raspy whisper: "But they're Nazis, Larry. *Nazis!"*

Nazis! What Stern said there may be finally all that can be said of them, for the term has always held an appalling distinguishment, the distinguishment of a genocide that is, so far, the most fully documented, deliberate, and catastrophic human extermination that the world has known, and one that is, because of its sheer enormity, and the enormity of the fact that it happened at all, that it *could* happen at all, a historical event that has made the world a more terrible place than it had been before.

Yet the Third Reich's Final Solution is certainly not the first genocide. The warfare of Genghis Khan, as George Steiner once noted in a review in the *New Yorker,* was always genocidal in its tactics, but Khan, it seems, left no one alive on those mountain passes to record it fully. Steiner also notes that genocide itself,

---

When Mr. Levis wrote this essay he had available to him the entire working copy of *The Führer Bunker* cycle as it existed in 1988. This is the first essay to respond to portions of the cycle written after the 1977 BOA edition of *The Führer Bunker.*

dormant for a few centuries despite incessant conflicts, reappears again in this century as a characteristic of warfare as early as 1915, with the Turkish massacre of Armenians; it continues not only with Hitler but also with the exterminations under Stalin. In fact, it is a symptom of a world grown more terrible because of the Holocaust that smaller genocidal incidents, the exterminations of Gypsies, for example, can be more readily forgotten and ignored, as if a crime of incalculable scale makes the same crime on a smaller one invisible.

In the case of the United States limited genocides (limited, one might venture to say, because of demographics), have occurred with or without open declarations of war against indigenous North American Indian populations until the end of the nineteenth century. In this century, during World War II, the United States has displayed manifestly pregenocidal conditions with the internment of Japanese Americans; such internments, it should be noted, were what constituted the Third Reich's *Second* Solution to the "Jewish Problem." In *The Pursuit of Loneliness* Philip Slater argues that the United States has persisted in the use of genocide as a military tactic, again in an undeclared war, as recently as the 1960s in its aerial bombardment of Vietnam. Such military actions, Slater charges, constituted a genocide against all Vietnamese and had to constitute this, since the sophistication of "cluster bombs" destroyed life, Vietcong and otherwise, in swaths a mile long and a quarter-mile wide.

The logical implications of Slater's assessment, however, suggest that the nature of modern warfare itself is genocidal, since the Allied bombing of Europe was hardly confined to Nazis.

As practiced by the Nazis, however, the totalitarian use of genocide appears different, more deliberate because of its propaganda, and more pervasively insidious because of the organizational methods, especially gassings and the use of ovens, which were accomplished in camps rather than on battlefields.

Even if modern warfare makes all nations accomplices in genocide, my opening question becomes oddly more rather than less insistent: Why won't the Nazis *stay* dead? Snodgrass begins his cycle of poems with two epigraphs. The first is from Joseph Goebbels: "Even if we lose this war, we still win, for our spirit will have penetrated the hearts of our enemies." The second is a confirmation of the first and comes from a very different source: "Mother Teresa, asked when she first began her work of relief and care for abandoned children, replied, 'On the day I discovered I had a Hitler inside me.'" Snodgrass's examination of this theme is not new. One can find the same prediction in Mailer's early fiction, in its implications that the legacies of the totalitarian mind will continue and prevail; one can find it in Marcuse's *One Dimensional Man*. And such a warning sounds throughout that most precise and least specious examination of all, Hannah Arendt's *On the Origins of Totalitarianism*.

If I drive a few hours north of where I'm writing this, to a place called Hayden Lake, Idaho, I can pass by a roadside attraction more alarming than any snake farm. For, when it is convened at Hayden Lake, there is another nation within this one, one that openly calls itself the Aryan Nation. If it has no politically sanctioned existence, it nevertheless lives frighteningly enough in the minds of its believers. No matter how ridiculously vestigial and reprehensible their ideology, no matter whether they display swastikas or scorn them, they are Nazis in mutational form, "Aryans" whose propaganda, for what it is worth, urges separatism, not genocide. How many are there in such a nation? A few hundred? More?

And how many Nazis were there when the party began? Shirer informs us that when Hitler joined them there were seven who met in a small beer garden off a Munich side street. Of course, they possessed no Uzis nor M 16s nor Berettas then. In this respect at least, they differed from their late followers at Hayden Lake.

Part of the problem with totalitarian groups is that it is difficult to take them seriously, and, in the worst of times, one doesn't feel much anxiety about them until it is too late. The same is true of the Aryan Nation, whose spokesmen, when interviewed, display such pathetic ignorance. Yet it is not astounding to learn that a dolt can assassinate someone, a radio talk show host for example, just as efficiently as a genius.

But, if the Aryan Nation does not generate much paranoia, it may be because it declares itself as racist and is so observable as to seem an almost pathetically nostalgic form of fascism.

The questions raised by the epigraphs and by the entire cycle of poems in *The Führer Bunker* is far more serious and unsettling. Hitler and his high command are dead. But their deaths seem not quite enough. The quantitative horror of their genocide demands more, and one of the questions one might legitimately ask is this: Are they extinct? Was there something even in their defeat and the destruction of Berlin, emblematizing for them the destruction of all known European bourgeois values, that constituted the seeds of their rebirth or renewal? And what forms will new totalitarianisms take? How will they mutate? Can one possibly identify all the forms of totalitarianism that even now exist? Some of these are, of course, obvious: there is the photograph of Mao (which seems doctored) swimming in the river; there is the pedestal in downtown Bucharest where the statue of Stalin once stood beside those of Marx and Lenin—his *space* now, that empty air, reminds everyone who notices it of his existence more surely than any effigy could have done. The fictionalized speculations of early Mailer and later Burroughs, Marcuse's essay on technological man, ask whether there are not hidden strains of totalitarianism, strains with sophisticated systems of adaptation, camouflage and concealment, that go unnoticed and are undetectable, like the AIDS cell duplicating a normal one. In this regard at least Snodgrass in *The Führer Bunker* is responsible enough to attempt an answer to such a question, and, if anything, his display of voices is not, as has been charged, the fulfillment of Goebbels's epigraphical prophecy, but its qualified renunciation. Snodgrass has replied to the charge in the following terms:

My poems say such more awful things about the Nazis than their enemies ever said. Goebbels predicts that the Nazi philosophy will survive, that their mythology about themselves is what will survive. I hope that what I am getting here is not the mythologized Nazis at all, but the real ones. . . .
Their awful tendencies of personality have survived, indeed, as in our desire to believe that the Germans were not human, which seems to me just like their desire to believe the Jews were not human. But Goebbels is predicting that their mythologized selves will survive. That isn't what I think. I think that, as a matter of fact, the realistic side of them is what has survived.[1]

In other words, Mailer's and Burrough's fiction indulges in paranoia in order to follow it, often enough, to its own self-devouring ends, and in this way such authors play the role of warning, but ultimately imaginative and deflecting, prophets of doom: to say it before it happens is a way of gelding it of possibility in fact, or so one might hope. But to speculate on the possibility of totalitarian hegemony in politics almost always makes one vulnerable to paranoia. The problem with paranoia is that there is really no ceiling to its potential growth, and so finally it, in itself and even in opposition to totalitarian forms, becomes a philosophical failure of nerve by which one sees a Nazi beneath every elm on the block, patches together a dubious history of lacunae in which the CIA assassinates Kennedy, and accuses the World Health Organization of developing the AIDS virus under laboratory conditions. Fact is always a casualty of paranoia, and in this regard its impaired imaginative licentiousness is more likely to resemble a product of totalitarianism than any capable antagonist of it. For the absence of fact is one of the fertile conditions for all totalitarian propaganda and conversion; as Hannah Arendt states: "its members' whole education is aimed at abolishing their capacity for distinguishing between truth and falsehood, between reality and fiction."[2] Hitler once said: "I am not here for the betterment of men; I am here to prey upon their weaknesses." And what is paranoia, even in opposition to such a man, but a symptom of being weakened by him?

Yet the totalitarian mentality does survive, partially or wholly, and *their awful tendencies of personality have survived* as well. It is interesting to think of the recent Iran or Contragate administrational use of lies and propaganda in the light of what Arendt concludes about the use of ideology by the elite in any totalitarian system: "The elite formations are distinguished from the ordinary party membership in that they . . . are not even supposed to believe in the literal truth of ideological cliches."[3] Oliver North, upon interrogation by a Senate committee, played to the cameras, to the crowds; in other words, he played past the laws of the land, demonstrating in those moments the superiority of totalitarian propaganda to legality, which had become lost in the movie in which Oliver North starred and in which the senators appeared as extras. But such an episode does not mean that a totalitarian structure has come to power in the Reagan administration; if it had, Bruce Springsteen would have felt compelled to endorse it when asked. It would seem that the alleged "failure" of American education has not interfered with the ability of the general population to smell a dead fish, if one notes this refusal by one of its *genuinely* popular representatives.

In the case of *The Führer Bunker* a reader might justifiably say to himself, "What am I supposed to feel about such monsters?" What Snodgrass rejects, early in the conception of the book, is the implicit judgment that the reader makes: that these are, in fact, "monsters;" the role the poet has taken up, in these circumstances at least, is the arduous demonstration that they are not, that they are, or were, human, and that being human is also, on occasion, a matter of being the perpetrator of evil, of a "tragedy of evil."[4] The probably inescapable element of kitsch in every modern culture is always too eager, too ready, to equate *human* with *good*. And perhaps this is why, after so many years of peeling off the layered encrustations of neurotic suffering to expose and witness the psyche, Freud, upon being asked in a letter what he thought of human beings in general, replied: "In my opinion, most of them are garbage."[5]

Another difficulty in these poems has to do with the reader's frustration upon encountering a group of lyrics that also constitute *history*, as Paul Gaston has noted. The difficulty occurs not because the reader is not used to something this new but more probably because he is no longer capable of experiencing something so *old*, for the methods of *The Führer Bunker* seem like dinosaurs when contrasted to the uses of the past that appear in Modernist texts, and I think they are meant to be so, meant to be ancient and formal and troubling—troubling because they are so unadorned by the juxtapositions wielded by any poet/priest, by spatial form or mythical method, and troubling too because the postmodernist lyric of the confessional poet is entirely absent here. For, unlike the thin veil that Prufrock was for Eliot, or the speaker of "Daddy" was for Plath, or the temporary shield that S. S. Gardons was for Snodgrass, these personae are as obdurate as Browning's, if not more so, and their devouring selves permit no one else to whisper reassuringly to us through their lips. If one comes to these poems looking for the real W. D. Snodgrass, there will be no one at home, and this absence is intentional. Snodgrass, as his own testimony insists, wanted to get "the reality" of the Nazis into the poem, a reality that constitutes not myth, but history, *record*. And to embark upon some specious dialogue with such speakers is to risk the contamination of the record, to say nothing of the risk to oneself. In concept, then, such strictures are defenses against the licentiousness of paranoia, against the impairment and limitation of imaginative act. Strangely enough, it is the kind of thing Conrad would have recognized as *restraint*. Of course, in a world that feeds habitually upon fantasies a restraint that displays for us the banality and horror of historical fact will be labeled sensationalism.

The crucial questions remain, however. Is the human tragedy of evil in these poems perceptibly and dramatically represented as human *enough*? And can history, without a violation of the available and by now unignorable facts (what one cannot possibly not know), still be transformed into poetry? If Adorno is correct in saying that "poetry after Auschwitz is a barbarous act," then is this collection meant at once to be both a renunciation of Adorno and also such a "barbarous act?"

The answer to the first question will be found not so much in the voice of Hitler, who *is* monstrous and insane here, but more often in the self-lacerating self-assessments of Goebbels, Göring, Eva Braun, Speer, and Magda Goebbels. The far more minor characters of Henrici and Weidling, generals who cling, or wish they could cling, to wholly military identities, are voices that are diminished reflections of Speer's, and in such a drama they serve much the same purpose as the chorus or the clowns of Shakespeare. However minor, they are important, for their appearance links them to traditional tragedy: their assessments of the battlefronts remind us of a world waiting outside the bunker, and their reminders are oddly comforting, for their employment here recalls to us not only a Renaissance convention but also its conception of Evil, sturdy enough and wide enough to encompass the evil we witness. For here the nature of Evil is unchanged from Shakespeare's notion of it; only its scale has undergone, in literal fact, enormous expansion. And this is, of course, the final problem for which there is no solution at all, neither in poetry nor in history.

The answer to the second question, although it may sound implausible at first, is involved with prosody itself, with *song* and with the expressive possibility of it, a possibility that can make one other than what he is even as it coerces from him a precise confession of what he has allowed himself to become.

Bound up with this is the role of the poet as craftsman, as *maker,* for his invisibility and seeming detachment, which are necessary, are in fact products of his immersion into these forms, and into the Other. Resplendent with a kind of ironic mimesis throughout, apparent first as poetic form replicating technology, where does the poet exist in *The Führer Bunker* but as a mute, voluntary victim of the Nazis in whom he must, for a while, dwell? In those instances in which the voice is neither compelling nor interesting, as in some of Speer's interior monologues, one senses, perhaps, the understandable withdrawal of that victim from his Other.

Snodgrass began his best work in opposition to some of the principles of the New Critics, and this work retains at least one congruency with that opposition: in *The Führer Bunker* the mimetic fallacy, or versions of it, rise like spring grass in a Panzer's track. Himmler's block letters on graph paper and left margin acrostics banal as the alphabet; Speer's poems that resemble shark fins or silly triangulated skyscrapers with enormous foundations like boot soles and nothing at the top, or vaults or mass graves built into the earth, colossal bunkers; all the homely odes, such as Göring's, of those who will never be poets, these examples of all that is amateurish, forlorn, and wrong, are hardly the texts that "humanize" the Nazi command; rather, they are documents abrim with self-loathing, in which a vestigial conscience, often enough reviled, assesses its own self-betrayal, its abandonment especially of choice and free will, without which there can be no possibility of human *good* and within which, since, as Hannah Arendt informs us, "there can be no radical evil," only the oldest Evil, the only one our culture has, is allowed to prevail. The discoveries these characters are permitted to make are still comparable to what Milton's Satan finds in book 4 of *Paradise Lost:* "I myself am Hell, Which way I fly is Hell." None of them have Satan's grandeur of course, and the fact that they are, by historical setting, limited to the confines of a concrete basement condominium, with the ultimate eviction notice of Allied bombs falling on the city above them, informs us of the petty scale of such a hell: to find that one has become a five-foot teninch Satan is to find the mockery of such miniaturization, one's true and final diminishment.

If the entire collection were merely an anthology of ineptitude, of amateur Nazi versification, one might dismiss it. But what explains the exquisitely perverse formal brilliance of Magda Goebbels's villanelles, the modified form itself mimetic of her mind in the act of hesitant decision, a decision that finally proclaims loyalty to Hitler only and, as such, is a betrayal literally of life itself? The final poem in the sequence finds the form both incremental and inexorable, but it is dependent upon the meditations of this third poem:

III

The children? They'll just have to come with me.
At their age, how could they find their own way?
We must preserve them from disloyalty.

They're too good for the world we all foresee.
If they were old enough, we know they'd say
It's right and just they'll have to come with me.

My father left—divorced—when I was three
So how could I leave them alone today?
We must preserve them from disloyalty.

They've been the fist behind my policy
Since Joseph and that Slav girl ran astray;
It's right and just they'll have to come with me.

I slammed his door on him. "Of course you're free.
It's time they learned who cares and who'll betray."
We must preserve them from disloyalty.

My father came; he said Joseph would be
Ruin to us all. I turned him away.
It's right and just they'll have to come with me.

He begged to visit them. He will not see
Them till he dies. That's just the price he'll pay.
We must preserve them from disloyalty
And this false world. They'll have to come with me.

IV

You try to spare them the worst misery;
Who knows what cold force they'd be subject to?
How could we let them fall to treachery,

Disgrace, to brute foes? At the best, they'd see
Scorn in the face of every Red or Jew.
You try to spare them the worst misery.

In evil days, models of constancy
Are the one thing that will still see men through.
How could we let them fall to treachery

When they've once known our Leader? Yet if He,
If we go, just how many could stay true?
You try to spare them the worst misery

Of wanting this, that. From our own past, we
Know things they might have to say or do.
How could we let them fall to treachery,

To making base terms with an enemy,
Denying us and our best ideals, too?
You try to spare them the worst misery

But they'd still want to live. What if they'd be
Happy—they could prove all we thought untrue.
How could we let them fall to treachery
And their own faults? You end their misery.

The only survival of any possibly redeeming relativistic approach occurs in the irony of her questions and pathetic assertions: "In evil days, models of constancy / Are the one thing that
will see men through. / How could we let them fall to treachery
// When they've once known our Leader?" Throughout this
poem, and throughout the poems of the entire cycle, the horror
is that of a possible betrayal: "But they'd still want to live. What
if they'd be / Happy—they could prove all we thought untrue."
It is this denunciation of all futures, all possible flux and change,
that most characterizes her, and *relativism* itself is martyred here
for a spurious, delusional immortality.

The coercive possibilities of form are even more evident in
the actual murder of the children, where the triple and envelope rhymes in the eight line tetrameter stanzas, undercut by
the truncating three stress accentual lines in the fourth and final
positions, underscore the finality of the decision. This finality
is further reinforced by the almost primerlike mode of the
poem, its childlike style relieving even its speaker of existential
freedom:

MAGDA GOEBBELS

—30 April 1945

*(After Dr. Haase gave them shots of morphine, Magda gave each child an ampule
of potassium cyanide from a spoon.)*

This is the needle that we give
Soldiers and children when they live
Near the front in primitive
    Conditions or real dangers;
This is the spoon we use to feed
Men trapped in trouble or in need,
When weakness or bad luck might lead
    Them to the hands of strangers.

This is the room where you can sleep
Your sleep out, curled up under deep
Layers of covering that will keep
    You safe till all harm's past.
This is the bed where you can rest
In perfect silence, undistressed
By noise or nightmares, as my breast
    Once held you soft but fast.

This is the Doctor who has brought
Your needle with your special shot
To quiet you; you won't get caught
    Off guard or unprepared.
I am your nurse who'll comfort you;
I nursed you, fed you till you grew
Too big to feed; now you're all through
    Fretting or feeling scared.

This is the glass tube that contains
Calm that will spread down through your veins
To free you finally from all pains
    Of going on in error.
This tiny pinprick sets the germ
Inside you that fills out its term
Till you can feel yourself grow firm
    Against all doubt, all terror.

Into this spoon I break the pill
That stiffens the unsteady will
And hardens you against the chill
    Voice of a world of lies.
This amber medicine implants
Steadfastness in your blood; this grants
Immunity from greed and chance,
    And from all compromise.

This is the serum that can cure
Weak hearts; these pure, clear drops insure
You'll face what comes and can endure
    The test; you'll never falter.
This is the potion that preserves
You in a faith that never swerves;

This sets the pattern of your nerves
    Too firm for you to alter.

I set this spoon between your tight
Teeth, as I gave you your first bite;
This satisfies your appetite
    For other nourishment.
Take this on your tongue; this do
Remembering your mother who
So loved her Leader she stayed true
    When all the others went,

When every friend proved false, in the
Delirium of treachery
On every hand, when even He
    Had turned His face aside.
He shut himself in with His whore;
Then, though I screamed outside His door,
Said He'd not see me anymore.
    They both took cyanide.

Open wide, now, little bird;
I who sang you your first word
Soothe away every sound you've heard
    Except your Leader's voice.
Close your eyes, now; take your death.
Once we slapped you to take breath.
Vengeance is mine, the Lord God saith
    And cancels each last choice.

Once, my first words marked out your mind;
Just as our Leader's phrases bind
All hearts to Him, building a blind
    Loyalty through the nation,
We shape you into a pure form.
Trapped, our best soldiers tricked the storm,
The Reds: those last hours, they felt warm
    Who stood fast to their station.

You needn't fear what your life meant;
You won't curse how your hours were spent;
You'll grow like your own monument

To all things sure and good,
Fixed like a frieze in high relief
Of granite figures that our Chief
Accepts into His true belief,
  His true blood-brotherhood.

You'll never bite the hand that fed you,
Won't turn away from those that bred you,
Comforted your nights and led you
  Into the thought of virtue;
You won't be turned from your own bed;
Won't turn into that thing you dread;
No new betrayal lies ahead;
  Now no one else can hurt you.

In this sort of derangement murder is alchemy; murder is pres-
ervation; small corpses are the statuary left in the wake of the
Third Reich. That they are seen in this way, that Magda Goebbels
actually *did* this, that the mass murder of her own children stands
in microcosmic relation to the Holocaust and exists as one of the
small, horrible curios of history, is Snodgrass's exhaustive display
of delusion in which the "reality," rather than the "mythology," of
the Nazis becomes increasingly obvious.

The critical point here is whether this reality has not already
been far too obvious to mention, or, in Stern's phrase: "But
they're Nazis . . . *Nazis!*" What such a cycle demands is what
length in any work always and inevitably demands: either narra-
tive or drama. Here the narrational aspect, while not absent, is
clearly limited by the time and place in which the voices speak.
The pure *action* of *The Führer Bunker* poems more or less follows
Trevor-Roper's account of it in his 1947 study, *The Last Days of
Hitler.*[6] The principal plot revolves around betrayal and the threat
of betrayal by Göring, Himmler, and others. But the drama, the
kind of interior change and suffering that at least a few important
characters undergo, is something quite different and is finally the
only redemptive value posited by such poems. For, if the nihil-
ism mutating into Evil here prevents any human knowledge of
what it is, then in fact there is the possibility that the world,
which is always and finally the tormented human psyche rather
than the Russian front in these poems, will come to nothing. It
may come to nothing anyway, but the central dramatic question
is whether one can know it as it does so. The themes of the
betrayal of life and the brief triumph of Evil and of its goal,

"nothing," are nowhere as ironically clear as they are in Eva Braun's testimony, shortly after her marriage to Hitler. Shortly after this meditation, of course, she will, since character and the timidity of character is still Fate, join Hitler in suicide. But she will not die as the obsequious bimbo of the Third Reich; she will die with awareness of what she has married. The intimation here that she can, and has, confronted such terrible knowledge is, if consciousness is a value in itself, reprehensibly redemptive.

EVA ß HITLER, GEB. BRAUN

—30 April 1945

(After her improvised civil wedding and the brief reception, Eva sits on the bed in her room alone. Hitler has gone with Traudl Junge, his secretary, to dictate his will before their mutual deaths in a few hours. Fragments of the Mass and the formal Catholic marriage service run through her mind.)

Consummatum est.

It is accomplished.
   My mother's will be done.
                        Is done.

         The Dodd Girl, the Valkyrie,
         Ley's wife, Geli above all—
              how many died
      so I could carry her
         His name. When we were kids
            we looked at the eclipse
   through snapshot negatives. They held
      their longing up to Him; their sight
            flashed out. Twice
      I tried to kill myself.

                  To Thee do we cry, poor banished
                        children of Eve.

      At the photographer's I called Him
         "Herr Wolf"; we met
            disguised. Later,
      He'd slip me an envelope
   with enough to live on. Never
      a love note; never a word

in public. I sat at my dresser
kissing His picture through glass;
in April weather, the sun
outside my windows
sneered at me. We drove
to the Munich Station; His train
had gone; all we saw
was tail lights. He
was never there. Only my first "suicide"
brought Him in. Tonight
the third. This one
for dead sure.

What God hath joined together
let no man put asunder.

A boy, He wouldn't listen
to the priest; they'd find Him
catching sunlight
in a pocket mirror, playing it
around the trees, the courtyard. Even now
He has gone off with Traudl
to dictate His will. Since He cannot
have His will. He leaves me
this concession
I once was:
my crossed-out name, my
new name on a piece of paper:
Eva ß Hitler, geb. Braun.

Therefore shall a man leave father
and mother and cleave to his wife.
They shall be one flesh.

And even if He came, He
would be missing; He
would not hear me. I
could look through Him
like a worn-out lantern slide. The priest
held up the monstrance
they said held the Host
before the people, right and left,
while we cast down our eyes. But one day I

crept up in the empty chapel,
      to the holy case. There
the sacred vestments, the gold
        chains, the monstrance
        rayed out gleaming
like the May sun. And in the
      center, the tiny glass bead,
      I could see nothing.
      Nothing.

And yet I have these albums, these
      pictures proving it all so.
    We danced together; we
  sat together over tea; even
    the wedding ceremony . . .
          My grandmother's brocade—
I left it at the mountain;
I had to wear my long black taffeta.
    This ring delivered for me
  by the Gestapo . . .
I am black but beautiful
    ye daughters of Jerusalem.

                With this ring I thee wed;
                This gold and silver I thee bring.

. . . this ring torn off some Jew's hand.

in templo sancto tuo in Jerusalem.

      I am the Black Bride that will be
      devoured, that will pass
    down into Him like used water
    down a drain, a film stuck,
    burning through, or reeling
      back into itself.
    Like all the women, all
    the foreigners, our beautiful
young men—all small
    as red ants under
the magnifying glass
    He reads His maps by.

Consummatum est.

To be so soon consumed and
never consummated.

O Thou who hast created
all things out of nothing . . .

Now each one has the nothing
they fought for. We have earned
our deaths. And yet,
my mother, not even she
would will me this. She only wants
it all to mean
her meaning. Something instead
of life. To tell the neighbors.
And that I give her. She
can rest.

Ite. Missa est.

My mother's will be mine.
Is
mine.

It is accomplished.

Such testimony, because her interior monologue is hardly like the high style of Faulkner or Beckett, can be overlooked. But it should not be, for the modesty of her unraised voice is a dramatic climax and the acceptance of despair; as such, it shows us most clearly, without falsification of character, the trait and earmarks of tragedy. For this bride and suicide is falling from a high place, not because she is Hitler's wife but because she is at this point taking leave of all she once was, a common but still potentially valuable product of bourgeois European culture. But by joining Hitler she has joined one who seems to have been faith and culture's nemesis from an early age: "A boy, He wouldn't listen / to the priest; they'd find Him / catching sunlight / in a pocket mirror, playing it / around the trees, the courtyard. . . ." It is Hitler's oedipal jealousy, not only familial but projected to all fathers, any *authoritas* (Shirer informs us that his hatred of Jews began in Vienna as a sexual jealousy of what he saw as their prowess with young Austrian women), that becomes the devouring Evil, the kind of fantasy of burning the world with a pocket mirror and of deflecting the attention of a congregation, in the muteness of childhood, with a silent and distracting light. And so in the chapel, in the monstrance becoming tiny glass bead Eva peers into, she discovers the result of her loyalty to Hitler: "I see nothing. Nothing." Like Conrad's Kurtz, there will be nothing left of such a child but a "voice," in which beliefs and values have become mere expediency.

One can recall, in this context, Richard III, who carries a looking glass so that he might see his shadow as he passes. Like Hitler's boyhood mirror, it is a device of distortion and abnegation of all but the devouring Self. In such a conception the inexorable nature of Evil allows that Self one activity only, the destruction of the world, or of its order, its culture, its "restraint." Conrad's diminishingly modest term is sadly definitive in the more modern, uncrownable context. Quite logically, Evil, both literally and metaphorically in the *Bunker,* reaches its end in the devouring even of itself, or of those hosts for whom it has become the overwhelming parasite; when the psyches it feeds upon are gone it also must vanish.

All that is *not* Nothing, all that is the inheritance of culture, informs Hannah Arendt in her identification of such Evil:

It is inherent in our entire philosophical tradition that we cannot conceive of a "radical evil," and this is true both for Christian theology, which conceded even to the Devil himself a celestial origin, as well as for Kant, the only philosopher who, in the word he coined for it, at least must have suspected the existence of this evil even though he immediately rationalized it in the concept of a "perverted ill will" that could be explained by comprehensible motives. Therefore, we actually have nothing to fall back on in order to understand a phenomenon that nevertheless confronts us with its overpowering reality and breaks down all standards we know. There is only one thing that seems to be discernible: we may say that radical evil has emerged in connection with a system in which all men have become equally superfluous. The manipulators of this system believe in their own superfluousness as much as in that of all others, and the totalitarian murderers are all the more dangerous because they do not care if they themselves are alive or dead, if they ever lived or never were born. [7]

The Nazis form that final nihilism, then, in which even the instinct for physical self-preservation is absent. This is why Kurtz and Hitler are voices, not bodies. And to lack a body, or to despise it for its mortality, is to speak posthumously in the present. Such incarnations are not the triumph of any private mythology nor of philosophy either; they are errors. To the extent that such errors are allowed to grow into systems they can become large errors, as Arendt suggests above, and an enormous *quantitative* increase (the Holocaust), becomes, as Marx noted, a qualitative, phenomenological change. Arendt identifies the prerequisite conditions for such a change, or "radical evil," in specific terms: "The concentration camps are the laboratories where changes in human nature are tested, and their shamefullness therefore is not just the business of their inmates and those who run them according to strict 'scientific' standards; it is the concern of all men."[8]

Yet even the "emergence of a radical evil" has its origin in prior manifestations of Evil and in the concept of Evil. It is ironic that in a cycle of speeches from those who are presumably supermen, iconoclastic toward all bequeathed values, the recognition of the contagion of "Nothing" and its infestation is so clearly traditional, even bourgeois.

REICHSMARSCHALL HERMANN GÖRING

—23 April 1945

(After the conference of April 20, Hitler's birthday, Göring drove south to Berchtesgaden with a convoy of forty vehicles. Having set up headquarters there, he imagines the splendors of his erstwhile parties.)

Dear friends, the moment's come to ask
What lies beneath the glittering gear
And costumes radiantly displayed
At the Reichsmarschall's masquerade;
Find who romanced and danced us here,
To face the face behind the mask.

Who can adapt to each new role
And change costumes so cunningly
With each day's new conditions that
He wears a lantern on his hat
When he must run downstairs to see
The man who comes delivering coal?

Whose self-made uniform asserts
Clear blue, horizon to horizon,
Like azure skies no enemy

Dares invade; where instead we see
Medals like close-drilled stars bedizen
An ever-expanding universe?

Who wears this tent-sized dressing gown
All day, bought forty business suits
So he could change each hour or two
For fear his sour sweat might soak through?
Is this our famous Puss-in-Boots
Or just some knock-down, drag-out clown?

Who steps up now to the forefront
Wearing this pair of lederhosen,
A dagger tucked in his wide belt
And rough-cut vest from a deer's pelt
To signify himself the chosen
Chief of Reich Forests and the Hunt.

Who flaunts this frilly satin blouse,
These velvet knickerbockers, that
Alluring jacket of green suede
And in such fluff and frou-frou played
The true effete aristocrat,
The idle lord of an old house?

Who wears this modern well-ironed version
Of a toga he must hope dangles
Over his circular abdomen
Like an Athenian lord or Roman,
But with his nail paint, rouge and bangles
Looks more like some debauched Persian?

Who, at the Fuehrer's staff confab,
Accused of crimes just short of treason,
Got Hitler's leave to flee Berlin
And drive south, while he stood there in
The smartest fashion note this season:
Garb of American olive-drab?

Who wears this thick flesh, layer on layer—
Loose outposts of a weakening heart?
Who seems a one-man population
Explosion, or expanding nation,

Then, at the showdown, gives you a start:
He lifts his mask and no one's there.

Göring, who finds himself a betrayer of Hitler as well as a betrayer of himself and all possible choices, focuses his self-loathing portrait upon the style, the costumes, the adornments of Nazism that cover and camouflage his own absence: "He lifts his mask and no one's there." All the concrete specificity of the "glittering gear," the satins, velvets, lederhosen, ironed togas, display the obsessions of the fetishist, the fascination with what *encloses* mythology but is not the mythology. It appears as if their insignias, their style, has outlived (except for the American Nazi party and the Aryan Nation) any specific ideology of the Third Reich. As Susan Sontag has noted in "Fascinating Fascism," the style, the black leather boots and jackets of the Nazis, has survived and attained a kind of popularity that has nothing to do with Nazism but with the sexual theater of sadism and masochism, which values spectacle and the frankness of an extreme sexuality for the purposes of staging it; its thrill is the manner in which eros and thanatos combine, especially when witnessed by an audience, however imaginary. Such a style is hardly the proclamation of fascism, for the insignias mock the rigidity of their inventors, mock whoever strolls past in ox-blood Bass Wejuns, and mock, lightly, the wearer also: For what is the value of such knowledge of the sensual except that it must be repeated, with variations, endlessly? Like any form of *ecstasis,* it wants no results, no production, no generative future; appearing to have leapt parentless into the adornment of the viciously cool, it has no need of politics and therefore proclaims its estrangement with the world's conditions, its neutrality toward them. Like the little carved *X*'s on the forehead of Charlie Manson's "girls," these are costumes meant to take one *out* of this world as most people experience it.

If Snodgrass demonstrates at some length that what survives of the Nazis is their realistic side, and if their mythological dimension is revealed as delusion either by *The Origins of Totalitarianism* or *The Producers,* why has Snodgrass ended his collection with a restatement of theme by Goebbels?

DR. JOSEPH GOEBBELS

—1 May 1945, 1800 hours

(The day after Hitler's death, Goebbels and his wife climbed the steps into the garden where both committed suicide.)

Say goodbye to the help, the ranks
Of Stalin-bait. Give too much thanks
To Naumann—Magda's lover: we
Thank him for *all* his loyalty.
Schwaegermann; Rach. After a while
Turn back to them with a sad smile:
We'll save them trouble—no one cares
Just now to carry us upstairs.

Turn away; check your manicure;
Pull on your gloves. Take time; make sure
The hat brim curves though the hat's straight.
Give her your arm. Let the fools wait;
They act like they've someplace to go.
Take the stairs, now. Self-control. Slow.
A slight limp; just enough to see,
Pass on, and infect history.

The rest is silence. Left like sperm
In a stranger's gut, waiting its term,
Each thought, each step lies; the roots spread.
They'll believe in us when we're dead.
When we took "Red Berlin" we found
We always worked best underground.
So; the vile body turns to spirit
That speaks soundlessly. They'll hear it.

How much importance, dramatic importance, should be at-
tached to the sequential placement of the poem here, as finale to
the cycle? Is it meant as the poet's warning, as his way of assum-
ing the role of a deflecting prophet of doom? In this possibility,
saying the prophecy, especially in the voice of a diminished per-
sona, would be to preempt it from happening in fact and in a
future. Or is this simply a signal that the poet has himself be-
come overwhelmed by the persona he inhabits and therefore his
own voice has become muted and gloved with another's? The
second, mocking possibility, with poet as deflecting seer, seems
most likely if one examines what Goebbels says here. Of course,
he and others of the Nazi high command "will pass on, and
infect history." But hasn't history always been infected in such a
way by tyrants? And haven't those past infections vanished
through the world's forgetfulness? It is difficult to get very upset
about Genghis Khan now. Furthermore, that Goebbels speaks

Hamlet's last words in ironic and reprehensible appropriation is simply true to his character, a character limited by what he has allowed himself to become, through loyalty and an indifference he mistakes for freedom. And, if the "vile" body turns to spirit, it turns into none other than what it has already been found to be, the disembodied voice of Hitler or Kurtz. Certainly it will be heard, though this does not ensure it an audience. In fact, it seems more probable that an audience for Kurtz's and Marlow's and Conrad's fabulation of evil may exist far longer than one devoted to the historical fact of Hitler.

This is a problem of some dramatic proportion here. Unlike Iago or other fictionalized villains, whose evils spring from individual blights upon their psyches, Hitler and others of the high command take up evil as indiscriminately and single-mindedly as feeding sharks or as vanished gods taking sides on a battlefield in the interest of sport or revenge. And they remain just as alien to us as either. For the Nazis, by institutionalizing evil, by making a system out of it, and an impersonal pursuit, became one-dimensional "supermen"—that is, they became boring, and not a little of their banality finds its way into this dissection of their "realistic side." Even Hitler's guide to kinky sex, in one of his speeches, is not shocking in its testimony to sexual degradation, although, if his character were mixed with anything else except this sort of unrelieved, monomaniacal ill will, it might be both shocking and interesting. That his character is not capable of providing more is an obstinate historical fact.

And now it seems proper to recall Stern's rejoinder: "But they're Nazis, Larry, *Nazis!*" The best clarification of Stern's emphatic insistence upon this is clear from one of Arendt's concluding paragraphs, and what she notes there suggests a quite large and immovable obstacle for any reader of these poems:

> Until now the totalitarian belief that everything is possible seems to have proved only that everything can be destroyed. Yet, in their effort to prove that everything is possible, totalitarian regimes have discovered without knowing it that there are crimes which men can neither punish nor forgive. When the impossible was made possible it became the unpunishable, unforgiveable absolute evil which could no longer be understood and explained by the evil motives of self-interest, greed, covetousness, resentment, lust for power, cowardice; and which therefore anger could not revenge, love could not endure, friendship could not forgive. Just as the victims in the

death factories or the holes of oblivion are no longer "human" in the eyes of their executioners, so this newest species of criminals is beyond the pale even of solidarity in human sinfulness.[9]

It is alarming to note that at this time Arendt herself feels the need to enclose the word *human* in quotation marks. But nowhere does Arendt say that this "newest species" is not human; she says that it is beyond the pale of "human sinfulness." Do the members of the death squads in El Salvador and the Marines at My Lai qualify for membership in this newest club? But the Holocaust was a quantitative horror, and participation in a single atrocity does not move one beyond the pale of human sinfulness—it moves one deeply into it. When Snodgrass maintains that the Nazis in fact were human, and writes a book that is both poetry and history in demonstration of this, he insists upon a reappraisal of what it is to be human.

The task for Snodgrass, in which the imagination license is narrowed, and in which it must pace the cage of the speaker's psychic confines, is difficult, and the overall dramatic conception becomes crucial. For had he included only Hitler, Göring, Goebbels, Himmler, and Borman in such a history, it would be an aberration rather than a diminished tragedy of evil. But throughout the form of the book testifies to the conceptual ability of tragedy to confront these men, and it does so, just as Renaissance tragedy could do, by providing us with others, with perspectives, with degrees of conscience and Reason apparent in the voices of Eva Braun, Speer, Heinrici, and other officers—all of whom remind the reader of that other and larger world lying outside the bunker, a world sturdy enough, perhaps, to withstand the madness inside it.

A further difficulty is apparent in all this because historical fact remains immutable throughout the cycle. In such history fact becomes ethical necessity, and the poet, rather than offering a specious compromise in which one can consign these Nazis to the category of monsters and/or oblivion, assumes a troubling role. For what really irritates the reader is the lack here of discursive comfort, of answers, of a poet who refuses to enter the fabric of the whole in any lyrical, explanatory way at all. Therefore, the reader finally participates in the sort of ugly awe that "anger could not revenge, love could not endure, friendship could not forgive." Snodgrass simply isn't there, as Pound is sometimes absent, and this too is part of the book's examination, its way of prolongedly wondering whether "poetry after Auschwitz is a barbaric act."

The violation that the Nazis perpetrated upon the Jews, the fact that they could do it and therefore behave as if humans, other humans, were superfluous, is the central act of the century. Therefore, such poetry brings with it an implicit historical justification, and Snodgrass's *Bunker* can be critically defended for any number of reasons. It is obviously an important book, not only because of the events it takes up but also because of the genius of its author. But finally, if the end is somehow difficultly in the beginning, the origins of these poems, as related by Paul Gaston, are revealing:

> The most immediate impetus for *The Führer Bunker* may have come, however, from two experiences Snodgrass had while participating in panel discussions. As a member of one panel, he found himself with Allen Ginsberg and LeRoi Jones (now Imamu Amiri Baraka). Snodgrass recalls the experience vividly: "They were calling me every filthy name and talking about what a rotten fascist I was and how dreadful and horrible." When the moderator attempted to restore order by asking the panel to articulate what they thought wrong with American civilization, Jones pointed to Snodgrass and said, "He's what's wrong with American civilization." Snodgrass's reaction? "What a compliment!" I started thinking about that and decided: if only it were true! If one could identify with *all* that evil, he ought to be one hell of a poet. And I suppose the *Bunker* is one way to try that.[10]

Why? An identification with "all that evil" need not make anyone "one hell of a poet" nor even a better poet. The same is true of an identification with the "good." Snodgrass continues in this notion, however, by saying: "being willing to identify with what you think is evil is perhaps what is most crucial to the making of a work of art that has some kind of breadth."[11] But isn't breadth made greater through a renunciation of either kind of one-sided identification, as it appears in Keats's *Odes* or in much of Wordsworth's *Prelude* or in Yeats's notion of a radical innocence after the experience of maturity? I believe that *The Führer Bunker* may be Snodgrass's large, Hardyesque gesture of "taking a long look at the worst" before that later breadth is fully achieved. For, despite the admiration I feel for the uncompromising concealment of the lyrical self, for the submergence, however rancorously undertaken, of that Self into muteness in these poems, the absence here of the poet of *Heart's Needle, Remains,* and *After Experience* is a palpable loss. And what is the mute immersion of the Self into the Other, into personae, good for unless it is a promise, after all the chorusing of carcasses here, of its buoyancy and resurfacing in another embodiment?

If the Nazis in their systemization of evil have made evil more ubiquitously possible in this age, especially under totalitarian regimes, and if these poems are demonstrations of the banality of evil, of its limited nature, of the horror and boredom that it has begun to elicit from us as its later surviving witnesses, then, in the poetry at least, the problem of the mimetic fallacy remains. And the anxiety that has led Snodgrass, after the modest exhibitionism of his early and enduring work, to abandon the lyric and its tensions, no matter how rancorous and shrewd his reasons for doing so, allowing this evil to be displayed in its pure state, unrelieved by Reason, produce here, as a curious by-product of the poet's absence, a lack of tension. In such a cycle the reader has the reality of the Nazis, but only by a careful reading of the irony in their voices is he aware of that spirit, manifested here as the intrigue of form that allows each voice to indict itself, which opposed and defeated them, and did so not because of any inherent virtue it had, but out of simple and terrifying necessity. I am afraid that the invisibility of the poet in this cycle will be mistaken for a mimetic fallacy, and for what has been called a "humanizing" of the Nazis, especially by a careless reader who will miss the irony of this work. If one can learn anything from the history of World War II, it is this: one does not compromise with Nazis. The poet who willingly goes into their voices, dwells there to dissect and destroy them with their own words, is not compromising with them and is not compromised by them. But I would advise him that, with his task finished, he ought to get out of this bunker as fast as he can.

NOTES

1. Paul Gaston, *W. D. Snodgrass* (Boston: Twayne, 1978), 154.
2. Hannah Arendt, *Origins of Totalitarianism* (New York: Harcourt, Brace, 1951), 385.
3. Arendt, *Origins,* 384.
4. Gaston, *W. D. Snodgrass,* 147.
5. Ernest Becker, *Denial of Death* (New York: Free Press, 1973), 256.

6. Gaston, *W. D. Snodgrass*, 144.
7. Arendt, *Origins*, 459.
8. Arendt, *Origins*, 458.
9. Arendt, *Origins*, 459.
10. Gaston, *W. D. Snodgrass*, 146–47.
11. Gaston, *W. D. Snodgrass*, 147.

PART SIX *Anecdotal Essays*

DONALD HALL

Seasoned Wood

W. D. Snodgrass won the Pulitzer Prize for *Heart's Needle* in 1960. Perhaps, in the memorable language of Richard Nixon, he peaked too soon. When he brought out his second collection, *After Experience* (1968), although it was a better book, it received less attention. *The Führer Bunker* of 1977 was sometimes denounced by strategies of misreading. Ten years ago it was commonplace, in summary accounts of contemporary verse, to blame Snodgrass for the abuses of confessional poetry. Thus are the sins of the third generation visited upon the progenitors. One must admit that *Heart's Needle*, with its miseries of divorce and child loss, started things: Robert Lowell credited his Iowa pupil Snodgrass with showing him the way to *Life Studies*.

Perhaps Snodgrass's *Selected Poems 1957–1987*, beautifully produced by Soho, will find this paleo-conservative new readers among the young, as younger poets look to rhyme and meter again: for Snodgrass is a master of prosody. His meters are flabbergasting and multiple, counting whatever can be counted. Within these meters, and without them, when he tries a poem free of number, his rhythms are resolute and expressive. He begins with the noise of the 1950s, "Stone lips to the unspoken cave," but continues to explore the thousand things available to formal genius, like this stanza that ends "Lobsters in the Window":

> I should wave back, I guess.
> But still in his permanent clench
> He's fallen back with the mass
> Heaped in their common trench
> Who stir, but do not look out
> Through the rainstreaming glass,
> Hear what the newsboys shout,
> Or see the raincoats pass.

The first half of this essay (slightly revised) reviewed *Selected Poems 1957–1987* in the *Partisan Review*, Summer 1988. Reprinted by permission of the author.

This poem, from *After Experience,* I would submit to any skeptical eye; the title poem is another.

Snodgrass is one of nature's rhymers. No one in this century has used rhyme so structurally or so semantically or with more serious wit. From the beginning he made rhyme on the offstress, demanding distortion for meter's necessity: "The hills, the little houses, the costumes" rhymes with "A tourist whispering through the priceless rooms." He rhymes vowels, consonants, dissyllables; he rhymes impossible words with his ear's exactness. Does rhyme lead him to song or song to rhyme? Elizabethan song is audible in early poems, Provençal in later; one remembers that Snodgrass has spent years making rhymed translations (of songs) according to original impossible schemes.

At the start his poetry recounts personal loss and betrayal. Loss and betrayal continue but turn general as Snodgrass perceives human error (selfishness, treachery, deception, narcissism, murder) first in himself and then in everybody. Appropriately, the personal situates itself in the historical—so does the historical. Behind the intimate *Heart's Needle* is Korea; behind the objective or historical *Führer Bunker* is Vietnam. His vision of humanity, bleaker than Calvin's, accounts for some nervous rejections of his work. His work is hard to take.

Hardest is *The Führer Bunker,* in which Hitler himself, Eva Braun, Goebbels, Göring, Himmler, and the rest of the cast speak poetic monologues during the last days of the Reich. This poetry of outrage continually reaches past shock to obscenity, making a catalog of sin like Dante's Hell without a Purgatory, much less a Paradise. The fundamental vision, constantly misread, damns not merely *them*—Germans or Nazis *out there*—but the viciousness we share with them. In no way does Snodgrass let these people off his hook: we find it offensive that we feel the same hook caught in our own jaw.

His protagonists defend themselves, of course, consciously by evasion and rationalizing, unconsciously by splitting attention: indentations in some monologues present minds wandering distractedly among topics and obsessions, most powerfully Eva Braun's soliloquy when she keeps hearing "Tea for Two." Then there is Hitler's monologue, which zigs and zags from a description of coprophagy to immediate perceptions to plans for suicide and to sentimental memory of "the cake my mother made me . . ." (!)

Form buys speech back. Against expressive evil Snodgrass builds tight grids of shape; the grid itself turns expressive—

reflexive, ironic—when Himmler fits his self-justificatory blather onto graph paper. Magda Goebbels poisons her children in ninety-six lines of rhymed stanzas mimicking children's verse. The conflict form engenders is itself obscene, obscenity doubling obscenity with fierce energy to construct a murderous cradle song:

> This is the needle that we give
> Soldiers and children when they live
> Near the front in primitive
>   Conditions or real dangers;
> This is the spoon we use to feed
> Men trapped in trouble or in need,
> When weakness or bad luck might lead
>   Them to the hands of strangers.
>
> This is the room where you can sleep
> Your sleep out, curled up under deep
> Layers of covering that will keep
>   You safe till all harm's past.
> This is the bed where you can rest
> In perfect silence, undistressed
> By noise or nightmares, as my breast
>   Once held you soft but fast.

Long overdue, the *Selected Poems* (overselected; too little from *Heart's Needle*) gathers work out of print, poems printed in small editions, poems never before collected. The final section comes as a relief, more grid and song than pain—though injustice and suffering remain the song's burden. Finally, Snodgrass's poems exemplify and affirm endurance despite the horror of things. In some later poems the poet praises birds that keep on singing and trees that live on, seasoned wood and the people who season it.

Thus (with a few changes), I reviewed W. D. Snodgrass's *Selected Poems* for *Partisan Review* in 1988. In the meantime I kept an eye open for other reviews. In the *New York Times Book Review* Snodgrass had some luck. Reviewer was an English poet named Gavin Ewart, able to recognize skill when it clobbered him on the head. In mockery of facts and lists—but in real admiration—Ewart called Snodgrass one of the six best living poets. Because Americans cannot tell when an Englishman is joking, his publishers could advertise that the *New York Times Book Review* called Snodgrass "one of the six best living poets."

In the *Hudson Review* Robert McDowell came to Snodgrass afresh, as if for the first time, dazzled by what he found. This man, he said, is better than Lowell! Wayne Koestenbaum wrote a good review for the *Village Voice,* Bruce Bawer in *Book World;* otherwise, I've not seen the reviews I hoped for: reparations corrective of a rotten consensus. In 1988 reviewing is the scandal of poetry in America. Or maybe *judgment* is: the 1987 prizes came and went with no attention to Snodgrass. "We gave him the Pulitzer in 1961; what more does he want?" I know what I want: critical recognition of his priority as well as his excellence.

In 1954 I took a fellowship in writing at a university out west, one free year with no academic work, no grades or diplomas, time for writing. In a small way I devoted the time to editing as well, for halfway through 1953 I had become poetry editor of the *Paris Review;* in early issues I printed Geoffrey Hill, Robert Bly, and Thom Gunn. I tried to remain alert for new poets, especially (after two years in England) the best Americans of my own generation. Eventually, I wrote letters to strangers whom I admired as I read them: W. D. Snodgrass, James Wright, W. S. Merwin, Louis Simpson. They sent poems; some became friends.

First was W. D. Snodgrass. Toward the end of my fellowship year I read manuscripts submitted by poets applying for the grant a year hence. Here I found W. D. Snodgrass, whose poems took all my attention, early things later printed in *Heart's Needle.* The marriage of form and energy enraptured me. It was a time in American poetry when form meant rhymed iambic and everybody could do it. Merely scanning and rhyming, after all, is no harder than riding a bicycle—and no more artistic. For seven years I had admired Lowell's driving couplets from *Lord Weary* and lost my breath to Wilbur's gymnastics of stanza; more recently, I had appreciated the elegant but thinner performances of young Merrill and Hecht. In 1954 Snodgrass's skill put him quickly into the category of these poets—but he was no imitator, and he went places that they couldn't or didn't choose to go. He was darker than anyone except Lowell, even before he found (in the lyrics of "Heart's Needle") the tone or subject area that revolutionized poetry—and that allowed his teacher the major swerve of *Life Studies.*

Let me look at *Life Studies* and *Heart's Needle* from the other side, from the vantage of the 1940s, not the 1980s. The confessional *frisson* was to hear poets revealing conventionally discreditable or politely unmentionable things about themselves. I read at the Mandrake Bookstore (memory claims) an issue of *Partisan Review* with lines from our poet of classical allusion: "Tamed by *Miltown*, we lie on mother's bed. . . ." Nobody younger can imagine the shock. This poetry was personal in a way that did not resemble John Donne, Hart Crane, T. S. Eliot, Emily Dickinson, or John Keats. Wordsworth and Whitman had frequently confessed—to virtue, sensitivity, and imagination. In *Heart's Needle* the personal was intimate, miserable, and uncomplacent. In later years confessional poetry too often turned into a narcissistic whine, into scab scratching, into the complaint that the world was not more indulgent. Clearly, we enjoy hearing complaint; especially we enjoy disapproving of the brutes, rapists, and Fascists whom we darkly connect to our parents. Even in the best confessional work readers entertain complacency because the violence, hatred, and self-hatred happens outside them in another recognizably neurotic person. We watch, as she told us, the Sylvia Plath Show.

If Snodgrass complains, it is not over accidental circumstances but over the corruption of the human heart, including his own heart. Nor is this lament the whole of it. Snodgrass brings together the serious fury of extreme states (whether the subject be ostensibly personal, as in *Heart's Needle,* or ostensibly historical, as in *The Führer Bunker*) with the grid or staff that Wilbur plays his tunes on. Surely no one among our poets, not Lowell nor Plath nor Wilbur nor Ginsberg, so combines the sonnet and the scream.

Snodgrass was not offered the scholarship. I asked permission to write him, to ask for poems for the *Paris Review.* Not long ago I found the letter he wrote in answer, the beginning of a conversation that has continued for thirty-five years. Long letters in red ballpoint pen came from Iowa then from Cornell. It was years before we met. Then, as it happened, we took jobs near each other, "De" at Wayne State in Detroit and I at the University of Michigan in Ann Arbor. We picnicked, we played tennis, we met at parties; I went into Detroit, De visited Ann Arbor. During these years we talked poetry but never read each other's manuscript poems.

Then our private lives turned crazy. Remarried De moved to Syracuse, and for several years my children and I stopped with him each summer, at his house in the country, spending a night en route from Michigan to New Hampshire. We ate great meals and stayed up late talking. These were years when De worked with diligence at his apprenticeships to music and to wood, concentrating (as I suppose) on grids that held the precarious world together. I recognized his brave diligence, and it served me as model. When I remarried the four of us met each summer in Stratford, Ontario, to watch plays and picnic together. This time was a peaceful interlude for De, like Europe in the summer of 1914.

After I quit teaching and returned to New Hampshire De went through another divorce and displacement and our friendship entered another moment. In recent years we have seen each other less frequently—mostly when someone asks us to read together: Bridgeport, New York, Philadelphia, Washington, Norfolk—but our correspondence has flourished. Friendship between writers is the history of literature; so much of it—appropriately enough—is friendship enacted by words on paper. We send each other poems as we work on them—and we work over each other's poems. It gets harder, as you get older, to receive from others the necessary close readings, both negative and encouraging. Old friends die off, get cranky, or become too egotistical. Some younger poets help a lot—but many either love us (which makes them useless) or hate us (which makes them worse than useless). De's work on my poems is invaluable because of his literal mind. His intimacy with what words say, with *all* the baggage they carry whether they acknowledge the load or not, provides him a Johnsonian scalpel. When his thick envelope arrives I sigh deeply before I open it, knowing that I will find inside my work's just and courteous ruin. Then I open it.

ROBERT DANA

De

S. S. Gardons. Will McConnell. Kuzma Prutkov. De. All pseud-
onyms of gifted and mischievous W. D. Snodgrass, whom I
knew briefly at the Iowa Writers' Workshop in the 1950s.

Looking back, neither the workshop nor Iowa City seem
really to fit Robert Lowell's description of them on the dust
jacket of *Heart's Needle*. Lowell thought the Midwest the "most
sterile of sterile places." But Iowa City then was not unlike most
other American towns its size. Buttoned up and buttoned down.
Stores didn't stay open after five-thirty. Most didn't open at all
on Sundays. The bars, such as they were, were ordinary, except
for Irene Kenney's, where writers tended to gather. And no one
in his right mind would ever have used the word *cuisine* to de-
scribe food cooked in any of the restaurants there. It was your
steak and mashed potatoes town. But how could a Boston nabob
appreciate that?

In fact, one night, asked at his first literary party if he'd like an
old-fashioned, one young poet (not De Snodgrass) asked, "An
old-fashioned? What's that? A sandwich?"

If one can believe Philip Levine, Iowa City had no Jews until
he arrived. (Probably untrue, but true enough.) And, despite
their heroic play on a football team eventually Rose Bowl bound
when *bowl* meant one of three, Forrest Evashevski's black play-
ers had to get their hair cut in the dorms west of the river, no
matter how powerfully they submarined tacklers or how fast
they ran the hundred.

The "Korean police action" is a phrase that catches something
of the deep ambivalence of those days. General MacArthur, be-
fore he faded away like the hero of his own barracks-room bal-
lad, had starred daily in Walt Kelly's comic strip, *Pogo*. For a
while so had badger-browed Wisconsin Senator McCarthy,

DeWitt is W. D. Snodgrass's middle name, as in "Deewitt" rather than "Duh-
witt." Thus Mr. Snodgrass is known by many of his close friends as "De,"
pronounced with a long *e*.

whose first name hardly anyone now remembers. "Deck the halls with Boston Charley!"

A blurry period blurs even more in recollection. But this is something like it.

A very, very green newcomer to the famous workshop, I remained for a very long time at a respectful distance from its old hands. And De was an old hand. He was already working there and living with his first wife Lila and their small daughter in a barracks-like apartment on Finkbine Court when William Stafford arrived. And Stafford and Flannery O'Connor had already been gone a couple of years, leaving their legends behind them when my crowd showed up. In fact, when De finally left to take a teaching position at Cornell University, he had been in Iowa for nine years, finishing two masters and working on, though never completing, a Ph.D. I remember him being called on both in the workshop and in academic courses (classics, I think) to recite Homer in ancient Greek because he had some theory about the musicality of the verse.

His natural voice was precise and musical when he read aloud, even in English. It was also high and nasally boyish and had the jingle of laughter in it. He seemed, much of the time, and without any trace of condescension, to find the heavy seriousness of his younger contemporaries pleasantly amusing. When I think of him now I seem to see him, tall and thin, arriving, right on the stroke of two in the afternoon, at the old, corrugated tin barracks that served as the workshop's classroom and general headquarters. Or arriving perhaps a few minutes late, still dressed in hospital whites.

It was part of De's singularity that, with a wife and child, his financial responsibilities were heavy enough to require a second job (teaching assistantships paid about seven hundred dollars a year then). So he'd found employment as an orderly at the V.A. Hospital, sometimes handling stiffs (see "A Flat One" and "The Operation").

I don't remember his standing out by virtue of any brilliant pronouncements during those intense critical sessions that were the bread of Wednesday afternoon workshop classes. Perhaps because he'd already experienced a lot of that kind of intensity. Visitors to the workshop before my generation of aspiring poets arrived had included Dylan Thomas, Randall Jarrell, and Robert Penn Warren. Of Jarrell, Snodgrass once remarked, "It's fun to have a 'Gee Whiz' critic now and then, especially after these austere visitors." Warren, on the other hand, had been one of the first to recognize the promise in De's early work.

For me De was both central to the mood and character of that cold war–era Workshop and, at the same time, peripheral to it. He wasn't peripheral in the way that I was. He wasn't a new-comer. He certainly wasn't unread and unschooled in the subtle-ties of his art. He wasn't remote or careful, although there was a shy side to him. I'm not sure he'd ever been an insider in the sense that his contemporaries William Belvin, Donald Justice, or Donald Petersen were—one of those who enjoyed a high rank in the pecking order. He seemed slightly off to the side. This eccen-tricity was, and still is, I think, part of what gives Snodgrass his importance. There was a sort of "Aw, c'mon! Let's get real!" reaction among us when "These Trees Stand . . ." appeared on the worksheets. " 'Snodgrass is walking through the universe'?! Man, you can't get away with that!" But, clearly, he got away with it. And wonderfully.

There may have been other reasons De seemed on the periph-ery. It's possible he'd lost favor with Paul Engle because he was uninterested in achieving his Ph.D. Perhaps his divorce, in the buttoned-down 1950s, when divorce was not the conventional solution it is now, had put him in some special social category. Perhaps his insistence on writing in his own particular way, a way more gently lyrical, and more personal and good humored than that favored by the prevailing winds of style, had cost him rapport with his peers. There were prevailing winds then, even as there was a pecking order.

The dominant theoretical mode at the workshop, as it was almost everywhere in literary America in the 1950s, was, of course, the new criticism. Text was all. The text, passionate but austere. Eliot's argument for the poem as "objective correla-tive" had made the New Criticism *de rigueur*. The whole notion had been polished and augmented into a system by Brooks, Warren, and John Crowe Ransom. *Understanding Poetry* was the official casebook. The stifling neoclassicism of Yvor Winters's poetry and criticism were also part of this hard-line climate. The poems De wrote during this time, many of which appear in the opening section of *Heart's Needle,* owe a great deal of their polished control to this critical climate. But, ultimately, they are not of it.

Perhaps, as some critics claim, De did invent "the confessional school" of modern poetry. I don't know. Perhaps, as a graduate student, he did influence our onetime teacher Robert Lowell. It would be exhilarating to think so.

None of us, including De himself, I'm sure, ever thought in such terms back then. If we did, in some moment of unguarded euphoria or delusion, we would have certainly kept our mouths shut. We thought mainly of trying to write well. And some of us were still trying to decide what "write well" meant. De once said in an interview that his early work shares some of the characteristics of poetry written in the confessional mode. He also said he had no further interest in the question. Viva!

In order to recover the Snodgrass I knew and some of the pungency of the old Lowell-Berryman days, I've scavenged my back files and come up with two sloppy and priceless manila folders. In both the dittoed worksheets are beginning to yellow at the edges and become brittle. On many pages the poems are not accompanied by the poet's name. The luxury of anonymity was granted to the condemned. Nevertheless, we all knew whose poems we were discussing. On a few I had the presence of mind to pencil names. Beyond that the really remarkable poems are still remarkable. One remembers readily who wrote them.

The first folder contains poems by Henri Coulette, De, myself, Donald Petersen, Jane Cooper, Donald Justice, and William Dickey, to mention those I can positively identify. It also contains a copy of Allen Tate's "The Swimmers," which he'd handed out while he was still working on it and which he discussed with the class. On the back of it someone has written, "I think what your best achievement is is that you know what he's just been saying." The handwriting is completely unfamiliar, and I've no idea what the comment refers to or whether I'm the person addressed. There are, alas, other poems here whose authors have sunk down into obscurity, or whose lines, as they themselves would be first to admit, now seem eminently forgettable. In the second folder are two copies of De's "A Flat One" with my notes scribbled on them in pencil; four Donald Justice poems, including the powerful sestina "On a Painting by Patient B of the Independence State Hospital for the Insane"; and "Winter Stop-Over" by Peter Everwine.

There are things here far more remarkable than my amateur literary historian's delight in finding on the back and face of Justice's poems notes attributed to someone identified only as "B." The lines of Yeats's "A Deep Sworn Vow" are accompanied by the comment, "One of the greatest poems in English, I think—B"; and slanting across the upper left-hand corner of

Justice's "The Violent Ward: I," this priceless jab, "Byron, whose poems were iceboxes—B." Who the hell was B? Then in my mind's eye we are all, for a moment, together again there in the metal barracks, giant geraniums growing like Jack's bean-stalks in the hot, makeshift bay window, and a voice is talking mushily and brilliantly and enthusiastically about Justice's poems and ranging over the whole course of English poetry to focus them for us. Jesus! Who else? B. John Berryman, who followed Lowell as workshop whip.

There are four Snodgrass poems here, in the inimitable purple ink of pre-Xerox days. "A Flat One" and "Papageno" in one folder; "At the Park Dance" and "Mehtis . . . ou tis" (its Greek title hand-lettered, I presume, by the poet) in the other. What's remarkable about these poems is certainly not my notes on them, nor the list of Joycean vocabulary words carefully pen-cilled vertically in the margins (megalomania, eponymous, om-phorion, pseudopigraphic . . .). What's remarkable is the excep-tionally high quality of the poems, both in themselves and when measured against the rest of the poetry here, both good and bad. "He fed them generously who were his flocks, / Picked, shatter-brained, for food." Or

> My mouth was padlocked for a liar.
> Losing what old hands never seek
> To snare in their most cunning art,
> I starved till my rib cage was wire
> Under a towel. . . .

Or from "At the Park Dance":

> Beyond, jagged stars
> are glinting like jacks hurled
> farther than eyes can measure;
> on the dancefloor girls
> turn, vague as milkweed floats
> bobbing from childish fingers.

It's tempting here to quote some of the humdingers from poems the rest of us were writing at the time, but it would be perhaps unfair and unkind. Let's just say, noting the easy move-ment of this language within its complex meters, the careful adjustment of the poem's loose and delicate rhymes and asso-nances and the two exactly right, counterbalanced metaphors on

which the poem closes, that some of us were still in poetic kinder-
garten learning to tie our shoes. It's no accident of sloth that
three of these poems made their way into the pages of *Heart's
Needle* without a single revision, straight from the worksheets to
the Pulitzer Prize for poetry. They were already completely fin-
ished in 1954, five years before De won the award.

After he left Iowa I saw Snodgrass only twice until the Carter
White House Salute to American Poetry in 1980. In 1959 or 1960
he returned to the university to give a reading of his work before
a packed house in Shambaugh Auditorium. It was a triumph, of
course. Not only because he read well but because this prodigal
son of the New Criticism was the first poet from the Iowa Writ-
ers' Workshop to achieve really major literary recognition. Per-
sonally, I was as elated as if I'd won the damn prize myself. It
seemed to me that workshop politics had suffered a blow, and
good-humored independence and dedication to craft had found
its reward. What could have been sweeter?

In the early or mid-1960s De and I met accidentally in the field
house of the University of Iowa during a hectic registration. He
was just passing through town and had stopped to see friends.
I've no idea now what I was doing there, probably signing up for
courses toward the Ph.D. I later abandoned. "How's the writing
going," I asked. It's the secret handshake. The password. The
touchstone question all writers ask each other in one form or
another sooner or later when they haven't seen each other for
awhile. "I haven't written a thing in two years," he said. Too
many readings, too many lectures, too many public appearances
had carried him away from poetry. "I'm desperate to get back to
it. I'm in analysis right now, trying to break through." He
looked tired.

De, of course, did break through and went on to publish *After
Experience* in 1968, *Remains* in 1970, *The Führer Bunker* cycle in
1977, a number of smaller volumes of verse, and recently his
Selected Poems. So Snodgrass continues to walk naked through
the universe. Viva!

DeLOSS McGRAW

Two Statements on Collaborating with W. D. Snodgrass

On the Beginnings of the Collaboration

In December of 1981 I was encouraged by Joanne Dempsy to write a letter to W. D. Snodgrass, asking permission to use his name in the title of two etchings that I was making as a guest artist at Cranbrook Academy of Art.

Being acquainted with his work, primarily *After Experience* and *Heart's Needle,* I was presumptuous enough to think I was capable of visually commenting on the breadth of that work in those two etchings. The first image was a horizontal with a walking man outreaching toward a floating cherub. It was printed in light pink and turquoise. My desire was to make a high-key image comparable to the music of Corelli. This was inspired mainly by poetry selections from *Heart's Needle* and was titled "W. D. Snodgrass, You Sentimental Fool."

The second image was a vertical that pictured a violent storm with a figure bent over, "protecting" himself. The colors used were white and gray on black paper. It was titled, "W. D. Snodgrass, Silly Man, Come Out of the Storm." This image, no doubt, was a reflection of the poems from *After Experience,* published seven years after *Heart's Needle.*

The quality of his work that I was drawn to was irony—this ability he had to write about dire situations in his life and, as from *Heart's Needle,* laugh about them:

> If all this world runs battlefield or worse,
> Come, let us wipe our glasses on our shirts:
> Snodgrass is walking through the universe.

The poet, after receiving the prints and their titles, had a great enthusiasm for the project. His open and receptive response, I knew, was the "go ahead" for me to be able to paint from his work with an unconscious honesty. I didn't have to worry about offending the poet. I had responded in paintings to poets' work before, but the poets I used were dead. This was a wonderful opportunity for the possibility of a dialogue.

That dialogue did not really start until after I had my first one-person exhibition, "In Response to the World of W. D. Snodgrass," at Adrienne Simard Gallery in Los Angeles. In that series of paintings I used all of his writings to visually convey the poet's emotions. Two particular paintings from this series were the catalyst for our first collaboration.

The paintings, "W. D. Searches for Cock Robin" and "W. D. Attempts to Save Cock Robin," were made from the desire to comment on an aspect of the poet's attitude toward death. Many of his poems are concerned with death, but it was a statement in his prose work *In Radical Pursuit* that I found especially unusual. It relates the story of his sister, who, having asthma, was nowhere near death physically but, in W. D.'s view, woke up one fourth of July morning and merely decided not to live anymore.

To me there was something unusual about this view of death that was perplexing and to which I could not see how to make a visual statement. Finally, I realized what struck me was its simplicity and innocence—an almost childlike quality. Immediately, the nursery rhyme "Who Killed Cock Robin" came to me. This nursery rhyme introduces a child to the theme of death, and I knew I had a venue.

The two Cock Robin paintings mentioned above were the only ones included in the Simard exhibition. That following autumn Snodgrass left for Mexico. It was there he wrote the first Cock Robin poem, originally entitled "Dispersal" and later "Auction." I believe it was composed without seeing any image. This poem began the dialogue. Together with letters, poems, slides and the telephone we concocted some thirty-three poems and seventy paintings, titling the work "On the Death of Cock Robin." The collaboration's substance and exchange came not so much from the intellectualizing of ideas as from a "song" we were making, not unlike jazz musicians do.

The Cock Robin suite was successful for two reasons that I did not understand until later. The first is the incredible similarities in taste that we share. In visiting De and Kathy for the first time in their home in a very remote area (a remoteness I desire), I was struck by the fact that the furniture, the books, music (particularly of the medieval period), and even the musical instruments they love are all favorites of mine. Commenting on this, I stated "Isn't it odd—our similar tastes?" To which he snapped, "Of course not. Why do you think we have this relation?"

The second reason is that the original Cock Robin tale had such a self-contained structure: the introduction of numerous characters, the mystery of death, and the tale's familiarity to the public and to both W. D. and myself, gave us the supporting freedom to work independently yet within a cohesive form.

Artist's Statement on "Just Dancing" for Robert Kidd Gallery

In the last five years my collaboration with Mr. Snodgrass has resulted in probably two hundred paintings from his poetry and sixty poems from my paintings. Here's the way it works: I read a Snodgrass poem and it triggers an idea for a painting or paintings. I send him slides of the work, and in return he writes a poem off the painting and perhaps a poem off the poem. I receive the poem and respond, and on and on. What makes it work for me and, I believe, for us, is that we explain very little to each other concerning our content, and most often we read each other differently than our intent.

This exhibition. It began five years ago, when we made the series "On the Death of Cock Robin," some seventy paintings and thirty-five poems, and then ended for a couple of years. Later, as I was painting an exhibition of work based on J. D. Salinger's *Catcher in the Rye,* one of my dealers stopped by the studio to see the progression of the work. After studio talk he became silent for a moment and then said that his teenage daughter was going to have a baby and that she had refused to marry the father. As he spoke the thought occurred to me, "Isn't it unbelievable that as we all perform our jobs and pursue our goals, we carry around so many problems? It's actually a full-time job just trying to sort through life." I had this admiration for man (in general), that wouldn't go away. My friend, the dealer, caught a plane a few hours later, and I returned to my studio and removed all the paintings on *Catcher*—they looked hard and ungraceful. I felt the need for more grace in my work (and life), and I painted a picture titled "Lullaby: The Comforting of Cock Robin." A year later I painted an exhibition based on Mr. Snodgrass's poem (not the experience of my friend), and the exhibition went to London and was cataloged. The poet saw the catalog and wrote six or eight poems based on the paintings, set to the rhythm of different dances as the tango, tap, waltz, and fox-trot.

I thought it was a crazy idea (I loved it), and in turn his poems nudged me toward the music of the swing era and Cole Porter. In the meantime the opportunity came to exhibit at Robert Kidd Gallery. Ray Fleming said he loved my work, wanted a show, and wanted the work big. I don't believe I would have thought of this large format—the largest I have ever worked. Yet the format was the perfect size for the rhythm of the dances, and I simply had a wonderful time painting the exhibition.

The Size of Snodgrass

To sum up the work of William DeWitt Snodgrass is a daunting task, like trying to weigh Mount Rainier or the Mississippi: I want to fall silent and simply point. But respect for potential readers of this array of valuable criticism, especially for those who may lately have begun catching up with Snodgrass, compels me to try to sum up in a few words the stature of the man and of his work and to place it at least roughly in the context of recent American poetry.

Now that we have the *Selected Poems 1957–1987* it may be easier to see the wide sweep and fierce consistency of Snodgrass's poetry. Not long ago it gladdened me to see Gavin Ewart, writing in the *New York Times Book Review,* declare Snodgrass to be one of the best American poets alive, for, as far as I know, this obvious truth had not often been stated. (Actually, John Berryman once said so too.) When in 1960 the Pulitzer Prize fell to Snodgrass's very first book, *Heart's Needle,* the event must have taken most readers and critics by surprise, for until then his work had been relatively little noticed. In retrospect I can't help feeling smug. In 1958 sections of "Heart's Needle" (the poem) had caught my eye in a little magazine, and I had been startled to encounter a poet who not only said something moving and gentle and powerful but whose words were placed on the page in a fashion severe and masterly. His memorable name stuck in memory, and, as soon as his first book appeared, I bought it, devoured it, felt bowled over by it, and fired off to its author one of the few fan letters I have ever been prompted to write. In return I received a friendly note. And then—wonder of wonders—one evening in late 1959, on the door of my bachelor student pad, came an unexpected knock: it was W. D. Snodgrass himself. This mythical individual proved to be a tall, intense man only a little older than me, with a quivering mustache and a voice that, when excited, kept sliding into an upper register. He had lately taken a job at Wayne State University in nearby Detroit, happened to be passing through Ann Arbor, and had decided to look me up. His admirers must have been fewer back then—not too many to call on personally.

That surprise visit began what has been, over the years, not a close friendship but a steady and (for me) a cherished one. In the company of other young poets I was to visit Snodgrass several times at home outside Detroit, usually hearing him perform upon one of the beautiful string instruments he collects, and I will never forget my joy at Robert Lowell's reading in Detroit when Lowell broke the news of Snodgrass's Pulitzer. Time passed. Snodgrass gravitated to Syracuse, later to the University of Delaware. Soon after the triumph of *Heart's Needle,* metrical, form-bound poetry passed out of fashion, and at mention of the name of Snodgrass young poets no longer leaped up and cheered. A second book, *After Experience,* though it contained several excellent poems, drew less praise than had greeted the first. When in 1972 my wife Dorothy and I brought out a little magazine devoted to rhyme and meter (called *Counter/Measures*) and Snodgrass generously contributed "Owls" and "An Elm Tree," two of his finest poems of that era, I felt overwhelmed to receive—for an obscure little magazine that paid nothing!— poems of a caliber that the *New Yorker* might have welcomed, only a few years earlier, when traditionally formal poetry had predominated. That kind of generosity is characteristic. Never one to worry about marketing, Snodgrass has worked as he liked and published where he chose, trusting his audience to catch up with him.

Before Snodgrass metrical and syllabic poets had favored subjects from Greek mythology. They wrote self-conscious, decorative poems showing off their skills, addressed to an audience of critics. After *Heart's Needle* that kind of writing seemed no longer possible. For Snodgrass restored to formal poetry in America its ancient advantage of truth telling. Today he does not seem to have been a confessional poet, doing public penance but, rather, a poet bent on illuminating the shadowy corners of his mind and heart, for his own enlightenment. It must have been this quality of searching frankness that so impressed Robert Lowell. Lowell began as Snodgrass's teacher at Iowa and ended up being taught. Surely "Heart's Needle" made possible Lowell's escape from the overbearing rhetoric and garish nightmares of *Lord Weary's Castle* and enabled him to write that humane, truth-telling poem about himself, "Skunk Hour."

The sequence "Heart's Needle" still stands for me as the best long poem of its time; indeed, I know no such ambitious poem since *The Waste Land* that I love more. Snodgrass shows himself well aware of the world beyond his own skin, involved with it. There is no accident in the fact that the poem begins,

Child of my winter, born
When the new fallen soldiers froze
In Asia's steep ravines and fouled the snows . . .

and proceeds to imagine the "chilled tenant-farmer" and to liken the cold war to the poet's own crisis. Snodgrass takes to heart not only his own sufferings but those of humankind. He does so not only in *Heart's Needle* but also in *The Führer Bunker* and in other poems besides.

Among American poets of our time I believe him to be the one most clearly possessed of a tragic sense. Early on he recognized the truth of Ezra Pound's dictum that in poetry only emotion endures, and so his poems have gravitated to the most over-whelming emotions of all. It is his concern with suffering, his willingness to confront the most painful and oppressive matters, personal and universal, that sets his work off from the rest with distinction and dignity. In the beginning he distilled poems from his private anguish. At one time I wondered how he could continue to write poetry without finding new anguish of his own, and so I felt relieved when he gravitated to writing poems to be spoken by personae, poems of the Nazi Holocaust, that most enormous anguish of all. His recent devotion to serious nonsense, in the cycles of W. D. and Cock Robin, was foreshadowed by his consuming interest in the poems of Christian Morgenstern, which with Lore Segal he has so faithfully translated. Above all, Snodgrass is a consummate musician, intent on bringing the songs of the troubadours over into the American language. This devotion to sound is present in his smallest poem, for any who care to hear.

Snodgrass has always placed a colossal value upon sincerity, upon discovering what you truly believe and telling that truth. And, as his essay "Finding a Poem" reveals, shaping and polish-ing a formal poem is often a matter of devoting such close atten-tion to one's words that at last one discovers, beyond all the deceits of the mind, that truth to which one cannot help but cling. This attitude is far from that which detractors of meter sometimes attribute to metrical poets: that a form is a hollow box to be stuffed with words.

If I seem to place undue stress on the value of form to Snodgrass, I do so lest this essential be neglected. Poets who write in meter play a profoundly different game from poets who write in open verse. The language of a Snodgrass poem has been shaped with the utmost passion and devotion. It is language that comes from the poet's deepest reservoirs of feeling, language to be heard aloud, chewed, and digested. Whoever perceives, in reading a Snodgrass poem, nothing except the denotations of its words, has not even begun to read that poem at all.

I could not possibly exaggerate the importance of Snodgrass for me and many another writer back in those Dark Ages when Ginsberg's *Howl* was heard across the land, drowning out other voices, and when poets in droves were deserting the apparently sinking ship of traditional form. To write in what Kenneth Koch called the "pale skunky pentameters," or in syllabics, was to brand oneself a reactionary, quite out of it. With Anthony Hecht, Howard Nemerov, and Richard Wilbur, Snodgrass did not swerve from his convictions but continued throughout those years to write in form, whether or not readers cared for it. For more than a quarter-century when form was out of favor, his example stood before me and sustained me through many a gloom.

Let me close with a Zen anecdote. One night years ago, during metrical poetry's dark hours, when I was on a reading trip to Delaware, Snodgrass gave me a ride back to my guest room, and we found ourselves sitting and talking for a while in a bleak campus parking lot. I said something like, "De, doesn't it ever bother you that nobody appreciates the kind of poetry you write anymore? Thinks that if you go to the trouble to write in meter you're some kind of fusty crud, some back number? It bothers the hell out of me. Sometimes I feel like giving up." To this bleat Snodgrass made one brief reply: a slow and compassionate "Awwwww-w-w-w-w . . ." that tapered off into the quiet of the night.

What he didn't say spoke volumes. He did not say, "Keep the faith. Suffering makes you whole." He did not say, "How can you forget? The art of formal poetry stands in the tradition of Shakespeare, Milton, and Keats. Is not that tradition worth allegiance, worth the last ounce of a poet's blood?" He did not say, "Who cares what presentday readers think they want? Screw the bastards—write for the ages!" He did not actually voice those thoughts, and yet somehow I felt that something along those lines had been what he had believed and had made manifest in his own work all along.

COMPILED BY KATHLEEN SNODGRASS,
WITH CHARD deNIORD

W. D. Snodgrass Bibliography

Primary Works

Poetry

Books
Heart's Needle. 1959; reprint, New York: Knopf, 1983. Hessle, Eng.: Marvell, 1960.
After Experience. New York: Harper, 1968. London: Oxford University Press, 1968.
Remains: A Sequence of Poems. Brockport, NY: BOA Editions, 1985.
The Führer Bunker: A Cycle of Poems in Progress. Brockport, NY: BOA Editions, 1977.
Selected Poems: 1957–1987. 1987; reprint, New York: Soho, 1991.
W. D.'s Midnight Carnival. With DeLoss McGraw. Encinitas: Artra, 1988.
The Death of Cock Robin. With DeLoss McGraw. Newark: University of Delaware Press, 1989.

Limited Fine Press Editions
Remains: Poems. S. S. Gardons, pseud. Mt. Horeb, WI: Perishable Press, 1970.
If Birds Build with Your Hair. New York: Nadja, 1979.
These Trees Stand. Portrait series by Robert Mahon. New York: Carol Joyce, 1981.
Heinrich Himmler: Platoons and Files. Cumberland, IA: Pterodactyl, 1982.
Magda Goebbels. Winston-Salem, NC: Palaemon, 1983.
The Boy Made of Meat. Wood engravings by Gillian Tyler. Concord, NH: W. B. Ewert, 1983.
D. D. Byrde Callyng Jennie Wrenn. Concord, NH: W. B. Ewert, 1984.
A Locked House. Concord, NH: W. B. Ewert, 1986.
A Colored Poem. Color lithographs by DeLoss McGraw. San Diego: Brighton, 1986.
The House the Poet Built. Color lithographs by DeLoss McGraw. San Diego: Brighton, 1986.
The Kinder Capers. Illustrations by DeLoss McGraw. New York: Nadja, 1986.
The Midnight Carnival. Original etchings by DeLoss McGraw. San Diego: Brighton, 1988.
To Shape a Song. Illustrations by DeLoss McGraw. New York: Nadja, 1988.
Autumn Variations. New York: Nadja, 1990.

Pamphlets
Spaulding Distinguished Lectures. Durham: University of New Hampshire Press, 1969.
Lullaby: The Comforting of Cock Robin. New York: Nadja, 1988.

Broadsides and Posters
"After Experience Taught Me . . ." *Ligature 68*. Chicago: Madison Park, 1968.
"Coming Down from the Acropolis." Derry, PA: The Rook Society, 1976.
"Mutability." *Northern Lights*. Winston-Salem, NC: Palaemon, 1983.
"Owls." Graphics by Marta Anderson. Concord, NH: W. B. Ewert, 1983.
"Magda Goebbels: 12 April 1945." Winston-Salem, NC: Palaemon, 1984.
"Old Jewelry." *Fifty Years of American Poetry*. Winston-Salem, NC: Palaemon, 1984
"The Death of Cock Robin: Poems and Paintings." Long Beach: University Art Museum, California State University, 1986.
"Lullaby: The Comforting of Cock Robin." Hand-colored etching by De Loss McGraw. San Diego: Brighton, 1987.
"Three Versicles." Concord, NH: W. B. Ewert, 1987.
"Dance Suite: Minuet in F##." Concord, NH: W. B. Ewert, 1989.
"Dance Suite: Mexican Hat Dance." Concord, NH: W. B. Ewert, 1990.

Translations

Books
Gallows Songs. By Christian Morgenstern. Trans. with Lore Segal. Ann Arbor: University of Michigan Press, 1967.

Limited Fine Press Editions
Six Troubadour Songs. Providence, RI: Burning Deck, 1977.
Traditional Hungarian Songs. Baltimore: Charles Seluzicki, 1978.
Six Minnesinger Songs. Providence, RI: Burning Deck, 1983.
Antonio Vivaldi: The Four Seasons. New York: Targ, 1984.
Star and Other Poems. By Mihai Eminescu. Concord, NH: W. B. Ewert, 1990.

Broadsides and Posters
"Somnoroasa Pasarele" (Now the Songbirds, All Adrowse). By Mihai Eminescu. Trans. with Augustin Maissen. Concord, NH: W. B. Ewert, 1985.
"Star." By Mihai Eminescu. Baltimore: Charles Seluzicki, 1982.

Criticism

Books
In Radical Pursuit. New York: Harper, 1975.

Uncollected Reviews
"Elegance in Marianne Moore." *Western Review*, Autumn 1954, 57–64.
"Four Gentlemen; Two Ladies." Review of *Thrones: 96–109 de los Cantares*, by Ezra Pound; *The Self-Made Man*, by Reed Whittemore; *Selected Poems*, by Robert Duncan; *Scrimshaw*, by Winfield Townley Scott; *A Water Walk by Villa d'Este*, by Jean Garrigue; *Valentines to the Wide World*, by Mona Van Duyn. *Hudson Review* 13 (Spring 1960): 120–31.
"Gottfried Benn." Review of *Primal Vision: Selected Writings of Gottfried Benn*, ed. Ernst Basch. *Hudson Review* 14 (Spring 1961): 118–26.
"In Praise of Robert Lowell." Review of *The Old Glory*. *New York Review of Books* 3, no. 8 (3 December 1964): 8, 10.

"The Last Poems of Theodore Roethke." Review of *The Far Field* and *Sequence, Sometimes Metaphysical. New York Review of Books* 3, no. 4 (8 October 1964).

"Nobodies of Prominence." Review of *Greta Garbo*, by John Bainbridge; *Lawrence of Arabia: A Biographical Enquiry*, by Richard Aldington; *The Mint*, by T. E. Lawrence. *Western Review* 20 (Spring 1956): 231–39.

Review of *The Pattern of Hardy's Poetry*, by Samuel Hynes. *College English* 23 (January 1962): 322–23.

"Spring Verse Chronicle." Review of *Words for the Wind*, by Theodore Roethke; *Paterson, Five*, by William Carlos Williams; *95 Poems*, by E. E. Cummings; *The Magic-Maker: E. E. Cummings*, by Charles Norman; *Goodbye Earth and Other Poems*, by I. A. Richards. *Hudson Review* 12 (Spring 1959): 114–23. Partially reprinted in *William Carlos Williams: The Critical Heritage*, ed. Charles Doyle. London and Boston: Routledge, 1980.

"Voice as Visions." Review of *Man Now*, by William Burford; *The Dancing Bears*, by W. S. Merwin; *The Death Bell*, by Vernon Watkins. *Western Review* 19, no. 3 (Autumn 1954): 57–64.

Uncollected Essays

"After-Images: Autobiographical Sketches" (I. Good Housekeeping, II. Paralysis, III. Father). *Southern Review* 25, no. 2 (April 1989): 261–82.

"Against Your Beliefs." *Southern Review* 26, no. 3 (Summer 1990): 479–95.

"An Applecart Named Darwin." *Views* (University of Louisville) 3, no. 2: 55–58.

"Apple Trees and Belly Dancers." In *Singular Voices: American Poetry Today*, ed. Stephen Berg. New York: Avon, 1985.

Foreword to *For They Are My Friends*. By Tom Marotta. New York: ArtReflections, 1977.

Foreword to *The Hardeman County Sequence*. By Michael Jennings. Rochester: Heliographis, 1980.

Foreword to *The Roses and the Windows*. By Rainer Maria Rilke. Trans. A. Poulin, Jr. Port Townsend, WA: Graywolf, 1979. Reprinted in *The Complete French Poems of Rainer Maria Rilke*. Trans. A. Poulin, Jr. St. Paul, MN: Graywolf, 1986.

Foreword to *Syracuse Poems*. Syracuse: Syracuse University, Dept. of English, 1969.

Foreword to *Syracuse Poems*. Syracuse: Syracuse University, Dept. of English, 1972.

Foreword to *Syracuse Poems*. Syracuse: Syracuse University, Dept. of English, 1976.

Foreword to *Un Ghimpe In Inima si Alte Poezii* (Heart's Needle and Other Poems). Trans. Ioan A. Popa. Bucharest: Editura Univers, 1983.

"From the Journals of Woodchuck Charlie Robinson, Wilderness Guide and Trapper." *Bred Any Good Rooks Lately?* Ed. James Charlton. Garden City, NY: Doubleday, 1986.

"Giving Up Music." *Syracuse Scholar* 5, no. 1 (1984): 69–78.

"The House of Snodgrass," "Artist and Businessman," and "Grandfathers and Sons." *Salmagundi* 78–79 (Spring–Summer 1988): 176–205.

"The Immutability of the Quick-Change Artist: Donald Hall." In *The Day I Was Older: On the Poetry of Donald Hall*, ed. Liam Rector. Santa Cruz: Story Line, 1989.

Introduction to *Dance Script for Electric Ballerina*. By Alice Fulton. Philadelphia: University of Pennsylvania Press, 1983.

Introduction to *Leverage*. By Jonathan Holden. Charlottesville: University of Virginia Press, 1983.

Introduction to *Naming the Darkness*. By Jane Ellen Glasser. Fairfax Station, VA: Road Publishers, 1991.

"Lutemaker Is Real Craftsman." (Newspaper headline) *Atencion* (San Miguel de Allende, Mexico), 12 February 1988.

"Play Shows Struggle." Letter to editor on *Mister Roberts*. *Daily Iowan*, 27 May 1955.

"Poetry since Yeats: An Exchange of Views." Symposium with Stephen Spender, Patrick Kavanagh, and Thomas Kinsella. *TriQuarterly* 4 (1975): 100–106.

Preface to *Cedarhome*. By Barton Sutter. Brockport: BOA Editions, 1977.

"Pulse and Impulse." *Southern Review* 27 (July 1991): 505–21.

Interviews

Anstett, Patricia. *Chicago Today Magazine*, 22 March 1970, 6–7.

Arnett, Judd. "A Talk with a Poet: 'Success Is Hard to Digest.'" *Detroit Free Press*, 8 May 1960.

Beacham, Walton. "Richard Wilbur and W. D. Snodgrass: An Interview." *New Virginia Quarterly* 1, no. 1 (1979). Reprinted in *Conversations with Richard Wilbur*, ed. William Butts, 205–23. Jackson: University of Mississippi Press, 1990.

Boyers, Robert. "W. D. Snodgrass: An Interview." *Salmagundi* 22–23 (1973): 149–63.

DeVries, Hillary. "When Two Arts Interact: Poet W. D. Snodgrass and Artist DeLoss McGraw." *Christian Science Monitor*, 17 December 1987, 30–31.

Di Angelo, Mary Jo. "W. D. Snodgrass." *University of Delaware Magazine* 1, no. 3 (Spring 1989): 30–35.

Di Sesa, Debbie. "Talking with a Poet: Meeting Snodgrass." *Daily Orange* (Syracuse University), 23 October 1964, 1.

Dillon, David. " 'Toward Passionate Utterance': An Interview with W. D. Snodgrass." *Southwest Review* 60, no. 3 (Summer 1975): 278–90.

Gaston, Paul L. "W. D. Snodgrass and *The Führer Bunker*." *Papers on Language and Literature* 13 (Summer 1977): 295–311; 13 (Fall 1977): 401–12.

Gefen, Pearl Sheffy. "The Strengths You Own." *Jerusalem Post Magazine* (9 February 1973): 12.

Gerber, Philip L., and Robert J. Gemmett. " 'No Voices Talk to Me': A Conversation with W. D. Snodgrass." *Western Humanities Review* 24 (Winter 1971): 61–71.

Haven, Stephen. "An Interview with W. D. Snodgrass: Recent Work." *Crazyhorse* (Spring 1990): 76–92.

Herz, Bob. "An Interview with W. D. Snodgrass." *Seneca Review* 7, no. 2 (December 1976).

Johnson, Bruce. "Newark's Bearded Bard." *Delaware Today* 28, no. 2 (February 1988).

Mahoney, Thomas A. "Pulitzer Poet Hits Stereotypes." *Ferndale Gazette-Times*, 5 May 1960, 1, 3.

Mathieu, Bertrand. "Interview with W. D. Snodgrass." *Noiseless Spider* (University of New Haven) 8, no. 1 (Fall 1978): 2–25.

Nelson, Greg. "Interview with W. D. Snodgrass." *Phoebe: The George Mason Review* 14 (Fall 1984): 30–42.

Nickerson, Edward A. "Portrait of W. D. Snodgrass." *Delaware Today*, April 1983, 13–15.

Niikura, Schinichi. "Modern American Poet: An Interview with W. D. Snod-grass." *Modern Poetry Handbook* (Japan) 1 (January 1978): 26–30.

Packard, William. "Craft Interview with W. D. Snodgrass." *New York Quarterly* 18 (1976). Reprinted in *The Poet's Craft: Interviews from the "New York Quarterly,"* ed. William Packard. New York: Paragon, 1987.

Popa, Ioan A. "As sa vin din nou in Romania." *Tribuna* 16, no. 50 (14 December 1972): 8.

Raisor, Philip. "Framed Portrait: An Interview with W. D. Snodgrass." *Southern Review* 26, no. 1 (January 1990): 65–80.

Rosu, Dona. "Dialog cu Poetul American W. D. Snodgrass." *Revista de Istorie si Teorie Literara* (Romania) 36, nos. 3–4 (July–December 1988): 281–88.

Sollner, Werner. "Nur Mich Selbst Ausdrucken." *Neue Literatur* 9 (1976): 61–63.

Spires, Elizabeth. "W. D. Snodgrass: An Interview by Elizabeth Spires." *American Poetry Review* 19, no. 4 (July–August 1990): 38–46.

Vitale, Tom. *A Moveable Feast.* National Public Radio. WNYC, New York, 29 September 1987.

Watson, Catherine. "Snodgrass—Experience Is Change." *Minneapolis Sunday Tribune,* 14 April 1968.

Theatrical and Musical Productions

Biedermann and the Firebugs. By Max Frisch. Trans. and adapted by W. D. S. and Rosmarie Waldrop. Dir. David Hamilton. Regent Theater, Syracuse University, 29–30 April, 1 May 1966.

The Führer Bunker: A Cycle of Poems in Progress. Staged by Paul Dicklin. Riverview Playhouse, Old Dominion University, Norfolk, VA, 27 September 1978.

Dr. Joseph Goebbels, 22 April 1945. Performed with percussion in concert. West Gate Theater, New York, 6–7 November 1981.

The Führer Bunker. Adapted by W. D. S. Dir. Carl Weber. American Place Theater, New York, April–June 1981.

The Führer Bunker. Adapted and dir. Gary Fisher. Buffalo Entertainment Theater, 23 September 1982.

The Führer Bunker. Adapted by W. D. S. and Annette Martin. Dir. Annette Martin. Eastern Michigan State University, Ypsilanti, MI, 3–11 April 1987.

Midnight Carnival. Faustwork Mask Theater. Dir. Wynn Handman. American Place Theater, New York, 5–16 December 1990.

Secondary Works

Books

Gaston, Paul L. *W. D. Snodgrass.* Boston: Twayne, 1978.

Articles

Barolini, Antonio. "Un Poeta Americano." *Il Mondo,* 3 December 1963, 11.

Bede, Jean-Albert, and William B. Edterton, eds. *Columbia Dictionary of Modern European Literature.* 2d ed. New York: Columbia University Press, 1980.

Berke, Roberta. In *Bounds Out of Bound: A Compass for Recent American and British Poetry,* 81–85. New York: Oxford University Press, 1981.

Bradbury, Malcolm, et al., eds. *Penguin Companion to American Literature.* New York: McGraw, 1971.

Cantrell, Carol Helmstetter. "Self and Tradition in Recent Poetry." *Midwest Quarterly* 18, no. 4 (1977): 343–60.

Carroll, Paul. "The Thoreau Complex amid the Solid Scholars." In *The Poem in Its Skin*, 174–87. Chicago and New York: Follett, 1968.

Curtis, Simon. "Recent Poetry." *Critical Quarterly* 21, no. 2 (1979): 75–84.

Farrelly, David. "Heart's Fling: The Poetry of W. D. Snodgrass." *Perspective* 13 (Winter 1964): 185–99.

Goldstein, Laurence. "*The Führer Bunker* and the New Discourse about Nazism." *Southern Review* 24, no. 1 (Winter 1988): 100–114.

Gray, Richard. *American Poetry of the Twentieth Century*, 227–29. London and New York: Longman, 1990.

Helterman, Jeffrey. "W. D. Snodgrass." In *Dictionary of Literary Biography: American Poets since World War II*, ed. Donald J. Greiner, 266–74. Detroit: Gale, 1980.

Heyen, William. "Fishing the Swamp: The Poetry of W. D. Snodgrass." In *Modern American Poetry: Essays in Criticism*, ed. Jerome Mazzaro, 351–68. New York: McKay, 1970.

Hoffman, Stephen K. "Impersonal Personalism: The Making of a Confessional Poetic." *ELH* 45, no. 4 (Winter 1978): 687–707.

Howard, Richard. "W. D. Snodgrass." *Alone with America*. New York: Atheneum, 1969.

Leary, Robyn. "Pulitzer Prize-Winning Poet at University of Delaware." *Delaware State News*, 3 July 1988.

Lyttle, David. "Snodgrass Walking." *Approach* 41 (Fall 1961): 13–16.

McClatchy, J. D. "W. D. Snodgrass: The Mild, Reflective Art." *Massachusetts Review* 16 (Spring 1975): 281–314. Reprinted in *White Paper: On Contemporary American Poetry*. New York: Columbia University Press, 1989.

Mah, Marsha, and Lyn Foltz. "Success Secrets." *Delaware Today* 25, no. 12 (December 1986): 65.

Mavor, Ronald. "An American Poet Steals the Show." *Scotsman* (Edinburgh), 26 August 1965, 6.

Mazzaro, Jerome. "The Public Intimacy of W. D. Snodgrass." *Salmagundi* 19 (Spring 1972): 96–111.

Milburn, Michael. " 'Sacred Beings': Writers in Recorded Conversation." *Poetry* 146, no. 2 (1985): 101–11.

Monteiro, George. "Snodgrass Peoples His Universe." *Papers of the Bibliographical Society of America* 56, no. 4 (1962): 494–95.

Moritz, Charles, ed. *Current Biography 1960*. New York: Wilson, 1961.

Miller, Elsie. "The Artist and the Poet." *San Diego Magazine* 35, no. 11 (September 1983): 146–51.

"People on the Way Up." *Saturday Evening Post* 235, no. 22 (2 June 1962): 26.

Phillips, Robert. "W. D. Snodgrass and the Sad Hospital of the World." *University of Windsor Review* 4, no. 2 (Spring 1969). Reprinted in *The Confessional Poets*. Carbondale and Edwardsville: Southern Illinois University Press, 1973.

Popa, Ioan A. "Intre Folclor si Poezia Moderna." *Contemporanul* (Romania) 35 (27 August 1982): 16.

Seulean, Joan. "Romanian Ballads Translated into English." *Romanian Bulletin* 7 (January 1978): 11–12.

Shaw, John MacKay, ed. *Childhood in Poetry*. Detroit: Gale, 1967.

Soulsman, Gary. "UD Poet Recalls Anne Sexton's Mania." *Sunday News Journal* (Wilmington, DE), 15 September 1991, H1+.

Survey of American Poetry. Vol. 10. Great Neck: Roth, 1984.

Torchiana, Donald T. "Heart's Needle: Snodgrass Strides through the Universe."

TriQuarterly 2 (Spring 1960): 18–26. Reprinted in *Poets in Progress: Critical Prefaces to Thirteen Modern American Poets,* ed. Edward B. Hungerford. Evanston, IL: Northwestern University Press, 1962.

"UD Professor Full of Rhyme, Reason." *News Journal* (Wilmington, DE), 21 May 1991, A11.

Vourvoulias, Sabrina. "Pulitzer Winning Poet Summers in Chenango Valley." *Chenango Valley News,* 26 July 1991, 7.

Vreeland, Susan. "Painter as Poet: The McGraw-Snodgrass Connection." *Hill Courier* (San Diego) 2, no. 7 (August 1984): 12–13.

White, Gertrude M. "To Tell the Truth: The Poems of W. D. Snodgrass." *Odyssey* 3, no. 2 (1979): 10–18.

White, William. "Snodgrass Peoples His Universe: II." *Papers of the Bibliographical Society of America* 57, no. 1 (1963): 94.

Who's Who in America. 46th ed. 1989–90.

Williams, Edwin W. "W. D. Snodgrass." *Survey of Poetry: English Language Series.* Vol. 6. Ed. Frank N. Magill. Englewood Cliffs, N.J.: Salem, 1982.

Reviews

Heart's Needle
Bakhash, Alfred K. *Audience* 6, no. 4 (Autumn 1959): 103–8.

Bogan, Louise. *New Yorker* 35 (24 October 1959): 196.

Book Review Digest, January 1960.

Booth, Philip. *Christian Science Monitor,* 14 May 1959.

Carruth, Hayden. *Poetry* 95, no. 2 (November 1959): 118–21.

Church Times (England), 17 February 1961.

Davie, D. *Spectator* 206 (24 March 1961): 416.

Dickey, William. *Epoch* 9 (Spring 1959): 254–56.

Farina, Richard G. *Cornell Daily Sun,* 28 May 1959.

Fasel, Ida. *Wichita Falls Times–Feature Magazine,* 6 September 1959, 7.

Fiscalini, Janet. *Commonweal* 70 (14 August 1959): 429–30.

Furbank, P. N. *Listener,* 30 March 1961, 583.

Hall, Donald. *New York Herald Tribune Book Review* 35 (19 July 1959): 3.

Hamilton, Ian. *Oxford Opinion* 47 (8 May 1961): 28.

Hoffman, Daniel G. *Sewanee Review* 68, no. 1 (Winter 1960): 122–23.

Hollander, John. *Partisan Review* 26, no. 3 (Summer 1959): 503.

Holmes, John. *Saturday Review* 42 (23 May 1959): 21+.

Jerome, Judson. *Antioch Review* 19 (Fall 1959): 429–32.

Kliatt Young Adult Paperback Book Guide 18 (Spring 1984): 29.

Kohler, Dayton. *Louisville Courier Journal,* 17 August 1959.

Legler, Philip. *New Mexico Quarterly* 29 (1959): 449.

Meredith, William. *New York Times Book Review* 64 (26 July 1959): 25.

Picton, John. *Vancouver Sun,* 23 May 1959.

Robie, B. A. *Library Journal* 84 (1 June 1959): 1897.

Robson, W. W. *Observer,* 12 March 1961, 28.

Rosenthal, M. L. *Nation* 189 (24 October 1959): 257–58.

Schroetter, Hilda Noel. *Durham Herald,* 2 August 1959.

Simpson, Louis. *Hudson Review* 12, no. 2 (Summer 1959): 308.

Skelton, Robin. *Critical Quarterly* 3, no. 2 (Summer 1961): 187.

Sorrentino, Gilbert. *Yugen* 7 (1961): 5–7.

Thompson, Frank. *Prairie Schooner* 35, no. 2 (June 1961): 182.

Thompson, John. *Kenyon Review* 21, no. 3 (Summer 1959): 488–90.
Times Literary Supplement, 7 April 1961, 218.
Turco, Lewis. *Voices,* January–April 1960, 47–50.
Virginia Quarterly Review 33 (Summer 1959): cxxx.

Gallows Songs
Seymour-Smith, Martin. *Spectator* 221 (6 September 1968): 328–29.

After Experience
Beall, De Witt. *Chicago News,* 27 April 1968.
Bogan, Louise. *New Yorker* 44 (28 December 1968): 63.
Booklist 64 (1 May 1968): 1018.
Book Review Digest, January 1968.
Boyers, Robert. *Partisan Review* 36, no. 2 (1969): 306.
Brady, Charles A. *Buffalo News,* 18 May 1968.
Brownjohn, Alan. *New Statesman* 77 (10 January 1969): 52.
Conarroe, Joel. *Shenandoah* 19, no. 4 (Summer 1968): 77–88.
Dale, Peter. *Agenda* 7, no. 2 (Spring 1969): 79–81.
Dickey, R. P. *Missourian* (Columbia), 2 June 1968.
Dodsworth, Martin. *Listener* 81 (27 March 1969): 433.
Donoghue, Denis. *New York Review of Books* 10 (25 April 1968): 17.
Geran, Juliana. *Maroon* (Chicago), 1 March 1968.
Harrison, J. *New York Times Book Review* 73 (28 April 1968): 6.
Hine, Daryl. *Poetry* 113 (October 1968): 52.
Homberger, Eric. *Cambridge Review,* 17 January 1969, 206.
Howes, Victor. *Christian Science Monitor,* 29 May 1968, 11.
Jacobsen, J. *Commonweal* 88 (21 June 1968): 417.
James, Clive. *Times Literary Supplement,* 2 January 1969, 7. Reprinted in *The Metropolitan Critic.* London: Faber, 1974.
Jerome, Judson. *Saturday Review* 51 (1 June 1968): 32.
Johnson, R. P. *Minneapolis Tribune,* 14 April 1968.
Kavanaugh, P. J. *Guardian Weekly* 101 (2 January 1969): 15.
Kirkus 35 (15 December 1967): 1519.
Lask, Thomas. *New York Times,* 30 March 1968, 31.
Layton, R. F. *Library Journal* 93 (15 January 1968): 193.
Leibowitz, Herbert. *Hudson Review* 21, no. 3 (August 1968): 553.
Lieberman, L. *Yale Review* 58 (Autumn 1968): 137.
Martz, William. *December* 10, no. 1 (1968): 197.
Mazzaro, Jerome. *Nation* 207 (16 September 1968): 252.
Moss, S. *New Republic* 158 (15 June 1968): 35.
News-Leader (Richmond, VA), 20 March 1968.
Pearre, Howell. *Nashville Banner,* 24 May 1968.
Porter, Peter. *London Magazine* 8, no. 12 (1968): 85–87.
Publishers Weekly 192 (25 December 1967): 54.
Simpson, Louis. *Harper's* 237 (August 1968): 74.
Smith, Ray. *Minneapolis Star,* 19 April 1968.
Swenson, May. *Southern Review* 7 (1971): 954.
Twentieth Century 176, no. 1039 (1968): 90.
Virginia Quarterly Review 44 (Summer 1968): ciii.
Walsh, Chad. *Washington Post Book World,* 14 April 1968, 6.
Worcester, Mass., Telegram, 31 March 1968.

Remains
Heyen, William. *Western Humanities Review* 25, no. 3 (Summer 1971): 253–56.
Phillips, Robert. *Poet Lore* 68, no. 1 (Spring 1973): 102–6.

In Radical Pursuit
Asselineau, Roger. *Etudes Anglaises* 31, nos. 3–4 (1978): 423–24.
Atlas, James. *American Poetry Review* 5 (March 1976): 35.
Booklist 71 (1 April 1975): 787.
Choice 12 (May 1975): 387.
Daniel, Robert W. *Sewanee Review* 84 (Summer 1976): xc–xciii.
Fisher, Benjamin Franklin IV. *American Book Collector* 26 (March–April 1976): 4.
Hall, Donald. *American Poetry Review* 4 (May–June 1975): 28.
Horwich, Richard. *New Republic* 172 (15 February 1975): 31.
Isaacson, David. *Library Journal* 99 (1 October 1974): 2482.
Kirkus 42 (15 September 1974): 1051.
Publishers Weekly 206 (25 November 1974): 41.
White, Gertrude M. *Criticism* 17 (Fall 1975): 373–75.
Wood, Michael. *New York Review of Books* 22 (17 April 1975): 15.
Yale Review 65, no. 3 (Spring 1976): viii–x.

The Führer Bunker: A Cycle of Poems
Asselineau, Roger. *Etudes Anglaises* 31, nos. 3–4 (1978): 424.
Bloom, Harold. *New Republic* 177 (26 November 1977): 25.
Booklist 74 (15 April 1978): 1321.
Chicago Daily News, 27 August 1977.
Choice 14 (January 1978): 1499.
Cotter, J. F. *Hudson Review* 31 (Spring 1978): 212.
Fremont-Smith, Eliot. *Village Voice* 22 (26 December 1977): 75.
Keith, Harrison. *Carleton Miscellany* 17 (Winter 1977–78): 147.
Kenner, Hugh. *New York Times Book Review,* 1 January 1978, 11.
Library Journal 102 (15 December 1977): 2166.
Morris, John N. *Ohio Review* 19, no. 1 (Winter 1978): 110–12.
North American Review, Spring 1978.
Peters, Robert. *American Book Review* 1 (December 1977): 14. Reprinted in *The Great American Poetry Bake-Off.* Metuchen, NJ, and London: Scarecrow Press, 1979.
Publishers Weekly, 26 December 1977.
Quest, May–June 1978.
Rochester Democrat and Chronicle, 11 September 1977.
San Francisco Review of Books, November 1977.
Selzer, David. *Poetry Review* (England) 67, no. 4 (1978): 49–51.
Simpson, Peter L. *St. Louis Post-Dispatch,* 20 December 1977, 3B.
Small Press Bookclub, Christmas 1977.
Stony Hills 4, no. 2 (1978).
Von Hallberg, Robert. *Chicago Review* 31, no. 3 (Winter 1980): 116–20.
Yenser, Stephen. *Yale Review* 68, no. 5 (Fall 1978): 86–90.

Six Troubadour Songs
American Book Review 1 (December 1977): 14.
Bloom, Harold. *New Republic* 177 (26 November 1977): 26.
Booklist 74 (15 December 1977): 663–64.

Carruth, Hayden. *Hudson Review* 31 (Summer 1978): 383.
Choice 15 (March 1978): 80.
Harrison, Keith. *Carleton Miscellany* 17 (Spring 1979): 234.
Kenner, Hugh. *New York Times Book Review* (1 January 1978): 11.
Library Journal 102 (15 December 1977): 2473.
Virginia Quarterly Review 54 (Spring 1978): 58.

If Birds Build with Your Hair
Gioia, Dana. *Hudson Review* 35 (Autumn 1982): 483.

Selected Poems: 1957–1987
Bawer, Bruce. *Washington Post Book World,* 3 January 1988.
Ewart, Gavin. *New York Times Book Review,* 13 September 1987, 52.
Geier, A. Woodrow. *Sunday Tennessean,* 27 March 1988, 9F.
Goldgar, Harry. *St. Petersburg Times,* 3 January 1988.
Gwynn, R. S. *Dictionary of Literary Biography: 1987.* Ed. J. M. Brook. Detroit: Gale, 1988.
Hall, Donald. *Partisan Review* 55 (Summer 1988): 505–7.
Harris, Jana. *Seattle Times,* 18 October 1987.
Jerome, Judson. *Writer's Digest,* March 1988, 13.
Koestenbaum, Wayne. *Village Voice* 32, no. 46 (17 November 1987): 63.
Laizik, S., and Mark Bing. *Philadelphia Inquirer,* 6 March 1988, F3.
Levis, Larry. *American Poetry Review* 18, no. 1 (January–February 1989): 9–14.
Logan, William. *Parnassus* 16, no. 1 (Summer 1990): 72–86.
Lovelace, Yann. *Oasis 38* (England), January 1990.
McDowell, Robert. *Hudson Review* 40, no. 4 (Winter 1988): 677–85.
McDuff, David. *Stand* 29 (Autumn 1988): 66–67.
McGovern, Martin. *Houston Post,* 17 January 1988.
Pinson, Ernest. *Jackson Sun* (Jackson, TN), 1 November 1987, C4.
Roffman, Rosaly DeMaios. *Library Journal* 112 (August 1987): 130.
Stuttaford, Genevieve. *Publishers Weekly,* 12 June 1987.
Virginia Quarterly Review 64, no. 3 (Summer 1988): 98.

W. D.'s Midnight Carnival
"Word and Image at Play." *This World (San Francisco Chronicle),* 30 October 1988, 10–11.

The Death of Cock Robin
Chappell, Fred. *Georgia Review* 45 (Summer 1991): 383–94.
Virginia Quarterly Review, Summer 1990, 100–101.

Theatrical Productions
Ann Arbor News, 7 April 1987, D5.
Barnes, Clive. *New York Post,* 3 June 1981, 16.
Eastern Echo (Ypsilanti, MI), 1 April 1987, 5.
Evans, Jeremy. *Show Business,* 10 June 1981.
Feingold, Michael. *Village Voice,* 10–16 June 1981, 93–94.
Gilman, Richard. *Nation,* 27 June 1981, 803–4.
Gussow, Mel. *New York Times,* 3 June 1981, C21.
Kissel, Howard. *Women's Wear Daily,* 4 June 1981.
Post-Standard (Syracuse), 30 April 1966, 7.

Raidy, William A. *Star Ledger,* 4 June 1981.

Sauvage, Leo. *New Leader* 64, no. 13 (1981): 22.

Simon, John. *New York,* 15 June 1981, 67.

Wynne, Peter. *Record,* 3 June 1981.

Dissertations

Blankenburg, Gary Dean. *A Rhetorical Approach to Confessional Poetry: Plath, Sexton, Lowell, Berryman, and Snodgrass.* Carnegie-Mellon, 1983. Ann Arbor: UMI, 1984. 84-06438.

Goodman, Diane Beth. " 'Heart's Needle': A Guide to the Original Manuscript." Case Western Reserve, 1989.

McClatchy, J. D. *Bloody-Hot and Personal: The Tradition of Contemporary Confessional Poetry.* Yale, 1974. Ann Arbor: UMI, 1975. 75-15336.

Bibliography

Gaston, Paul L. "Selected Bibliography." *W. D. Snodgrass,* 167–70. Boston: Twayne, 1978.

White, William. *W. D. Snodgrass: A Bibliography.* Detroit: Wayne State University, 1960.

POETS ON POETRY Donald Hall, General Editor

Poets on Poetry collects critical works by contemporary poets, gathering together the articles, interviews, and book reviews by which they have articulated the poetics of a new generation.